THE LANGUAGE MYTH IN WESTERN CULTURE

Edited by
Roy Harris

LONDON AND NEW YORK

First Published in 2002 by Curzon Press

First issued in paperback 2013

This edition published 2013 by Routledge
2 Park Square, Milton Park, Abingdon, Oxon OX14 4RN (UK)
711 Third Avenue, New York, NY 10017 (US)

Routledge is an imprint of the Taylor & Francis Group, an informa business

Editorial matter © 2002 Roy Harris
Individual chapters © 2002 the respective authors
Typeset in Times New Roman by Mews Photosetting, Beckenham, Kent

All rights reserved. No part of this book may be reprinted or
reproduced or utilised in any form or by any electronic,
mechanical, or other means, now known or hereafter
invented, including photocopying and recording, or in any
information storage or retrieval system, without permission in
writing from the publishers.

British Library Cataloguing in Publication Data
A catalogue record of this book is available from the British Library

Library of Congress Cataloguing in Publication Data
A catalogue record for this book has been requested
ISBN: 978-0-7007-1453-7
ISBN: 978-0-415-86521-0 (Paperback)

Contents

Contributors		vi
Preface		vii
1	The Role of the Language Myth in the Western Cultural Tradition *Roy Harris*	1
2	The Language Myth and Historical Linguistics *Nigel Love*	25
3	The Language Myth and Standard English *Hayley G. Davis*	41
4	The Language Myth and Linguistics Humanised *Edda Weigand*	55
5	The Mythical, the Non-mythical and Representation in Linguistics *Philip Carr*	84
6	Folk Psychology and the Language Myth: What Would the Integrationist Say? *Talbot J. Taylor*	100
7	The Language Myth and the Race Myth: Evil Twins of Modern Identity Politics? *Christopher Hutton*	118
8	The Language Myth and Mathematical Notation as a Language of Nature *Daniel R. Davis*	139
9	The Language Myth and the Law *Michael Toolan*	159
10	The Language Myth and Western Art *Anna Tietze*	183
11	The Language Myth, Schopenhauer and Music *George Wolf*	201
Index		221

Contributors

Philip Carr is Professor of Linguistics in the English Department at the Université Paul Valéry, Montpellier.

Daniel R. Davis is Assistant Professor of Linguistics in the Department of Humanities, University of Michigan-Dearborn.

Hayley G. Davis is a lecturer in the English Department, Goldsmiths College, University of London.

Roy Harris is Emeritus Professor of General Linguistics, University of Oxford.

Christopher Hutton is Senior Lecturer in linguistics in the Department of English at the University of Hong Kong.

Nigel Love is Associate Professor in the Department of Linguistics and Southern African Languages, University of Cape Town.

Talbot J. Taylor is L.G.T. Cooley Professor of English and Linguistics at the College of William and Mary, Virginia, and Co-Editor of *Language & Communication*.

Anna Tietze teaches in the Department of Historical Studies, University of Cape Town.

Michael Toolan is Professor of Applied English Linguistics at the University of Birmingham.

Edda Weigand is Professor of Linguistics at the University of Münster.

George Wolf is Professor in the Department of Foreign Languages at the University of New Orleans.

Preface

The International Association for the Integrational Study of Language and Communication held its first plenary conference at Goldsmiths College, University of London, on 3–6 July 2000. It was attended by participants from Australia, Denmark, France, Germany, Hong Kong, India, Spain, South Africa, Switzerland, U.K. and U.S.A. The eleven papers included in the present volume are revised versions of the principal presentations at this conference. They provoked lively responses and debates which, unfortunately, it proved impractical to try to summarize here. It would probably be fair to say, however, that no one went away feeling that the last word had been said on any of the highly controversial topics raised. This publication has as its main purpose the prospect of enabling a wider audience to share that continuing discussion.

Furthermore, although the conference agenda deliberately cast a wide cultural net, touching on such diverse matters as politics, race, education, psychology, mathematics, law, painting and music, there was a strong sense that in a few days at Goldsmiths we had done no more than make a rapid survey of the tip of an iceberg. For if the main contentions of integrationists concerning human communication have any substance at all, that already suffices to make an important difference not only to the question of how, academically, one should 'do' linguistics, but how one should 'do' such subjects as anthropology, philosophy, social studies, literature and history, to say nothing of the natural sciences. All these subjects depend on the construction of a discourse, a set of language-games. And virtually every discourse in Western academia, if integrationists are right, is to some degree moulded by assumptions derived from the language myth. Integrationism thus has its own distinctive contribution to make to the contemporary current of thinking that is often called 'postmodern'. There is, consequently, no shortage of issues that remain to be addressed at future meetings.

The IAISLC Committee would like to express its appreciation to Hayley Davis for all the organizational work which made the conference so successful and to Elsevier Science for financial support in awarding travel bursaries to graduate students, particularly from overseas.

R.H.

1 The Role of the Language Myth in the Western Cultural Tradition

Roy Harris

1. Introduction

The title of my paper might already seem to invoke so many question-begging terms as to call for some preliminary explanations. What is myth? What is culture? What is tradition?

As an integrationist, I may perhaps be allowed a certain measure of diffidence about definitions. I shall simply take it that we are dealing with a cultural tradition wherever a society has achieved a sufficient degree of self-awareness to discuss its own beliefs and practices by reference to authorities long since dead and to ideas which those predecessors held, or are alleged to have held. Gandhi was once asked what he thought about Western civilization and replied that he thought it would be a good idea. But I doubt that even Gandhi would have refused to acknowledge the existence of a Western cultural tradition, however civilized or uncivilized.

Nor do I suppose he would have had any more difficulty than I do with the notion that a cultural tradition may incorporate myths. But 'What is a myth?' is a much trickier question than 'What is a cultural tradition?' For my purposes a myth is a cultural fossil, a sedimented form of thinking that has gone unchallenged for so long that it has hardened into a kind of intellectual concrete.

My contention is that there is, and long has been, a language myth deeply entrenched in Western culture. The origins of this myth can be traced back over two millennia and more to the Classical period of ancient Greece. It is a myth of which we are all today – whether we regard ourselves personally as 'Western' or not – both beneficiaries and victims. We are beneficiaries insofar as the myth promotes certain values and practices that Western culture would be the poorer without. We are victims inasmuch as the myth inculcates certain attitudes and prejudices that prevent Western culture from realizing its full human and humane potential. For both kinds of reason, positive and negative, a fuller understanding of the way thinking about language has become fossilized in the Western tradition is worth serious attention.

2. The language myth

The myth I am referring to appears in various versions at different times throughout that long tradition; but, allowing for minor differences of detail, it usually takes something like the following form:

> Individuals are able to exchange their thoughts by means of words because – and insofar as – they have come to understand and to adhere to a fixed public plan for doing so. The plan is based on recurrent instantiation of invariant items belonging to a set known to all members of the community. These items are the 'sentences' of the community's language. They are invariant items in two respects: form and meaning. Knowing the forms of sentences enables those who know the language to express appropriately the thoughts they intend to convey. Knowing the meanings of sentences enables those who know the language to identify the thoughts thus expressed. Being invariant, sentences are context-free, and so proof against the vagaries of changing speakers, hearers and circumstances, rather as coin of the realm is valid irrespective of the honesty or dishonesty of individual transactions.

This preliminary characterization was first proposed nearly twenty years ago in a book I called *The Language Myth* (Harris 1981). Today I see little reason to alter that initial account in any substantive detail. The book then goes on to explain as follows how linguistic communication is supposed to work.

> Suppose A has a thought that he wishes to communicate to B, for example, that gold is valuable. His task is to search among the sentences of a language known both to himself and to B, and select that sentence which has a meaning appropriate to the thought to be conveyed; for example, in English, the sentence *Gold is valuable*. He then encodes this sentence in its appropriate oral or written form, from which B is able to decode it, and

in virtue of knowing what it means, grasp the thought which *A* intended to convey to him, namely that gold is valuable. (Harris 1981: 10)

This way of thinking about language seems to me to have become fossilized at a very early date in the Western tradition; fossilized in the sense not only that it is accepted by those who write authoritatively on linguistic topics, but also in that any challenge to it is regarded as an affront to common sense.

If you present the language myth by reference to examples like *Gold is valuable*, then sooner or later – and sooner rather than later, in my experience – someone is bound to ask: 'Is this a myth at all?' Is it not, rather, a very reasonable – albeit condensed – account of what actually happens in our daily verbal transactions? On what other basis could we in practice conduct our affairs? Do we not in fact resort to saying, for example, 'Gold is valuable' when we want to tell someone just that; namely that gold is valuable? How else could we proceed?

There may be those who regard some components or versions of the language myth as more mythical than others (Carr, this volume). Sceptics might even feel inclined to argue that if the language myth is a myth, then a conference such as this is self-stultifying, since it both presupposes and practices successfully that very form of communication declared to be mythical. But it seems to me that even if integrationists are misguided in their characterization of the myth, the mere possibility that they might be right, or even partly right, is already enough to pose questions about Western culture that cannot just be dismissed out of hand.

My original choice of the term *myth* was provocative, and what I hoped to provoke was a debate among linguists concerning the theoretical basis of their discipline. It seemed to me, in the late 1970s, that not since the articulation of the Sapir-Whorf hypothesis had there been any serious challenge to the monumental complacency of mainstream linguistics. My attempt to provoke a debate was not very successful; but its failure taught me two things. By their reactions, many linguists seemed unwittingly to confirm the mythological character of their own assumptions. For instead of trying to meet the challenge head-on and defend those assumptions, what they typically did was simply deny that they believed in the myth (just as they had previously denied their linguistics was Whorfian) and then carry on exactly as before. Which struck me as rather like denying one's belief in the Virgin Birth and immediately lighting another candle to Holy Mary. It was almost as if the denial somehow strengthened the original act of faith. And in retrospect I saw that is very characteristic of myth. Myths are not just common-or-garden illusions that can be empirically disproved and discredited. Nor, by the same token, can they be upgraded into 'science' overnight by dint of producing research that allegedly 'supports' them.

Anyone is doubly confused who supposes that findings from modern psycholinguistic experiments demonstrate conclusively the non-mythical character of the basic tenets of traditional Western thinking about language. That would be rather like concluding that there was no Oedipus myth after all, because research has lately discovered evidence of a historical person called 'Oedipus'. Trying to prove, one by one, the 'real existence' of words, meanings, sentences, consonants, vowels, dialects and all the other familiar bits and pieces of the mythical linguistic apparatus would be as Quixotic a conceptual enterprise as trying to prove the real existence of square roots, odd numbers, quotients and divisors (D. Davis, this volume) in order to justify what we do with elementary arithmetic; or establish the actuality of a certain state of my brain in order to verify the truth of my statement 'I believe that my name is Roy Harris' (Taylor, this volume). Linguists committed to analogous validation programmes in respect of linguistic elements create their own problems, for they have taken on a task which is as pointless as it is impracticable. ('Cantonese is a bit of a worry, you know: we haven't yet got irrefutable evidence about whether there really *is* a seventh tone.') Even more curious would be trying to prove that these really existent linguistic entities are 'really' subject to change over time (Love, this volume), as if showing that the 'real' Oedipus grew old, or eventually lost his teeth, corroborated the claim that the mythical Oedipus was not, after all, a mythical figure. The irony in the linguistic case is that these moves designed to 'validate' belief in a myth by denying its mythical status are typically surrogational moves: they show us the language myth in the process of trying to gain credit by offering its own terminological IOUs as security. ('A syllable, sir? Yes, I can show you one right here on my spectrogram.' 'A language? I have an excellent description of one in this grammar book.' 'A linguistic change? How about Latin *causa* becoming French *chose*? It's vouched for in the very latest etymological dictionaries!') Here is the mythological term: there the alleged item it stands for. Or, failing the item itself, a 'representation' of it. What more is needed? What more could be required, if you already believe in a surrogational semantics? Anything lost on the representational swings can always be recouped on the representational roundabouts. What this sad state of affairs reflects is a culture whose scholars are still 'bewitched' (as Wittgenstein once put it) by language, not least those whose scholarship is supposedly focussed on language itself.

The engagement of myth with reality – or its failure to engage – is of a quite different order from that of illusion or factual error. Once you recognize an illusion as illusory, or a factual error as erroneous, you are no longer taken in by it; but myths can command credence and respect even from those who recognize, however reluctantly, their essentially mythical character. Myths are often regarded as capturing some higher or symbolic truth, which transcends their superficial lack of factuality, or makes it irrelevant. They are held to have what the Greeks called *hyponoia*.

Myths also have a popular appeal as explaining certain things that would otherwise be mysterious. Lévi-Strauss once described the function of myth as being 'to provide a logical model capable of overcoming a contradiction' (Lévi-Strauss 1963: 229). He added: 'an impossible achievement if, as it happens, the contradiction is real'. This seems to me to apply exactly to the myth we are considering. (I shall return to the question of 'overcoming a contradiction' shortly.) A myth, then, unlike illusion or factual error, characteristically takes a form in which there is no straightforward way of testing its credentials. That, indeed, is one source of its power as a myth. On all these counts what I call 'the language myth' qualifies for inclusion. Nor do I think it can be excluded on the ground that it lacks the personifications and narratives in which myth is often clothed. For such trappings do indeed feature in some Western accounts that allegorize parts of the myth in question (e.g. the nomenclatorial exploits of Adam in the Garden of Eden, and the no less hypothetical activities of the primordial 'Namegiver' invoked by Socrates, not to mention those attributed to Hermes Trismegistus).

Now it is readily understandable that linguists should not take kindly to being told that what they are presenting to their students as up-to-date science is actually no more than recycled myth. Anyone bearing that message is not likely to be very popular initially, any more than Copernicus was popular among the orthodox astronomers of his day. But the question then becomes whether one prefers popularity with one's colleagues to the advancement of serious intellectual discussion. From reactions to my book I also learned something that I had only dimly realized before. When you challenge the kind of assumptions that I had identified as the 'language myth', you are challenging much more than people's beliefs about language. That is why they refuse to engage in debate, or reject the terms of debate out of hand, or say you are absurdly misrepresenting their position. For you are calling in question not simply a set of propositions of the kind that turn up in grammar books or works of linguistic theory. You are calling in question something about the way they conduct themselves not just in their professional capacity as linguists, but also as educated persons, law-abiding citizens, good neighbours, and in many other aspects of their social being. That is what offends them. You are challenging a whole cultural picture at a much more basic level than you might at first have supposed.

3. The communication myth

In recent years I have come to wonder whether the role of the language myth in the Western tradition was ever simply or mainly to justify certain ways of talking about words, sentences, nouns, verbs, and so on. In this paper I shall propose that it is possible to see the role of the language myth as being to interrelate and underpin certain wider assumptions concerning both the place of human beings in society and human knowledge of the natural world. From this perspective, many different facets of the intellectual development of Western culture can be viewed in terms of the adoption of, or adaptation to, the two essential components of the language myth: (i) the doctrine of telementation and (ii) the doctrine of the fixed code.

The language myth, as I have characterized it so far, can be viewed as just one version of a more general myth about communication. In its more general form, the myth would run as follows:

> Certain forms of communication involve a process of transmitting messages. Individuals are able to send and/or interpret messages whenever they have come to understand and follow the relevant procedure of transmission (public or private, voluntary or involuntary, natural or artificial). This is based on recurrent instantiation of certain invariant items. These items

are 'signs'. They are invariant items in two respects: form and meaning. Knowing the form and meaning of a sign enables one to identify and interpret the message it conveys.

Here a 'sign' can take any physical form whatever, verbal or non-verbal. It can include signs emanating from the natural world as well as signs emanating from human agents. Let us call this broader version of the language myth 'the communication myth'. As I have formulated it, it makes no claim to cover *all* forms of communication. Exactly what forms of communication it does cover can be left as an open question; and that is one of its important features. Because of this open-endedness, it was possible throughout the Western tradition to treat it as providing a general framework for theorizing about quite diverse kinds of activity. Treating *as many activities and relationships as possible* in terms of communication is, as I now see it, one of the most conspicuous features of that tradition.

4. The transmission process

The explanatory potential of any myth depends on certain basic features of its internal structure. In the case we are considering, the transmission of a message is represented as linear (in one sense of that debatable term) in that it involves a non-reversible process in time. But in the case of language this process is conceived of as linking at least two matching items. Starting from the thought that 'Gold is valuable' in A's head, we proceed via the utterance of the sentence to a matching thought in B's head. As a result of the one-way transmission, we get a second pattern that, although spatio-temporally discrete, copies the original. Thus in its simplest and most abstract form the transmission has a structure like this:

● > ●

For want of any better term I will call this a 'pattern transference' model. The original pattern has somehow been transferred to or re-created in a new location.

The first point I want to make is that if we wish to understand the language myth we must realize that it operates with a pattern transference model; and the second point, no less important, is that pattern transference itself is not a hypothesis but a natural phenomenon. A footprint in wet sand, of the kind that Robinson Crusoe one day discovered on his island shore, leaves a pattern corresponding to the configuration of the foot that made it. The recognition of pattern transference as a natural phenomenon is of enormous value to hunter-gatherer communities. It is important to be able to recognize the difference between the tracks of a predator and the tracks of various species of game. How primitive societies conceptualized the difference between such 'messages' accidentally left by passing animals and the messages deliberately projected by human agents, or whether they recognized it at all, we do not know. What we *do* know is that some such distinction must have occurred to the precursors of Plato, who already takes it for granted that verbal messages are signs of a different kind from natural signs. But in what exactly the difference consists he is not entirely sure.

Pattern transference, it hardly needs to be stressed, is quite fundamental to traditional Western conceptions of drawing and painting. A portrait of Queen Victoria is expected (or would have been expected in her day) to 'look like' Queen Victoria. A 'flower painting' would have been expected to depict things visually recognizable as flowers. There was a time – but perhaps it is now past – when any apprentice painter would have been laughed out of the studio if incapable of producing a plausible 'likeness'. In such cases, a pattern originating on the retina of the artist's eye is deemed to have been transferred, via the medium of paint on canvas, to the retina of the person looking at the picture. This is analogous to the transference that, according to language-myth accounts, allegedly takes place via the medium of sound in the case of words. Mimesis, as traditionally interpreted from Plato onwards, is a semiological concept underpinned, however vaguely, by pattern transference. Just how ubiquitously this pervades Western drawing and painting is evident from the way in which it overrides any biomechanical controls on 'likeness'. Thus, for example, it is – or was – supposedly possible for a competent painter to depict the archangel Gabriel, or the patriarch Noah, without ever having set eyes either on the heavenly messenger or on the builder of the Ark. In such cases we see how readily the Western artist substitutes mere names ('Gabriel', 'Noah') and associated verbal narrative for authentic visual experience. The substitution would hardly be feasible – and might even be held to be impossible – in a society which rejected outright the semiological assumption that description and depiction are head and tail of the same communicational coin. As is indicated in the famous dictum attributed to Simonides of Ceos (that painting is mute poetry and poetry a speaking picture), it has long been assumed in the Western tradition that two apparently disparate forms of communicational enterprise – pictorial and verbal – go hand-in-glove: there is a deep level of collusion between them. But it is a cultural collusion, built up over many centuries by social demands and practices; not a correspondence automatically built into our brains, or the brains of our primitive ancestors. Nevertheless, so familiar has it become in Western thinking that it now passes unnoticed (or, which amounts to the same thing, is regarded as 'natural').

In discussing pattern transference I shall deliberately skip over such questions as the exact topological and qualitative correspondence between patterns. We all know that Rembrandt had to draw in reverse on the plate to make his etchings, that a reproduction in colour is different from a reproduction in black-and-white, and so on. But these are complications which do not matter for present purposes. All that matters is that the transfer process should not so deform the pattern as to make it unrecognizable. That applies as much to game tracks in the Kalahari as to Rembrandt's etching or to radio broadcasts in London.

Random pattern transference of the kind that occurs naturally, as in the case of animal tracks, or as when the receding tide leaves a unique pattern of ripples marked out on the shore, although it may be important as a source of information, is theoretically of limited interest. Pattern transference becomes much more interesting when it can be controlled; that is, when consciously designed patterns can be reliably repeated at will. And this is the point at which all serious Western thinking about human communication begins.

There are three basic types to consider.

1. In the simplest type of case, each transference requires another performance of the transfer process. As, for instance, when using a rubber stamp. This is a labour-intensive form of pattern transference, in that whenever a new document has to be stamped you have to go through the business all over again. There is a one-one relation between process and transfer, even though there is a one-many relation between prototype and transfer, assuming you use the same rubber stamp on each successive occasion. In spite of its technological advancement, the modern office photocopier still belongs to this very simple type. We take our original document, put it in the machine, press the button to trigger an irreversible process, as a

result of which, at a later point in time, there is produced another document which replicates – if the machine is working properly – all the desired features of the original. If we want another copy of the same document, the process has to be repeated. The fact that we can instruct the machine to make a dozen copies by just keying in the number '12' and leaving the document in the same position does not alter the fact that the machine has to go through the whole scanning-and-printing cycle twelve times. So the appropriate model to capture what happens in these cases is simply:

● > ●

● > ●

● > ●

● > ●

etc.

The machine can, in principle, produce as many copies as we wish, until it breaks down or wears out. Let us call this 'iterative transference'.

2. The type of pattern transference just described has to be distinguished from one in which the production of a number of copies does not depend on repeating the process over and over again. This second type, which can be called 'multiple transference', conforms instead to the model:

● > ● ● ● ● ● ● etc.

That is to say, in multiple transference copies are produced from the same original, but there is no need to repeat the transfer process. That is what happens in carbon copying. The typist ends up with several copies, but has typed the letter only once, and no other processing is required. A single operation suffices.

3. This in turn has to be distinguished from a third type of case, in which we take a copy of the original and make a copy *of that*. So, potentially, the same process repeated gives rise to successive generations of copies. This is 'lineal transference':

● > ● > ● > ● etc.

These last two models are important because they explain how pattern transference can be renewed *ad infinitum*, given the right material conditions, and thus extend across space and time.

5. Pattern transference and sense perception

Pattern transference processes are important in the early development of technology. The modern photocopier has exactly the same structural features as much earlier techniques of reproduction. For instance, replication by casting is a process that has been understood and practised for centuries. The principle of plaster casts was familiar to Pliny, who attributes its invention (implausibly) to Lysistratus. You take the original object, make a mould of it, and then fill your mould with soft material that will take the shape of the original and later harden into a copy. Then you can repeat this to make further copies again and again. That is exactly what goes on in the modern photocopier, only under a very accelerated and sophisticated set of transformations that depend *inter alia* on having and controlling light-sensitive materials.

As has been pointed out on many occasions, analogies from technology have always played an important role in constructing hypothetical accounts of structures and processes that are not directly available to observation. The most recent and perhaps most notorious case is that of the electronic digital computer applied to the human brain. Descartes employed a hydraulic model to explain how the soul and the body interact. Examples could be cited endlessly from the history of Western science. Pattern transference technology is one such source and the reason why I am harping on about it is that if you wish to understand the plausibility of the language myth you have to realize that it employs the same iterative transference model as one of the most popular and long-lived Western explanations of how we know what is going on in the world around us.

The classic example is Aristotle's pattern transference model of sense perception (although he did not call it that). He held that the mind acquires copies or likenesses (*homoiomata*) of things in the external world (*De Interpretatione*, 16a). And in *De Anima* he gives the following general explanation of how our senses work.

> By a 'sense' is meant what has the power of receiving into itself the sensible forms of things without the matter. This must be conceived of as taking place in the way in which a piece of wax takes on the impress of a signet-ring without the iron or gold; we say that what produces the impression is a signet of bronze or gold, but its particular metallic constitution makes no difference: in a similar way the sense is affected by what is coloured or flavoured or sounding, but it is indifferent what in each case the substance is; what alone matters is what *quality* it has, i.e. in what ratio its constituents are combined. (*De Anima 424a*. Smith's translation.)

The wax impress is not a brilliant analogy because presumably these copies or likenesses would in many cases have to be smaller than their originals. There isn't room inside my head for a full-scale replica of Mount Olympus. But this is just where a pattern transference model comes into its own: the visual pattern presented by Mount Olympus gets inside my head on a much reduced scale. Exactly how this process works Aristotle does not explain, but he evidently thinks that it works in exactly the same way for all human beings. In short, the external world is the same for all observers, and their mental impressions ('affections of the soul' as Aristotle describes them) of the external world are likewise the same.

Aristotle's theory of sense perception was not without competitors. Plato puts forward in the *Theaetetus* a quite different account. According to this, the sensible qualities perceived – for example, the whiteness of snow – reside neither in the original object nor in the perceiving sense-organ. Whiteness somehow arises as the joint product of an interaction between eye and object. In other words, it is not a case of pattern transference at all. The reason I mention this is to point out that if Plato's theory had triumphed, that interactional model would not have done at all for purposes of explaining telementation. A chasm would then have opened up between the favourite Western explanation of sense perception, on the one hand, and the favourite Western explanation of verbal communication on the other. But with transference models these two things go together. They are both examples of basically the same kind of process.

Locke has a much more complicated theory than Aristotle, but it still at bottom relies on a pattern transference model. According to Locke, only certain elementary kinds of information from the outside world 'enter by the senses simple and unmixed'. Examples he gives are the hardness and coldness of a piece of ice, the smell and colour of a lily, the taste of sugar. Experience of such cases produces what Locke calls not 'affections of the soul' but 'simple ideas'; and simple ideas provide 'the materials of all our knowledge' (Locke 1706: II.2.i-ii). Like Aristotle, Locke never explains exactly how the senses manage to bridge the gap between the outside world and the inner recesses of the brain, but it is evidently some kind of pattern transference. When we feel the coldness of the ice, it is not that the temperature inside the head has suddenly dropped, but somehow the sensory pattern that we eventually recognize as coldness has been transferred from the finger-tips. Perception, for Locke, is something that happens only in the mind. You do not feel heat or cold until the message reaches the inner sanctum: 'whatever impressions are made on the outward parts, if they are not taken notice of within, there is no perception' (Locke 1706: II.9.iii).

I do not need to dwell on the horrendous problems that both Aristotle and Locke create for themselves in proposing this kind of account. My point is that what we see in the Western tradition is the development and sustainment of a view in which the senses are conceptualized as transference channels, channels of communication. Bacon, for example, writes explicitly of human beings having knowledge of the external world via what he calls 'the reports of the senses'. The individual is assumed to be totally isolated from the rest of the universe until messages are received about what is going on in the immediate environment. The senses – sight, touch, hearing, etc. – have communication as their basic function. They provide links between our inner selves and the great outside. And messages are coming in all the time. At every waking moment, and even during sleep, our sense-organs are being bombarded with a flow of information emanating from 'out there'.

So it might seem on first inspection that before there is any question of a language myth, or any account of words, there is already in place a no less mythical account of sense perception. But that is too simplistic. From Aristotle down to Locke and beyond, accounts of sense perception and accounts of language go side by side, each supporting the other. Some accounts are simpler and some are more complicated, but their interrelationship remains constant. It has been recycled time and again over the centuries. It appears in different versions, but without ever departing radically from its archetype. That is, typically, the mode of existence of a cultural fossil.

13

6. Somatic particularism

If this approach is on roughly the right lines, then we should be able to learn a great deal more by examining just how the language myth fits in with explanation of our knowledge of the external world. Again, Aristotle provides us with a very simple account that already contains all the basic features. It starts from certain unstated assumptions about the kind of life that human beings lead, assumptions which are also incorporated in a fairly transparent way into the language myth. To begin with, there is the assumption that the human agents involved in communication are individuals with an independent and unique existence. By 'independent and unique' I mean no more than we all believe ourselves to be creatures whose own experience and biohistory belong to no one else. I cannot digest your food, feel your tooothache or think your thoughts for you. I cannot see through your eyes or have your memories. I cannot be responsible for your decisions nor you for mine. In this sense, the assumption is that each of us is an island.

Now we can imagine a culture in which such assumptions were *not* entertained. Whether or not such cultures exist or have existed is beside the point. For purposes of comparison, it will do to conjure up a science-fiction culture, in which the basic belief is that all experience is common to the members of a family or a group. In such a culture there would be no room for concepts like '*my* feelings' or '*my* beliefs'; nor even for '*my* house' or '*my* mother and father'. For it would be assumed that whatever relationships an individual entered into were *ipso facto* entered into by everyone else in the collectivity.

But that is not the usual assumption in the Western tradition. In fact, in a Western perspective it does not make much sense. For even if one adopted an extremely egalitarian or communistic attitude towards material possessions and private property, how could my body – with its own arms, legs and other equipment – possibly be your body as well? That impossibility may seem to be built into the very use of words like *my* and *your*. (If you say that, unfortunately, you nowadays run the risk of being dismissed either as a latter-day Whorfian or as a naive linguistic realist.) To put the point less contentiously, Western thinking about the individual and society, from Plato onwards, seems to be based fairly firmly on 'somatic particularism', i.e. the thesis that individuals are differentiated one from another on the basis of each having a unique body. For those who believe in the body/mind distinction, it then becomes a corollary of somatic particularism that unique bodies have unique minds. Which is why Western psychology has such trouble with notions like 'sympathy' and 'empathy'. These concepts are rebarbative to that postulate of individual independence on which mainstream Western thinking about human behaviour is based. Such phenomena have to be explained away as somehow surmounting the natural barriers of human isolation. And so too does communication in general. The whole problem of communication as construed in Western philosophy is a problem about how somatic particularity – the natural state of isolation of the individual – can be overcome.

Here we come very close, I believe, to identifying one of those contradictions which, according to Lévi-Strauss, it is the purpose of myth to overcome. Its source in this instance is the thesis of somatic particularism, and the contradiction resides in our conviction that nevertheless individuals *can* share experience, which theoretically they ought not to be able to do. We need a model (however implausible *per se*) which will help us get over the difficulty.

To put the point another way, the crux of Western thinking about communication has always been the belief that in order to escape from a natural state of isolation, the individual has no recourse except to other equally isolated individuals. Hence the problem. How can one isolated individual plus one other isolated individual add up to any more (or less) than two isolated individuals? What has to happen in order that the two cases of isolation are cancelled out, or at least reduced?

It is here that the communication myth comes in to provide much-needed reassurance, and the concept of pattern transference is the trump card in that account. Applied to the case of human communication in general, what the transference model yields is the notion that if only an idea in A's mind can be copied into B's mind, by whatever means, then the limitations of somatic particularity have *pro tanto* been overcome. B will now have a replica of A's idea. The relevant pattern will have been transferred from one location to another. Furthermore, C, D, E and F – as many recipients as you like – can likewise in principle acquire a replica of A's idea by the processes of multiple transference. Moreover, each of these recipients can in turn pass on A's idea to others by the process of lineal transference. So instead of a lot of isolated individuals we end up with what is (significantly) called a *community*.

7. The implications of 'transference'

It is worth pausing at this juncture to draw attention to three things. The first concerns the kind of 'transference' that these models presuppose. If I transfer a sum of money from my bank account into yours, then the money is no longer where it was originally. It cannot be in two places at the same time. But that is not the kind of transference envisaged in our models of communication. If a speaker manages to convey an idea to a hearer, it is not supposed that the speaker no longer has it. On the contrary, what is assumed that *both* speaker *and* hearer now have the mental pattern in question. Sending a copy to you does not require me to give up the original. Similarly, making my thumb-print on the surface of the paper does not leave me without any configuration of lines and whorls left on my thumb. If making a photocopy automatically erased the original, the photocopier would not be a very useful machine.

The second point concerns the way the mental transference model already imposes certain requirements on our conception of what an 'idea' is. We do not have to buy Aristotle's notion of 'affections of the soul', or Locke's notion of 'simple ideas' either. Nevertheless, an idea, *ab initio*, has to be something that can be passed on from A to B. If something happens in A's mind that just *cannot* be passed on to B's mind, by whatever means, then it cannot be an idea; in other words, it fails to meet the criteria implied by the structure of the model. Thus before there is any question of finding out exactly *what* is passed on, an essential property of those units (and whether we call them 'ideas' or not is irrelevant) is determined in advance; namely, their patterns must be transferable.

This holds irrespective of any particular *mechanism* of transference. We are here in the domain not of linguistics but of philosophy of mind and philosophy of perception as well. Indeed, along this route we cannot get into linguistics at all *except* via the philosophy of mind, or the philosophy of perception, or both. Locke and his successors clearly saw this. But what they did not always see so clearly – and what I do not think even Locke saw – is the point that my discussion so far has been leading up to. It is this. The telementational concept of interpersonal communication – the notion that certain forms of communication consist in transmitting ideas from one mind to another – conceals a built-in circularity. For it assumes from the outset that ideas *are* transferable patterns of some kind. It thus becomes vacuous to claim that what a speaker conveys to a hearer are the speaker's ideas, for *ex hypothesi* there is nothing else that could be conveyed *except such patterns*. There is no physical object that moves its location. The hearer does not somehow acquire some of *A*'s brain cells, nor *A* lose them. Whatever may go on in the speaker's head that fails the criterion of pattern-transferability is ruled out by definition: for that which is incommunicable could not possibly be an idea.

The third point is that, *mutatis mutandis*, the same applies to messages from the external world. This leads directly to the thesis espoused by some eminent Western thinkers; namely, that reality – full reality – is unknowable. All that can be known is what our senses tell us. Any patterns in the external world that our senses cannot transfer we are destined to remain in ignorance of.

This model, therefore, does leave room for the unknowable and the incommunicable, but at a price: it simply denies that anything so essentially private or unique as to be incommunicable counts as an idea anyway. As regards Nature as a source of messages, the parallel conclusion is that we are slaves to our senses. They inform us about reality, at the same time as they limit our grasp of it.

Locke sensed the conceptual difficulty here, but failed to analyse it correctly. Instead, he left us with what he regarded as the problem of justifying the belief that communication is successful (i.e. that *B* does indeed grasp *A*'s idea). For this he has been called (perhaps not altogether fairly) a 'communicational sceptic' (Taylor 1992: 30). This puts the emphasis in the wrong place. For it is not that Locke was sceptical about the *fact* that communication is possible. (As a Christian, he believed that God provided mankind with the means of achieving it. It would have been a mockery on God's part to provide the illusion of communication instead of the real thing: and perhaps a form of heresy – for Locke – to suggest that God had. Similarly, one presumes, it would have been a mockery for God to allow human beings to believe that grass is green if, in fact, it is orange. Why not, after all, let them see grass in its true colour? I leave this as an inscrutable puzzle for theologians, while pointing out that it cannot be solved – or even raised – except within the context of the communication myth.)

The more general epistemological problem never went away. It is still with us. It is the problem that orthodox linguists show such reluctance to face up to. Saussure, for one, had an original approach to it, although operating with essentially the same model of communication as Locke. Saussure too sensed the same difficulty. His way of dealing with it is both cruder and more sophisticated than Locke's. He plunges in and denies that, prior to language, we have any clearly formed ideas at all. Our thought is just an amorphous mass (Saussure 1922: 155–6). This at one blow upsets the whole Aristotelian applecart. It is a crude approach in the sense that the denial of pre-linguistic ideas is given no supporting evidence or argumentation. Saussure merely announces it as if it were a self-evident truth. On the other hand, it is sophisticated inasmuch as it recognizes that – at least for purposes of the theorist of human communication – (i) the only mental items worth considering are those which are communicable, and (ii) to be communicable is to be expressible by means of signs, of which the most important are linguistic signs.

8. Mediated transference

From Aristotle down to Saussure, however, there is a consensus on at least two issues. One is that in speech it is not the idea that is copied directly from A's mind into B's. The idea is first translated into sound. What is actually transmitted intersomatically between A and B is the sound. Or, more precisely, the physical vibrations set off by the action of A's vocal cords. So what you end up with in the case of speech is a theory involving a double symmetry or double transference. Not only is A's original idea eventually replicated – at least, under ideal conditions – in B's mind, but in between, as it were, there is a section of the process in which a sound or sounds conjured up in A's mind is also replicated in B's mind. The hypothesized vehicle of this intermediate symmetry is what Saussure called the 'image acoustique'.

This, in short, is a 'mediated-transference model'. Such a model can be applied not only to speech but to many forms of communication. All that will differ is the medium through which the transfer is effected. It is a type of explanation that leaves the thesis of somatic particularism intact. Necessarily so; since *unless that thesis is presupposed, the explanation offered has no intellectual purchase at all.*

Secondly, there is also a consensus as to where the difference lies between two types of communication. Nature has already supplied us with the equipment for interpreting messages from the external environment, whereas messages from our fellow human beings require, in many cases, a knowledge of some specific code; and these codes may vary from one community to the next. They are based on what Nature has already supplied, but they are not immediately intertranslatable, because *on top of what Nature supplies to everyone* human beings have erected special arrangements to suit themselves.

This is the intellectual and psychological basis for the distinctions that run throughout Western thinking between what the Greeks called *physis* and *nomos*, natural order and conventional order. These are communicational concepts. The fundamental difference does not, however, impede thinking of natural messages in terms of human messages. This is what underwrites the figurative construal of Nature as one vast text to be interpreted.

Thrice happy he who, not mistook,
Hath read in Nature's mystic book.

It would be naive to imagine that only poets ever thought in this way about the natural world. The concepts of a natural sign and a conventional sign are intimately related throughout the Western tradition: one would be meaningless without the other. In the former case the relevant laws of cause-and-effect take the place of convention. Indeed the whole notion of 'laws of Nature', as has frequently been pointed out, is derived from that of legislation, i.e. from 'laws of society'. The crudest version of that derivation is when the laws of Nature are thought to be 'commands of the gods' (Magee 1973: 18) Here we have another myth, recognizable by its constant recycling and its imperviousness to empirical disproof. The laboratories of the Western world are still home to scientists who believe that what happens in their test tubes or cloud chambers was all ultimately ordained by God. Atheists who will have none of this and replace God by the forces of Nature are not *eo ipso* rejecting the legislative concept of the way things work: they are merely adding the proviso that these are laws that cannot be broken by any agency, human or superhuman.

However, just as we find poets (and others) prepared to move in that direction, so we find linguists nowadays keen to adopt a rhetoric that moves in the opposite direction by assimilating linguistic convention to natural law. (They presumably think this rhetoric reinforces their claims to be practising 'science'.) Thus I read Professor Steven Pinker assuring me that because of language he can *cause* me, his reader, to 'think some very specific thoughts' (Pinker 1994: 15). It is as if he were threatening that, with a sharp knife and the right opportunity, he could cause me to feel some very specific pains. Doubtless he could. But in the case of thinking specific thoughts I am less convinced, particularly when he begins to produce examples. One is: 'When a male octopus spots a female, his normally grayish body suddenly becomes striped.' I must confess I am unclear as to whether Pinker regards this as all one thought or more than one. But perhaps that does not matter. What worries me more is what would happen if it turned out that I had never before encountered the word *octopus*. Would he still be causing me to think a 'very specific thought'? And how could he possibly know that? Or suppose my knowledge of marine biology was so limited that it failed to encompass the possibility that there were males and females of the octopus? Or suppose it turned out that in practice I could not distinguish between an octopus and a squid? The more one ponders Pinker's assertion the more apparent it becomes, I suggest, that his rhetorical claim to wield these causally efficacious powers is a thinly disguised version of the assumption that *he* knows exactly what thought(s) this sentence captures (i.e. what it means) and can transfer the same thought(s) to anyone with the same knowledge. The sign conveys the idea if and only if the recipient already knows what idea the sign conveys. The immaculate circularity of the language myth re-emerges in triumph. (Actually, I doubt that even Professor Pinker knows what ideas an utterance or inscription of the word *octopus* cause to arise in his own mind; and which, if any, of these is the 'meaning' of the word is another question again.)

9. Ramifications of the language myth

Although it is convenient to talk of 'the language myth' as a specific set of beliefs or assumptions, in fact we are dealing with a mythological complex with ramifications which reach deep into the ways we live, or think we live. There seem to me to be at least seven areas of Western thinking and practice where the basic rationale relies, directly or indirectly, on the assumptions encapsulated in that myth. These are: (i) education, (ii) social and political theory, (iii) religion, (iv) the arts, (v) the physical and biological sciences, (vi) psychology, and (vii) competitive games. Here I shall do no more than pick out a few representative examples.

The Western concept of legislation, from which that of 'natural law' comes, is underpinned by the myth (Toolan, this volume). It makes no sense to think of laws as codifiable unless, indeed, a code is available to do this and supporting mechanisms of iterative and lineal transference available. Legislators would labour in vain if no one else but they knew what their laws decreed; although exactly what a given piece of legislation means is often disputed. When that happens it is customary (in Western culture) to blame the legislator and thus protect the sacrosanctity of the language myth.

But legislation itself is a social concept. And this brings us to an even more fundamental level at which the myth shapes our understanding of the world in which we live. Our notion of society makes little sense without presupposing that it is possible for groups of individuals to be united by sharing a common language, even before they proceed to formulate laws for the conduct of affairs. Plato had already made this capitulation to the language myth when he wrote his last work, *The Laws*.

Or take Rousseau's theory of the social contract, the essential precursor of Durkheimian sociology. The social contract is a myth in its own right. No one believes in it as a historical event, or even as a plausible piece of prehistory. But, like other examples I have cited, it is a double-decker myth. When we examine its structure we find one unprovable set of assumptions superimposed on another. Contractual explanations of society presuppose the communication myth as their foundation. Individuals cannot enter into contractual relations with others unless they have found some way of overcoming the isolation imposed by somatic particularism. Furthermore, contractual relations do not even make sense unless underpinned by the kind of folk psychology (Taylor, this volume) which assumes that individuals have thoughts and intentions which they can express by the linguistic means available to them.

My remarks about other aspects of Western culture will be even briefer. I take it there is no need to labour the role of the language myth as the basis for European education. It is what underwrites the pedagogic emphasis on reading and writing, and the study and transmission of texts. It promotes the ideal of a standard language, from which all deviation is banished (H. Davis, this volume). It invests that ideal with political power, as the correlate of a unified nation-state, or as backing for the even more sinister concept of a 'people' or 'race' (Hutton, this volume). It gives the community *ex hypothesi* a 'common mind', a collective understanding which is not shared by those outside the community. (It also generates a long-lived sub-myth about the relationship between writing and speech, which I have analysed in detail elsewhere: Harris 2000)

As regards the non-verbal arts, I shall mention only two: painting and music. In both cases I doubt whether anyone can study their history in the Western tradition without coming to realize something very curious about that development. The recognition of their importance as serious human enterprises is interlocked with debate as to whether, and to what extent, they operate with conventions analagous to those of a linguistic code. Is Beethoven's Fifth Symphony an expression of feelings or emotions that the sympathetic audience can somehow decode and thus share? Or is it merely a configuration of sounds, to which we can ascribe any meaning or none, as we please? Does the Venus de Milo in the Louvre require us to understand any convention at all? Does it not suffice to recognize the resemblance between certain shapes in carved marble and certain features of the human body? The theory of natural mimesis is the only serious competitor the theory of a fixed code has ever had in Western aesthetics. And whereas literature thrives on lineal transference, the value of certain works of art is held to depend on their qualities being essentially untransferable. (A colour reproduction of the Mona Lisa, however good, is not the Mona Lisa. But one can imagine a culture in which it was equally prized.) It is interesting in this connexion to note that a typically segregationist approach (Tietze, this volume) sees no problem in divorcing aesthetic experience from everyday life or in denying that non-verbal art has anything to do with language; whereas an integrationist approach (Wolf, this volume) sees no way of keeping them apart.

In the natural sciences, the pattern transference model of communication continues to hold sway virtually unchallenged, giving rise to numerous progeny. One relatively recent manifestation is the myth of the gene, based on lineal transference. This too is a double-decker myth. Like the myth of the social contract, it trades on the more basic myth of communication. We see this fairly clearly in all the unchallenged talk about DNA 'encoding' instructions for the perpetuation of certain biological processes. The gene was mythically supposed to be a 'unit of heredity'. It was the pattern that was allegedly 'passed on' from one generation to another in the cycle of reproduction. According to some, the gene was 'selfish', concerned solely with its own replication and indifferent to the fate of the unfortunate organisms acting as its host (Dawkins 1976). But none of this would have sounded remotely convincing, even as metaphor, to a culture not already accustomed to the notion that messages get passed on in space and time, irrespective of what happens to those who send or receive them. The case of DNA is an adaptation of the familiar communication myth, but an adaptation in which the sender and receiver are no longer human agents acting freely for a purpose. They have been replaced by biological agents, acting deterministically. Here again convention has become hopelessly conflated with cause-and-effect. The gene, in short, is a translation into biological terms of the concept of an autonomous unit of communication belonging to some universal code.

The case of games provides at least one interesting anecdotal example of how the myth becomes self-reinforcing. Saussure appeals to the analogy of chess in order to explain how a language works. That he could do this is a remarkable irony in itself. For actually the boot is on the other foot: we need the language myth in order to explain how chess works. What makes chess a playable game is that its signs and meanings, and permissible combinations of these, conform to a set known by all players. How could players grasp this unless they had the everyday analogue of verbal communication as an unquestioned exemplar? Can we imagine a languageless society that nevertheless had chess as an institutionalized form of social intercourse? The tail of Saussure's explanation wags the dog.

Concerning religion, I shall merely observe how remarkable it is that the most successful religion in the history of Europe was a text-based religion that had at its intellectual core the concept of communication between God and humanity. The revered figure in that religion is a messenger, a messiah. The most bitter disputes in its history are about the interpretation of the divine message; and, in particular, about whether or not that message is accessible to all, in their own language, without mediation by a specially authorized class of interpreters. This conference would doubtless have been richer for the participation of a theologian willing to discuss the ways in which religious orthodoxy in the Western tradition is indebted to the communication myth; perhaps, even, the extent to which the Western concept of a benevolent deity is itself constrained by the assumption that such a figure must be a Communicator.

10. Conclusion

Although I have cited only a few examples and explored none of them in detail, I hope they will suffice to reinforce my more general point: that it would be rash to imagine that the myth on which this conference is focussed is simply a myth about speech or writing, and hence of interest only to linguists. On the contrary, it is a myth which, in its most general form, pervades the whole of Western culture. It shapes Western understanding of (i) the human being as a creature with a body, a mind and senses, (ii) society as a collectivity of such creatures, engaging in collective enterprises, and (iii) the natural world as the mysteriously organized but partially controllable environment in which, like it or not, the human being is destined to live. The language myth plays the anchor role in our comprehension of how all these different facets of the human condition interrelate.

References

Dawkins, R. (1976) *The Selfish Gene*, Oxford: Oxford University Press.
Harris, R. (1981) *The Language Myth*, London: Duckworth.
Harris, R. (2000) *Rethinking Writing,* London: Athlone.
Lévi-Strauss, C. (1963) *Structural Anthroplogy*, trans. C. Jacobson, Harmondsworth: Penguin.
Locke, J. (1706) *An Essay Concerning Human Understanding*, 5th edn, London, ed. A.C. Fraser, 1894, repr. New York: Dover, 1959.
Magee, B. (1973) *Popper*, Glasgow: Fontana.
Pinker, S. (1994) *The Language Instinct*, New York: Morrow.
Saussure, F. de (1922) *Cours de linguistique générale*, 2nd edn, Paris: Payot.
Taylor, T.J. (1992) *Mutual Misunderstanding*, Durham, N.C.: Duke University Press.

2 The Language Myth and Historical Linguistics
Nigel Love

For present purposes 'historical linguistics' is a convenient cover term for both linguistic historiography and the history of languages. That is to say, the topic is not only how the language myth affects an institutionalised academic practice, but also the ways in which the myth is entwined in the object of study itself and how that object is conceived.

'The most important act of theoretical integration that could be performed in historical linguistics is somehow establishing (if it is possible in principle) a clear and intelligible nexus between short-term individual behaviour and long-term linguistic evolution' (Lass 1997: 363, n. 28). This is one way of stating the fundamental theoretical problem that besets historical linguistics, and the purpose of the present discussion is, if not to perform the act of theoretical integration Lass is calling for, then at least to outline an approach to doing so.

The problem Lass is alluding to is that historical linguistics seems to comprise two theoretically discontinuous aspects. On the one hand there is a tradition of comparative and reconstructive studies based on the observation of systematic correspondences between linguistic items separated by time, space or both. To take a simple example:

pan	*Pfanne*
path	*Pfad*
peach	*Pfirsche*
penny	*Pfennig*
pepper	*Pfeffer*
pipe	*Pfeife*
plant	*Pflanze*
plaster	*Pflaster*

plum	*Pflaume*
plough	*Pflug*
pound	*Pfund*

The differences here are at least partially systematic. Apart from other similarities between each pair of forms, an initial bilabial plosive in the first column invariably corresponds to an affricate in the second. And the meanings correspond too: the English word on the left would in each case serve to gloss the German word on the right. Correspondences as regular as these could not have come about by accident or coincidence. How then? The preferred answer is to suppose that each pair are in some sense variants of the 'same' word, to identify by whatever means a unique 'underlying' form that embodies that sameness (which may or may not be identical to one of the variants under analysis), and to project the analysis historically by supposing that the unique underlier was ancestral to the modern variants, having given rise to them by differential processes of linguistic change (which, in the case where a variant is identical to the underlier, will be zero). Given the level of abstraction from actual speech events at which such inquiries are pursued, there emerges a 'speaker-free' tradition of linguistic historiography focussed on reconstructing past language-states and issuing in an essentially figurative discourse in terms of which languages and the component parts of languages are treated as agents of their own evolution through time.

On the other hand, granted that there are such things as linguistic changes, and that they must somehow be a product of the linguistic activities of individuals, there arises a complementary, 'speaker-centred' study dealing with how changes originate in speech events and come to be diffused through linguistic communities.

Lass observes that it may not be possible in principle to integrate these two modes of inquiry, although he doesn't make any suggestions of his own as to why not. What may make it impossible is the concept of a 'linguistic change' itself. For whatever linguistic change might be, it is not simply an observable fact, even if there is a tradition whereby the contrary is either overtly stated or implied at the outset of a general discussion of the topic. 'Every language is undergoing, at all times, a slow but unceasing process of linguistic change' (Bloomfield 1935: 231); 'one of the most important facts about language is that it is continuously changing' (Milroy 1992: 1); 'languages are always changing' (Keller 1994: 3); 'languages change constantly' (Lehmann 1962: 1); 'the fact of language change is a given; it is too obvious to be recorded or even listed among the assumptions of our research' (Labov 1994: 9). But this is simply false: language change is not an observable fact, but a proposed *explanation* for the regularity of certain perceived linguistic differences.

Whether it is a good explanation would seem to depend on there being an intelligible account of what a linguistic change *is*. But when we turn to the micro-level, speaker-centred studies whose avowed aim is to provide such an account, we find that they encounter a fundamental problem. For there seems to be no such thing as a linguistic change, if by 'a linguistic change' we mean an identifiable episode in the world of first-order linguistic events. The difficulty is not merely that linguistic changes are not recognisable events in any one individual's experience of using language. A language-user may invent a new word, pronounce an old word in a novel way, give it a new meaning, etc., but to do any of these things is not *eo ipso* to bring about a change in the language. That much is of course common ground among historical linguists interested in the social origins of linguistic change. Milroy, for instance, puts the point thus: 'while investigators may observe something quite close to *speaker innovation*, they have no principled way of determining whether what they have observed is the beginning of a linguistic change in the system' (Milroy 1992: 222). For Milroy that is merely because 'a change is not a change until it has been adopted by *more than one speaker*' (223). How many more than one are required Milroy does not tell us, but at any rate there is a clear implication that, given the observation of sufficient instances, changes could in principle be pinpointed. But if so, what stands in the way of pinpointing them?

The lack of any agreed answer to that question is just one manifestation of the theoretical crisis in historical linguistics. There are others. One way of gauging the state of the art in a given field is to look at introductory handbooks for students, with reference to how the subject matter is organised, the role of general theoretical preoccupations, what is taken for granted *vs* what is treated as open to further debate. Textbook-writing traditions emerge, and whatever the differences between one such work and another there will tend to be a family resemblance as regards the overall approach to issues of this kind. Where historical linguistics is concerned, a good recent exemplar of (at least part of) the tradition is April McMahon's *Understanding Language Change* (McMahon 1994). This is a highly competent and well-received introduction to its subject, and it is

27

precisely for that reason that it makes a useful stalking-horse for the following discussion.

First of all, the fact of language change is treated as a pretheoretical given, and its study as complementary to the comparative and reconstructive investigations that constitute the other side of the coin of historical linguistics. (Reconstruction works backwards through time; language change is the phenomenon in terms of which the resulting family trees have a 'forward' interpretation.) In turn, historical linguistics as a whole is treated as complementary to synchronic language study. But it is synchronic linguistics that has the whip-hand theoretically:

> I shall be ... adopting the view that studying language change involves the examination and comparison of distinct language states and systems, which may be profitably analysed using models and theories developed in synchronic studies; conversely, these models can be usefully tested against historical data, and cannot be considered complete if they do not allow for the incorporation of change into the grammar (McMahon 1994: 9).

That is to say, although synchronic models and theories have to be *compatible* with the phenomenon of language change, there is no question of a theory of language change having priority, with 'synchronic data' being relegated to the role of testing-ground for it. Synchrony is in charge, and diachrony has to fit in as best it can. All this is par for the post-Saussurean course in historical linguistics. But it does mean that whatever understanding of language change might emerge, it is guaranteed from the outset to be one that treats it as epiphenomenal on the deliverances of currently received doctrines about synchronic language-states.

One result is that what synchronic theorists have to say about diachrony is presented as being on all fours with what diachronists themselves say. So, in accordance with the tradition, McMahon presents 'three views on sound change': the neogrammarian, the structuralist and the generativist (cf. Bynon 1977), without reference to the fact that whereas the first of these is a view of sound change *per se*, the second and third are *attempts to accommodate* sound change within theoretical frameworks designed for quite other purposes. Furthermore, since the focus in a work on language change is understandably not on the synchronic theories themselves, differences

The Language Myth and Historical Linguistics

between their ontological commitments, epistemological presuppositions and overall scope and purpose are simply ignored. But given that structuralism and generativism are simply not theories of the same thing, it is unclear what might in principle be gained by juxtaposing for inspection their treatments of sound change. Moving on from sound change, we find Lightfoot's 'principles and parameters' approach to historical syntax jostling cheek by jowl with the Milroys' theory of social networks, Greenberg's work on universals and typology, and so on and so forth, in an eclectic jumble that seems guaranteed to defeat the ostensible purpose of the book as announced in its title. In fact 'explanation of change', far from being the real goal of this work, is merely a sporadically discussed *topic* in it, indexed as such in an entry whose eighteen subheads conclude, rather forlornly, with 'viability of, 44–6'.

The explanatory enterprise is not helped by the bewildering variety of the phenomena deemed to fall within the scope of the term 'language change'. For instance (with one of McMahon's examples in each case – the language concerned being English unless otherwise stated):

(i) adaptation ([kwæsɒŋ] as an English-speaker's pronunciation of *croissant*);

(ii) amelioration (*cniht* 'boy', 'attendant', 'servant' > *knight*);

(iii) analogical extension (*bec* > *books*);

(iv) analogical levelling (the [w] in the pronunciation of *swore* – contrast *sword*);

(v) assimilation (Latin *septem* > Italian *sette*);

(vi) backformation (the verb *laze*, from *lazy*);

(vii) bleaching (*had* 'state, quality' > *-hood*);

(viii) borrowing (French *canif* < *knife*);

(ix) contamination (the initial [f] in *four* – cf. *five*);

(x) decreolisation (Jamaican Creole > English);

(xi) dissimilation (Latin *peregrinum* > Old French *pelerin*);

(xii) epenthesis (Latin *schola* > Old French *escole*);

(xiii) exaptation (the development of a new rationale for, and distribution of, the *-e* ending of Afrikaans adjectives following the loss of the gender system);

(xiv) language murder (what has happened to Hungarian in Austria);

(xv) loan translation *(skyscraper* > French *gratte-ciel)*;

(xvi) metathesis *(acsian* > *ask)*;

29

(xvii)   metonymy (*jersey* < *Jersey*);
(xviii)   pejoration (*sely* 'blessed' > *silly*);
(xix)   recreolisation (English > Jamaican Creole among young blacks in contemporary London);
(xx)   semantic extension (Latin *panarium* 'bread-basket' > French *panier* 'basket');
(xxi)   semantic restriction (English *voyage* < French *voyage* 'journey');
(xxii)   suppletion (the establishment of Italian *peggiore* 'worse' as the comparative of *cattivo* 'bad');
(xxiii)   word formation (*chocoholic* < *alcoholic*);
(xxiv)   word order change (SOV > SVO – e.g. Latin > French).

There are a number of lines along which one might attempt to bring something more satisfying than alphabetical order into this collection of disparate phenomena. Large-scale changes (e.g. SOV > SVO) could be distinguished from small-scale changes (e.g. *schola* > *escole*), internal changes (e.g. analogical levelling) from external changes (e.g. language murder), and so on. But it seems *prima facie* unlikely that any one explanatory framework could accommodate the whole range of processes listed: whatever the common factor might be in terms of which they all come to be treated together, it must be forbiddingly vague and general. So the *a priori* subordination of diachrony as an object of theoretical inquiry joins forces with the hopelessly catholic interpretation of what falls within its scope to make it doubtful whether *understanding* language change, as opposed to merely itemising and contemplating its multifariousness, was ever really on the agenda.

The language myth is implicated in this state of affairs in a number of different ways. One, perhaps superficial, way has to do with the development of institutionalised linguistics in the twentieth century. There is no doubt that diachronic studies have been adversely influenced by the particular form in which the language myth came to be entrenched as the basis for a science of language. Any linguistics founded on the telementational theory of communication and the concomitant idea of a language as a system of invariant signs enabling telementation to take place poses obvious problems for an inquiry whose object of study is constituted by the fact, or alleged fact, that linguistic signs change through time. But on the face of it the problems seem no graver than those posed for the synchronist by the fact, or alleged fact, of linguistic change. Saussure's achievement

The Language Myth and Historical Linguistics

is not just that he turned the language myth into a linguistic theory, but that he did so in a way that outflanked, and theoretically subordinated, the diachronist. His insistence that linguistic units could only be *identified* in terms of their role in the structure of an idiosynchronic *état de langue*, and that because this holistic system was the primary 'psychological reality' of language-use its study had 'priority' over diachronic investigation, confronted historical linguists with a challenge they were unable to meet. For the long-range comparative and reconstructive studies that largely constituted the historical linguistics of Saussure's day operate with no very specific concept of a language. Saussure, in contrast, claims to be telling us what a language essentially *is*. (That is why his technical term for the idiosynchronic language-state is *langue*, which is after all no more than the ordinary French word for 'a language'.) The fact that the language myth yields an account of what a language essentially is, and that historical linguists have failed to tell a countervailing story giving pride of theoretical place to the 'fact' of linguistic change through time, is one reason why historical linguistics, as commonly treated today as a topic on the syllabus of university courses, languishes in an atheoretical limbo.

Why have historical linguists failed to tell such a story? Part of the answer is that, despite Saussure's strict separation of synchrony from diachrony, the concept of a 'linguistic change' is itself crucially dependent on the language myth.

As a glance at McMahon's examples shows, the general formula 'A > B' or 'B < A' seems to cover a multitude of different things. If there is some sense in which, for instance, *sely > silly* (xviii) means that *sely* 'becomes' *silly*, it seems rather different from the sense in which *bec* 'becomes' *books* (iii), and different again from whatever might be meant by saying that *skyscraper* 'becomes' *gratte-ciel* (xv). Of particular interest for present purposes are cases where the item on the right of the arrow might be held to be an 'internal' historical transformation of the item on the left, as in (ii), (v), (vii), (xi), (xii), (xvi), (xviii) and (xx).

Let us take the case of *sely > silly*. On the face of it we have on the left a certain form with a certain meaning and on the right a different form with a different meaning. To say that one has 'changed into' the other is to imply that despite these differences there is something that has endured and retained its identity through time. But what does this diachronic identity consist in? It seems like the knife that has had both a new blade and a new handle. In what sense is it the same knife? It might certainly be the same knife in the eyes of someone who has owned it throughout its history, and can therefore explain in what sense it remains the same. But it is hard to see that anything comparable can be said in the linguistic case: given the span of time involved, there are no English-speakers for whom *sely* > *silly* embodies a fact to which they can testify from their own linguistic experience. So what is the basis for the etymologist's recognition of a diachronic identity here? The only conceivable answer is the one Saussure would have given. It involves postulating an unbroken chain of communicative acts, such that each link in the chain is forged by the idea that what has been transmitted and received is the same linguistic sign. If we compare the two ends of the chain we find that faulty transmission and reception (the vagaries of *parole*) have changed both form and meaning, but at no identifiable point was there a discontinuity in the process of transferring the sign from one mind to another. If there had been, it is hard to see what sense it would make to connect the two.

Both aspects of the language myth (the telementational theory of communication and the fixed-code conception of a language) are involved here. The telementational theory is what makes postulating such a process of continuous transmission plausible at all. And the telementational theory crucially relies on the idea of linguistic signs as entities with a continuous existence through time. If the time-span is short enough there will be no discernible differences (at the level of generality on which descriptive linguistics operates) between two instantiations of the same sign by members of the same speech-community. If the time-span is longer, differences may show up. But the fact is that the notion of the linguistic sign as an abstract invariant, which is crucial to the idea of a describable *synchronic* language-state, is in itself a *diachronic* notion, in as much as the sign is held to remain constant across temporally different occasions of use. And the paradox of linguistic 'changes' of the kind under discussion is (a) that it is only if the sign in some sense remains constant through time that it is possible to identify *what* it is that has changed, while (b) if the sign really has changed, that is precisely what calls in question the diachronic continuity that the etymologist seeks to establish.

What are the prospects, in general terms, for a historical linguistics that breaks with the language myth?

The whole idea that languages undergo continuous historical evolution – i.e. the whole subject matter of historical linguistics – is con-

The Language Myth and Historical Linguistics

stituted by the proposition that utterances instantiate entities that persist through time. So it is important to insist at the outset that this is not an objective fact. Understanding what you say may involve recognising relevant similarities between your utterances and certain other utterances (which does not rule out the possibility that part of your utterance may be an innovation of some kind), and getting you to understand what I say may often involve conducting myself linguistically so as to maximise the likelihood that you will recognise relevant similarities between my utterances and certain others. But there are indefinitely many dimensions in which utterances may be similar to one another, and which of them are in play in given circumstances will depend on the context. What if I say [təmɑːtou] and you say [təmeirou]? The senses in which [təmeirou] and [təmɑːtou] are similar exist alongside a sense in which they are obviously different. But so long as the communicational context is one in which what matters is the similarity, the difference may be unimportant. On the other hand, if you spring [təmeirou] on me out of the blue I may not have a clue what you are talking about. Conversely, if the context is sufficiently helpful it may not matter if, as a Frenchman whose English fails him at the crucial point, you say [tɔmat]. And if you say *books* instead of *bec*, the relevant similarities will be with (i) the singular *book* and (ii) other plurals in -*s*.

Qua first-order language-user, I am not ineluctably obliged to entertain the notion that certain utterances are utterances of some mysterious but nonetheless identifiable entity that endures through time. To interpret recognising that two things are similar as a matter of recognising one thing of which both are instances is just that – an interpretation. And it is this interpretation, and the fact that it *is* an interpretation, that opens up the conceptual gap between 'short-term individual behaviour' and 'long-term linguistic evolution' which Lass seeks to close by establishing his 'clear and intelligible nexus'. For short-term linguistic behaviour is not simply and uncontroversially a matter of instantiating the items – sounds, forms, words, constructions, languages – which are held to undergo long-term evolution. The latter are not first-order phenomenal realities but products of metalinguistic processes whose connection with anything that might be involved in short-term linguistic behaviour needs to be elucidated.

There are two questions that have to be addressed. When I say '[təmɑːtou]' I am not *eo ipso* doing anything but saying '[təmɑːtou]' So the first question is why we should be inclined to suppose that

33

there is *anything* more abstract that my utterance is an utterance of. And the second question is why, granted that we are so inclined, one particular dimension of abstraction should be especially salient: i.e. the dimension that makes it 'obvious' that when I say '[təmɑ:tou]' I am uttering the English word *tomato*. For on the face of it, the abstraction in question might merely be the British version of the word *tomato* (which has an American variant). Or it might be an abstraction embracing the English word *tomato* plus etymologically related forms *tomate, Tomate, tamatie, tomaat* etc. in other European languages, as in '*tomato* is pronounced [tɔmat] in French'. Or many other things besides.

One of the fundamental factors here is that we are inclined to think of our utterances, like everything else in our environment, as things we can talk about. Talking about utterances involves identifying them. And there is no way of identifying them other than by (what amounts to) *repeating* them. To repeat an utterance is not, in itself, to identify it: repetition will serve the specifically metalinguistic purpose at issue here in so far as it is held to locate what I said in terms of a system of abstractions, as opposed to (or in addition to) constituting just another utterance. The metalinguistic purpose is especially obvious when the 'repetition' is supposed to identify what I *would* say, as when an English-learning foreigner points to certain plants in my garden and says 'what do you call *them*?' My answer 'tomatoes' is obviously metalinguistic in so far as I am trying, and intend to be taken as trying, to pin down an entity that exists over and above its particular manifestations in utterances and which is permanently available for use on appropriate occasions.

The point of all this is that a language, as a set of entities that endure through time, is an inherently metalinguistic construct. That is to say, it is the product of a concerted process of confabulation whose basis is the reflexivity of language and the use of writing as an analogue of speech, and whose purpose is to establish, or to seek to establish, a set of abstractions to which utterances can be referred and in terms of which they can be identified. To mistake a language, *qua* codified system of abstractions, for a first-order reality is the essence of the language myth.

In cultures such as ours a set of abstractions is codified in writing and subjected to elaborate descriptive analysis. Knowing English may involve not just knowing that English contains a word *tomato*, but also that it is a noun, that it can be both a mass noun and a count noun, that if the latter it forms a plural *tomatoes*, that it has cognates of similar form in many other European languages, that its final -*o* is a specifically English development, that it refers to the plant *Solanum lycopersicum* and especially to its fruit .... One problem for those who believe that speaking English is a matter of implementing this codification is to establish what, for such purposes, it consists in. The codification itself appears to form a seamless unity with descriptive facts about it. Which, if any, of the above facts relating to *tomato* and tomatoes are in play as far as first-order use of English is concerned?

To conclude that that is a false question is not to deny either (i) that these are facts or (ii) that all or some of them are known to many English-users. What makes it a false question is that *none* of them *need* be known to any *particular* English-user, that there is therefore no determinate subset of them that necessarily enters into first-order English-use, and that to suppose otherwise is to draw the line between the linguistic and the metalinguistic in the wrong place.

But if that is a false question, then *a fortiori* still more false is the question what it is for first-order language-use to *change* the codification. If a language itself is a metalinguistic construct then a change in a language is a metalinguistic event, or perhaps a metametalinguistic event. It is, in general, a reformulation of the code to take account of perceived discrepancies between what the code lays down and the system of abstractions that *might be held* to underlie actual linguistic practice. Very broadly speaking, as far as 'internal' historical changes are concerned, discrepancies arise via (i) linguistic creativity; (ii) language-users' laxity and conservation of effort.

The language myth asserts that linguistic signs are context-neutral invariants. On the contrary, the pragmatic exigencies of particular utterance situations, far from being disregardable, are all-important in determining what kind or degree of similarity is required between the instant utterance and other actual or potential utterances in order for it to play the required role in a particular communicational event. Furthermore, no two utterances are ever physically identical, and the meanings to be attached to them are not fixed in advance, but emerge in the course of communicational interaction between individuals no two of whom have identical linguistic experience. Therefore, even if there arises from communicational interaction the idea of a set of context-neutral invariants, language-use is not, and cannot be, a matter of implementing that set. Small wonder if ideas as to the abstract norms underlying utterances vary from individual to individual and are in a constant state of flux.

But small wonder too if, over speech-communities as a whole, the flux appears to have a certain direction. The goal of language-users is simply to communicate effectively, where effectiveness is measured against the particular demands of the particular situation. And many or most situations are quite undemanding linguistically, as regards the attention they require participants to pay to what is said, how it is said, and what exactly they mean and understand by it. Corners are cut; much of verbal behaviour becomes routinised, just as many of the situations in which that behaviour takes place become routinised; and eventually the code may be deemed to require amendment to take account of such processes as those identified by the language historian as phonological attrition, morphologisation, grammatical reanalysis, semantic bleaching.

Because amending the code is a public act, politics enters largely into the process. Some would-be 'changes' spend an indefinite period stigmatised as errors or solecisms. In other cases the power and prestige of the speakers involved require that the change be acknowledged as such, even if, as far as the speech-community as a whole is concerned, it is only partial. For instance, with respect to English as a whole, there has been no change as regards the presence of *r* in syllable codas (i.e. non-prevocalically). But it is not politically possible to treat non-rhotic speakers as deviant, so non-rhoticity is acknowledged as a norm for the speakers concerned. (This is done by setting up a separate language or variety whose norm it becomes – e.g. in this case, Southern British English.) Decisions of this kind may even be enshrined in spelling (e.g. Dutch *lucht* 'air', *post* 'post' *vs* Afrikaans *lug*, *pos*, where Afrikaans orthography 'normalises' a cluster reduction that regularly occurs in the Dutch forms too).

Finally, it may be worth emphasising that the conceptual incoherence of locating linguistic changes in the activities of the individual *qua* first-order language-user does not mean that the individual *qua* participant in a language-myth-imbued culture does not have a role to play. By way of trying to say something about that role I shall conclude with an account of my personal relationship with a linguistic change in English.

In recent years I have become aware that the plastic or plastic-encased device attached to a computer and used for moving items around on the screen is known as a 'mouse'. I do not know why it is so called. Various possibilities present themselves. Perhaps, given the

The Language Myth and Historical Linguistics

ubiquity of such word-formation processes in the computing context, it is an acronym or some similar formation (cf. *modem*). Perhaps, less plausibly, it is an adaptation of a Latvian word meaning 'pointer'. Perhaps it is a figurative extension of the word *mouse* (call it *mouse*₁) referring to a small rodent of the genus *Mus*. So, granted the admission to the English lexicon of the word for the device in question, what I am in doubt about is whether I am confronted with a new lexical item homonymous with an existing one, or an old lexical item that has undergone a semantic complication. That is to say, I am in this respect ignorant of the structural analysis of the vocabulary of English. Put more simply, I do not know, *pro tanto*, what the words of my language *are*. And my ignorance on this point is not like my ignorance of the many arcane or abstruse or obsolete words to be found in any large dictionary that I happen never to have encountered or used. On the contrary, from the operational point of view both *mouse*₁ and *mouse*₂ are perfectly familiar to me.

Matters are complicated by the fact that there seems to be doubt, and not just in my own mind, what the plural form of *mouse*₂ might be. The evidence I have on this question is equivocal. On the one hand, a display case in a Cape Town computer shop containing a quantity of the items in question is labelled MOUSES. And, when cunningly trapped into referring to them in the plural, my twelve-year-old son, who owns a number of the things, uttered (after hesitation) that same form. On the other hand, a computer manual in his possession insists that the correct form is *mice*.

But not only is the evidence equivocal in itself, its interpretation is far from straightforward. The English of public signs in Cape Town is unreliable, often being composed by persons for whom English is their second or third language. So MOUSES in the computer shop could be a simple mistake. My son, although a competent English-speaker for his age, is a somewhat shaky informant when it comes to morphological irregularities (he still has an overgeneralised past tense form *costed* for *cost* in the intransitive sense). On the other hand, I am fairly sure that *mice* would be his word for what he might find a nest of behind the skirting-board. And the computer manual's insistence on *mice* could either be (i) a simple statement of the 'fact' (wherever that might be alleged to have come from), or (ii) – given that it is no part of the author's brief to advise at random on points of English grammar – a prescriptivist's defensive recognition that he is fighting a lost cause, or (iii) – in keeping with the overall tone of the book – a joke (cf. referring to a family whose surname is Foot as 'the Feet').

In any case, even if it could be unequivocally established whether the plural of *mouse*$_2$ 'is' *mice* or *mouses*, that would not suffice to settle the point at issue. If *mouse*$_2$ has no connection with *mouse*$_1$, that would make a plural *mice* unlikely. But even if *mouse*$_2$ is *mouse*$_1$ lexematically, I would not necessarily expect its plural to be *mice*, any more than I expect the plural of *goose* 'tailor's smoothing-iron' to be *geese*. For the fact is that morphological anomalies frequently demonstrate their status as fossils by failing to carry over to figuratively extended senses of words.

None of this is to say that I have no ideas of my own as to the relation of *mouse*$_2$ to *mouse*$_1$. I am indeed inclined to think of *mouse*$_2$ as involving a semantic extension of *mouse*$_1$. But why I am so inclined is a difficult question. The English figures of speech involving mice that I am familiar with tend to turn on such notions as small size, timidity, frugality, meagreness. None of these seems compellingly relevant in this context. Could it be the shape? To me, a computer mouse looks more like a bar of soap than any other common object, but then, I am not coining the word but merely trying to decide how I shall apprehend it.

I have reason to believe that I am not alone in associating it with *mouse*$_1$. On my secretary's desk there is a pad providing a surface on which to manipulate her computer mouse which bears the legend 'ceci n'est pas un mousemat' together with a drawing of a mouse$_1$ sitting on a mat. The allusion to Magritte (reinforced by the style of the lettering) is equivocal: one possible interpretation is that the mousemat-designer is *denying* any connection between *mouse*$_1$ and *mouse*$_2$. But at any rate, the mousemat is at least evidence that somebody else has perceived the *possibility* of such a connection. In the end, however, whether the designer is denying a connection, commenting on a connection that he or she takes to be already established, or contributing to the creation of a connection, I do not know.

In fact I do not 'know', in the sense of having obtained reliable objective information on the matter, *anything* about this usage. Nor, I suspect, do the vast majority of English-speakers for whom *mouse*$_2$ is part of the common currency of their everyday talk. Nor do I know whether my interpretation agrees with theirs, any more than they know whether theirs agrees with mine. But this general ignorance, and the consequent indeterminacy in the structure of the

English lexicon, is no bar whatsoever to successful use of *mouse*$_2$ in countless acts of communication, which simply do not require answers, let alone authoritative or definitive answers, to the questions at issue.

But perhaps the most interesting point here is that I stand ready to present what is no more than my own private understanding of *mouse*$_2$ to any inquirer (e.g. a child or a foreign learner of English) as if it were a matter of established fact. A computer mouse, I shall firmly state, is so called because its shape is reminiscent of the rodent's. And this is not or not merely because I happen to suffer from a hypertrophied didacticism that leads me to make up answers to questions sooner than admit ignorance. It is because the answers to such questions are *created* by language-users' private understandings. There is ultimately nowhere else for them to come from.

Of course, given that *mouse*$_2$ is a recent coinage, it would no doubt be fairly easy to find out who first used it and thus establish what some might see as 'authoritative', perhaps even 'definitive', answers to the questions at issue. For all I know, lexicographers have already done so, and whether *mouse*$_2$ should be a separate dictionary lemma from *mouse*$_1$, and what its plural is, may have already been decided on that basis. But I for one have no intention of hastening to find a dictionary willing to pronounce on these issues, and still less to consider myself 'refuted' if, for instance, *mouse*$_2$ turns out to be an acronym after all. The originator's views on the matter have no more privilege than language-users are prepared to give them. In any case, in so far as the originator's intentions are recoverable, what that shows is that *mouse*$_2$ is a special case. But there is nothing special about my general approach to deciding how I shall understand it – i.e. deciding what it *is*. It is an approach that leads me to create a private codification of the relevant part of my language that stands a chance of influencing the public codification whether or not it turns out to conform to it. And *mutatis mutandis* what goes for *mouse* goes for every other unit that allegedly makes up my language.

References

Bloomfield, L. (1935) *Language*, London: Allen Unwin.
Bynon, T. (1997) *Historical Linguistics*, Cambridge: Cambridge University Press.

Keller, R. (1994) *On Language Change: The Invisible Hand in Language* (tr. B. Nerlich), London: Routledge.

Labov, W. (1994) *Principles of Linguistic Change, Vol. 1*, Oxford, Blackwell.

Lass, R. (1997) *Historical Linguistics and Language Change*, Cambridge: Cambridge University Press.

Lehmann, W.P. (1962) *Historical Linguistics: An Introduction*, New York: Holt Rinehart & Winston.

McMahon, A.M.S. (1994) *Understanding Language Change*, Cambridge: Cambridge University Press.

Milroy, J. (1992) *Linguistic Variation and Change: On the Historical Sociolinguistics of English*, Oxford: Blackwell.

3 The Language Myth and Standard English

Hayley G. Davis

In 1997, John Honey, former Dean of Teacher Education at De Montfort University, yet again waged war with linguists over the teaching of standard English in schools (*The Guardian* 9/8/97; *The Independent* 24/8/97). This recent controversy arose out of the publication of his book *Language is Power: The Story of Standard English and its Enemies*, and occurred fourteen years after a similar debate was published in *The Guardian* (February/March 1983).

The original 1980s debate appeared to revolve around the question whether standard English should be taught in schools or whether school children should be allowed to express themselves in local speech forms. Honey's more recent proposal is for a National Language Authority on the lines of the French Academy: 'what the English language needs is a form of authority that can easily be appealed to for guidance as to the uses which are acceptable compared with those which are not – an authority based not on an individual's likes and dislikes but on the genuine consensus of educated opinion' (Honey 1997: 163). Whether there can ever be a genuine consensus of educated opinion is something I'll discuss later in this paper.

However, both debates between Honey and the linguists, although appearing to focus on different issues, are alike in their conflation of a number of different uses and understandings of 'standard English'. In the first place, standard English is nothing like standard French, the latter being spoken by no-one. Second, in France, it is only the Ministry of Education and the National Assembly, that have any legal power to enforce linguistic prescriptions. But in practice such bodies do not lay down any 'linguistic rules' because such 'rules', being totally unenforceable, would be ignored by everyone.

Part of the problem with the present idea of standard English is that it is often unclear whether linguists are referring to a spoken linguistic reality, a written variety of English, or an idealisation, as evidenced in the following quotations.

> In order to be able to participate confidently in public, cultural and working life, pupils need to be able to speak, write and read Standard English fluently and accurately (DfEE 95, pp. 2–3).

> There is little doubt that standard written English should be taught in schools and that curriculum documents are right to stress its importance. Standard English consists of a set of forms which are used with only minimal variation in written English and in a range of formal spoken contexts around the world (Carter 1999: 163).

> From an educational point of view, the position of Standard English as the dialect of English used in writing is unassailable … As far as spoken Standard English is concerned, we could conclude that the teaching of Standard English to speakers of other dialects may be commendable – as most would in theory agree, if for no other reason than the discrimination which is currently exercised against non-standard dialect speakers in most English-speaking societies – and may also be possible – which I am inclined, for sociolinguistic reasons (see Trudgill 1975) to doubt [sic] (Trudgill 1999: 127).

> In theory, at least, standard English can be spoken in any accent of English though in practice it is seldom (indeed perhaps never) spoken in the broadest forms of regional accent (Honey 1997: 3).

Carter and Honey seem of the opinion that standard English is both a written and a spoken variety of English, whereas Fromkin and Rodman below claim Standard American English is neither, since it is only an 'ideal' variety (whatever that implies).

> SAE is an idealisation. Nobody speaks this dialect: and if somebody did, we would not know it, because SAE is not defined precisely. Several years ago there was an entire conference devoted to one subject: a precise definition of SAE. This meeting did not succeed in satisfying everyone as to what SAE

should be. It used to be the case that the language used by national broadcasters represented SAE, but today many of these people speak a regional dialect, or themselves 'violate' the English preferred by the purists (Fromkin and Rodman 1993: 284).

With this definition, another complication emerges: standard English has at least two standards – standard British English and standard American English. Some even go as far as to state that within the United States, 'every region supports its own standard; none is the locus (or source) of *the* standard' (Hartley and Preston 1999: 207). As Julia Falk writes

> In the United States there is no one regional dialect that serves as the model. What is considered standard English in New York City would not be considered standard in Forth Worth, Texas. Each region of the country has its own standard (ibid).

The mockery this makes of the idea of a standard language should be obvious. In addition, the use of the word 'standard' here is unlike its use by such educationalists as John Honey. Honey is obviously using it to refer to some level of excellence in speech that all should aspire to, whereas Falk and other such sociolinguists use it to refer to uniformity of language.

Two of my postgraduate students, former teachers, pointed out the discrepancy between the Department for Education and Employment (DfEE)'s definition of standard English and its aims as published in its Glossary of Terms included in the National Literacy Strategy, and Trudgill's definition in his chapter 'Standard English: What It Isn't'. The DfEE writes that standard English is

> The language of public communication, distinguished from other forms of English by its vocabulary, and by rules and conventions of grammar, spelling and punctuation. Contrasts with dialect, or archaic forms or those pertaining to other forms of English, such as American/Australian English. To communicate effectively in a range of situations – written and oral – language users need access to standard English as well as their own dialect, and other varieties, so they can select the most appropriate register.

It thus emphasises spelling and punctuation as the defining features of standard English. Trudgill, however, says that his model of standard English in school has 'nothing whatsoever to do with spelling or punctuation' (Trudgill 1999: 127). And whereas the DfEE refers to the role of standard English in selecting the most appropriate register, Trudgill makes the claim that 'one can certainly acquire and use technical registers without using Standard English, just as one can employ non-technical registers while speaking or writing Standard English' (Trudgill 1999: 122). Moreover, unlike the DfEE, Trudgill opposes the idea that standard English is synonymous with formal styles to be used in formal contexts. And neither, for him, are standard English speakers denied the use of slang and swearwords. Finally, in all the accounts given, there is a lack of consensus as to how to spell 'standard English' – i.e. which words, if any, should be capitalized. All this confusion has been largely occasioned by The Language Myth in Western Culture.

Identified by Harris in 1981, 'the language myth in its modern form is a cultural product of post-Renaissance Europe. It reflects the political psychology of nationalism, and an educational system devoted to standardising the linguistic behaviour of pupils' (Harris 1981: 9). This cultural process culminated in such events as the compilation of the Oxford English Dictionary, which had the effect of creating a finite, standardized list of the vocabulary of the literate. However, the first editor of the OED continually rejected the task of standardizing the language. He wrote 'It is a mistake to suppose that there is a 'correct' spelling of every word' ... Instead 'there are hundreds of words of which one spelling is historically as good as another, or which have had two forms from the beginning' (Mugglestone 2000: 191). Likewise Alexander Ellis, an advisor to the OED on pronunciation matters amongst other things wrote 'it might be as well to explain that every quotation you give is *a testimony to the use of the word in such a sense* or *your* authority for saying it is used, and not generally an authority or permission for people to use it in that way' (Mugglestone 2000: 192).

However, what encouraged the general reading public to believe in the existence of a standard language was the 'institutionalization' of the fixed code theory of communication originally inherited from Aristotle and passed on through the modistic grammarians, Locke and Saussure. This was further bolstered by the printing and dissemination of the OED. This fixed code theory is now seen to be commonsensical and an accurate description of the way 'language works'. One of the assumptions underlying this view of communication is that 'speech is a form of telementation, a means of conveying thoughts from one person's mind to another' and that 'every effective form of communication requires a fixed code' (Harris 1998: 32).

The first part of this communication theory, telementation, can be illustrated with some words, reminiscent of Saussure's description of the speech circuit, of a contemporary linguist:

> Something in Harry's brain that we might as well call a 'thought' results in movements of his vocal tract (lungs, vocal cords, tongue, jaw and lips), which in turn create a sound wave that is transmitted through the air. This sound wave, striking Sam's ear, results in Sam's having the same 'thought' (or a similar one) in his brain (Jackendoff 1993: 3).

The fixed code theory can also be illustrated by this extract from Jackendoff:

> In order for us to speak and understand novel sentences, we have to store in our heads not just the words of our language but also the patterns of sentences possible in our language. These patterns in turn, describe not just patterns of *words* but also patterns of *patterns*. Linguists refer to these patterns as the *rules* of language stored in memory; they refer to the complete collection of rules as the *mental grammar* of the language or *grammar* for short (Jackendoff 1993: 14).

The rules have to be fixed under this model in order for both sets of interlocutors to arrive at the 'same' interpretation of the utterance. It would be a sorry state of affairs if Jackendoff's Sam regularly couldn't distinguish between such verb phrases as 'running up' in 'Harry was running up a bill' and 'Harry was running up a hill'.

The model of communication I've just depicted is derived from attempting to place common-sense views of language on a scientific footing. As Taylor writes

> It is precisely because of its mundane appearance that code theory is such a powerful form of intellectual discourse. It implies, in effect, that what the layman has been saying all along does in fact have a technical (or 'scientific' in the *lay*

sense of that term) justification ... code theory shows that ... [our everyday metadiscourse] corresponds to *the way things really are*: that is to the truth (Taylor 1992: 71).

But these so-called 'common sense' views do not conform to the 'way things are'. In fact if we suppose that communication is essentially a matter of transporting thoughts from one person's mind to another's by means of verbal utterances, we are left with the impossible task of identifying a successful, or even unsuccessful, episode of communication. How do we know what the thoughts are behind 'are you doing anything tonight?' Code theory assumes that there must be 'some private unobservably successful criteria ... which account for what is observably successful communication' (Taylor 1981: 271). But it is unclear how we would be able to tell if we had been successful communicators or not if the criteria for successful communication were private and unobservable. This hypothesis actually contradicts our communicational experiences: it is not difficult to tell when and whether our and others' utterances have been successful or not. And even when we can pinpoint the cause of our successful or unsuccessful interactions by referring to a certain word or words ('I said *maybe* not *baby'*), this still does not underwrite the thesis that linguistic signs are fixed and determinate. The ability to talk about a certain word or even to say that this word is the same as that word, is a highly sophisticated ability facilitated by the availability of writing, printing and *standardization*. However, as I will be demonstrating, any form of standardization is always provisional.

The metalinguistic game of abstracting any utterance in order to subject it to any form of analysis is a highly sophisticated one relying on an arbitrary division between verbal and analytic description. Even with a simple utterance like 'shall I open a bottle of wine?' said by Sam to Pam, Pam could analyse it as meaning 'Sam's changed the subject', 'he's making up with me', 'he's trying to get me drunk', 'he's feeling better now' ... In fact, lay speakers frequently do ask metalinguistic questions 'what does metalinguistic mean' and make metalinguistic comments 'there's no such word as integrationism'. But herein lies the difference: it is the lay speakers who are making reasonable, purposeful comments and asking the sensible questions, while segregational linguists are just theorizing about material (language) which started off as, and remains, an individual act of interpretation. It is only when metalinguistic language games are taken as constants for the purposes of theorizing about a language that they lend support to the view that standard English is, in some sense, a reality.

The authority of the dictionary in addition reinforces the view that words have fixed forms and fixed meanings. The dictionary is usually the first court of appeal regarding our linguistic practices – whether it be for composing a formal letter, checking the spelling in an examination script, finding an equivalent word in French or deciding whether or not the President of the United States committed 'perjury' when he claimed that he'd 'never had sexual relations with that woman'. But since different individuals and even the same individual, will have and have had different experiences, and since, in their uses of words they will be attempting to integrate such experiences to achieve a particular goal at a particular time in a particular context, there is no question of any of the words or phrases they use being invariant linguistic units. Any question as to what a particular word is will therefore presuppose certain cultural practices, but the answer will depend on the language game into which the question is integrated.

The results of Clinton's impeachment trial clearly demonstrate the possibility of arriving at word meanings which appear to run contrary to those as set out in a standardised form. Although Clinton had recourse to a dictionary, he decided to opt for his own definitions of 'sexual affair' and 'sexual relationship'. Although Clinton admitted to engaging in a variety of sexual activities which resulted in ejaculation on more than one occasion, he still managed to deny he had had a sexual relation with Lewinsky. This shows (and a good thing too!) that what a sexual relationship is cannot be decided by a purely linguistic analysis of the phrase 'sexual relationship'. This argument also applies to the term 'standard English'. It is individuals who are in control of their language and are free to justify their use of one word over another and to freely define, in context, words as they see fit. None of this is a denial that we can recognise the 'same word' or the 'same phrase': however, the similarity is only provisional and arbitrary, occasioned by such cultural practices as writing and printing.

An integrational approach is thus in opposition to the segregational approach that has dominated the field of twentieth-century linguistics. A segregrational approach does not take into account an overview of the various criteria which we would customarily bring to bear showing that we have understood another's request, command, statement etc. From an integrationist perspective linguistics is accordingly seen as essentially lay-oriented.

In the late 1980s, I conducted an empirical survey, part of which involved the use of what Trudgill and Honey and co. would call non-standard language. I questioned 21 informants on a number of sentences and phrases, asking them how the underlined words were used. The sentences and phrases involved included *we was only playing, he aint a pig,* and *my husband and me.* Not one of my informants used the phrase 'standard' or 'non-standard', not even the two who were linguists. The 24-year-old linguist, let's call him Wayne, of doctoral status, said that the first two sentences *we was only playing* and *he aint a pig* were 'ungrammatical' and spoken by the 'uneducated'. He also thought that *we was* was 'wrong'. The other 50-year-old linguist, whom I'll call David said, regarding the word *aint,* that 'people from the upper classes don't use it ... they may have done in the past but they don't now'. And when discussing the sentence *we was only playing* David said that the sentence was 'a grammatical error'. When I asked him whether he thought it incorrect, he added 'I don't use those terms – correct incorrect you know', the reason being that 'as a linguist I'm not er – I can't use er I'm not allowed to use that sort of statement as I never do'. Wayne, on the other hand, thought that *my husband and me* was 'wrong, uneducated people say it'. However, Neville, a doctoral student of History, thought that *aint* was a form used by 'perfectly educated people' but *we was only playing* was 'ungrammatical'. He also considered *my husband and me* to be 'ugly and it's normally wrong em – unless of course it's used in the accusative er – if you said Hayley came to visit my husband and me then it would be absolutely correct because me is the object of the visit em – nine times out of ten if people say my husband and me they mean my husband and I'. I did not think it worth asking Neville how someone could mean 'my husband and I' while saying 'my husband and me' and vice versa. But Arnold, a doctoral student of Classics, said 'they actually mean the same thing but that em – the latter sentence regarded by – er certain people as being – er – grammatically and more conventionally correct – though I don't agree – I think that they mean the same thing'.

Thus which forms are stigmatised is a debatable matter, and the stigmatising is done on different bases: there is no one person or text that can tell Wayne, Neville, Arnold or David what standard English actually is.

A common answer given to me by my students is that standard English is what is taught to students learning English as a Foreign Language. But it is unclear whose English is being referred to here. Is it Wayne's, Neville's Arnold's or David's? After all, all are educated speakers and all have presumably written readable texts. And what is to stop them all from changing their opinion from one day to the next? All came up with perfectly justifiable reasons for their preferring one word over another, whether it be appealing to the sound, the part of speech or the type of speaker who would presumably use such an expression.

Another objection to my insistence upon the mythical status of standard English given to me by my students is that standardization assists in reading, and therefore comprehension. It is very difficult to convince such students, and presumably John Honey, that before Samuel Johnson, there was no standard spelling in the sense that a standardized spelling exists today. Indeed, Johnson wrote in his *Dictionary of the English Language* 'In adjusting the ORTHOGRAPHY, which has been to this time unsettled and fortuitous, I found it necessary to distinguish those irregularities that are inherent in our tongue, and perhaps coeval with it, from others which the ignorance or negligence of later writers has produced' ([1755] 1984: 308). I am sure that all of us encounter nonstandard spelling every time we set foot in our local Indian restaurant. In the Brockley Balti House you can order a Chicken *Sushlick* with *Pillau* Rice whereas in the Babu Saheeb we can eat *Pilao* and a Chicken *Sashlick*, the Two Sisters Tandoori offers punters a Chicken *Shashlick* and a *Pillaw* Rice, whereas the Babur offers a Chicken *Shaslick* with a *Pillao* Rice. The Collins English Dictionary of 1984, however, lists under the variant spellings of *Pilau* only one of these spellings – *Pillaw*. It mentions, however, another three not mentioned in any of the menus from the local restaurants put through my letterbox last month – *pillaf*, *pillaff* and *pilao*.

Even if some linguistic body attempted to claim that standardizing all linguistic forms, even transliterated forms, would be beneficial to teaching, speaking and learning English (something Honey may wish to see as part of his argument in *Language is Power*), this could still not happen in practice. In addition, it could even have counter-productive results. Cameron (2000) cites examples from communication training practices in certain companies whereby staff are trained to use 'standard formulas, and, at the extreme, to perform to a uniform script' (Cameron 2000: 16). Communication training is 'intended to eradicate, or at least reduce, the variation people exhibit in their ways of interacting, and to bring the communicational behaviour of individuals into conformity with norms defined by the organisation' (ibid.: 17). This is supposedly to help the staff to use spoken language 'better'. But as Cameron points out, it is impossible to create a 'standard discourse'. One can only introduce standard formulaic expressions, on a par with the American greeting 'have a nice day now'. 'Standardizing performance to make it uniform, then, is a goal of some prescriptive guidance on communication, but it is a fairly marginal one with limited localised effects'. (ibid.: 49). Moreover, these formulaic expressions often had a counter-productive effect. Citing a survey conducted in Safeways supermarket chain in America, where staff are trained to make suggestions about other possible purchases that could go with the items being purchased, it was noted that 'although the gambits themselves were perfectly straightforward, some customers appeared to have great difficulty framing a response to them, because they could not fathom the checkout operator's underlying intentions' (ibid.: 75). And thus Cameron concludes that 'Attempts to prescribe 'standard' ways of performing particular communicative tasks typically take no account of the fact that spoken discourse exhibits a high degree of contextually conditioned variation, which is functional for communication rather than presenting some sort of obstacle to it' (ibid.: 71). Cameron, following Milroy, claims that although standardization, in the sense of 'uniform performance' is always an ideal rather than an achieved reality and does not succeed in changing people's linguistic behaviour, it nevertheless can succeed in altering people's attitudes. However, as my empirical work has shown, people's attitudes are not affected in the same way. Furthermore, as Barbara Johnstone has shown in *The Linguistic Individual* (1996), speakers, even when explicitly trained to follow a script, generally have a desire to express their individuality. Johnstone refers to public-opinion surveys conducted over the telephone.

Here, respondents are often given multiple-choice questions and are required to produce verbatim one of the choices that has been read to them. For example 'would you agree or disagree with a law that would require a one-week waiting period before a handgun could be purchased? Agree Disagree Don't Know' (Johnstone 1996: 97).

But instead of just sticking to the required task, informants usually deviate from the questions. Some ask for clarification, others comment on the survey, and the majority insist on justifying their responses, even though the justifications are not used in the polls. The interviewers too usually express their own individuality, even though all are trained to stick to the script, as any deviations could lead to biased results. Johnstone cites examples of interviewers blessing respondents when they sneezed, congratulating women on their pregnancies, apologising for the length of the survey and commenting on their colds. And as Johnstone concludes,

> Respondents refused to behave like the clusters of demographic facts the poll required them to be, insisting instead on behaving as if they had unique motivations for their opinions – and expressing these motivations in individually varied ways (p. 103).

> What interviewers' unsolicited comments had in common ... is that they tended to highlight the fact that interviewers were not machines, that real individuals were speaking with other real individuals (Johnstone 1996: p. 115).

Thus Honey's desire for a National Language Authority mentioned at the outset of this chapter is unworkable on a number of counts. First, even though the National Curriculum has required students of English Language to be 'accurate users of Standard English vocabulary and grammar' for over a decade, they have never felt the need to define what standard English is. Even the committee set up to improve standards of English in schools wrote in the Kingman Report of 1988:

> All of us can have only partial access to Standard English ... As we grow older, and encounter a wider range of experience, we encounter more of the language, but none of us is ever going to know and use all the words in the Oxford English Dictionary, which is itself being constantly updated, nor are we going to produce or encounter all possible combinations of the structures which are permissible in English (para. 31, p. 14).

Here, the Report, by explicitly stating that no-one is ever going to encounter all the structures permissible in English, is admitting that standard English is indefinable. Even though teachers may feel that they have the skills and expertise to 'correct' their pupils' English, that, in itself, does not constitute the pupils being taught standard English. And in the 1995 School Curriculum and Assessment Authority, many examples are quoted of children's non-standard forms. But there is very little on their standard forms, and what there is is contradictory or circular. I quote a section from the chapter on standard spoken English

> SSE need not be formal. Since many speakers use SSE 'natively', i.e. at home and with their friends, it necessarily has the full range of styles including the most casual. For example, if a speaker said *Don't think so* (without the *I*), we counted this as SSE on the grounds that it could be used by native speakers of SSE ....
>
> ... SSE, like all other varieties of language, is constantly changing and being redefined. Some of these changes involve forms that used to belong only to NSE but which seem to be widely used by young people who in all other respects use only SSE; but others are completely new, as with the use of the verb *go* with the meaning 'say' .... This example is relatively straightforward because the innovation comes from outside Britain – it seems to have started in the USA, and has never been particularly associated with NSE.

The second reason why Honey's proposal is unworkable is seen, as Cameron has pointed out, in the fact that even in those cases where people are given explicit instructions on effective speaking, the instruction only counts for a handful of well-worn expressions. And, even then, hearers often mistrust the overuse of such standardized expressions, as it creates difficulties in framing responses. Barbara Johnstone also found that in the majority of cases, speakers and hearers found it difficult to stick to a linguistic script when engaged in interpersonal communicative exchanges.

The only way that 'standard English' as used by segregationalists could be said to have any existence is when seen as a concept which lends support to and is supported by the Language Myth. This Myth, attempting to 'explain' how language works, requires that speaker and hearer have identical understandings of the determinate linguistic forms expressed. But such uses of the term 'standard English' are conflicting and confusing. As Tony Crowley concludes in his recent attack on John Honey's *Language is Power:*

It is in fact a great pity that the standard English debate is marred by the sort of conceptual confusions and political posturings (no matter how poorly expressed) which I have outlined by looking at one contribution to the debate. For I think there are genuine questions to be asked about what we might mean by 'standards' in relation to speech and writing. There is a great deal to be done in this respect and proper arguments to be made, but one thing is clear for sure. The answer does not lie in some simple-headed recourse to the practice of the 'best authors' or the 'admired literature' of the past, valuable though that writing is. Nor does the answer reside in 'rules' for speech laid down by either the 'educated' of any official body held to be able to guarantee spoken 'correctness'. The answers to the real questions will be found to be much more complex, difficult and challenging than those currently on offer. For these reasons they might be more successful. (Crowley 1999: 279).

And it is here that we can see how the integrationist approach of asking real speakers is the important step forward to receiving successful and challenging answers to real questions about linguistic standards. Such answers will always be provisional according to the viewpoints of the participants in the communicational processes. It is this provisionality which ensures that the search for any determinacy – whether it be of form or of meaning – will never lead to linguistic standards that can be generalisable, teachable or even usable.

References

Cameron, D. (2000), *Good to Talk*, London: Sage.

Carter, R. (1999), 'Standard grammars, spoken grammars: Some educational implications' in Bex, T and Watts, R. (eds.) *Standard English: The widening debate*, London & New York: Routledge.

Crowley, T. (1999) 'Curiouser and curiouser: Falling standards in the standard English debate' in Bex, T and Watts, R. *Standard English: The widening debate*, London & New York: Routledge.

Davis, H.G. (1999), 'Typography, lexicography and the development of the idea of 'Standard English' in Bex, T and Watts, R. (eds.) *Standard English: The widening debate*, London & New York: Routledge.

Falk, J. (1978), *Linguistics and Language: A Survey of Basic Concepts and Implications*, 2nd edn, New York: Wiley.

Fromkin, V. & Rodman, R. (1993), *An Introduction to Language*, 5th edn, Orlando: Harcourt Brace Jovanovich

Hartley, L, & Preston, D, (1999), 'The Names of US English: Valley Girl, Cowboy, Yankee, Normal, Nasal and Ignorant' in Bex, T and Watts, R. (eds.) *Standard English: The widening debate*, London & New York: Routledge.

Harris, R. (1981), *The Language Myth*, London: Duckworth.

Harris, R. (1998), *Introduction to Integrational Linguistics*, Oxford: Pergamon.

Honey, J. (1997), *Language is Power: The Story of Standard English and its Enemies*, London: Faber.

Jackendoff, R. (1993), *Patterns in the Mind*, Hemel Hempstead: Harvester Wheatsheaf.

Johnstone, B. (1996), *The Linguistic Individual: Self-Expression in Language and Linguistics*, Oxford: Oxford University Press.

Johnson, S. (1984), *Samuel Johnson (The Oxford Authors)*, ed. D. Greene, Oxford: Oxford University Press.

Mugglestone, L. (ed.) (2000), *Lexicography and the OED*, Oxford: Oxford University Press.

Taylor, T.J. (1981), 'A Wittgensteinian Perspective in Linguistics', *Language & Communication'* 1, no. 2/3, 263-274.

Taylor, T.J. (1992), *Mutual Misunderstanding: scepticism and the theorizing of language and interpretation*, Durham, NC and London: Duke University Press.

Trudgill, P. (1999), 'Standard English: What it isn't' in Bex, T and Watts, R. (eds.) *Standard English: The widening debate*, London & New York: Routledge.

4 The Language Myth and Linguistics Humanised

Edda Weigand

1. The general problem

A discussion of the language myth from different points of view in the year 2000 should be orientated towards a double goal: first, *an analytic goal*, in which we reflect on the scientific situation in linguistics left after more than two millennia of traditional and orthodox linguistic thinking; second, *a constructive goal*, in which we make proposals for overcoming the 'language myth' which can function as guidelines for the new millennium. My proposal will be a conception of linguistics as a human science which contradicts the view of linguistics as a natural science.

Like Roy Harris, I do not consider the language myth to be a particular case. In its general form, it pervades Western culture and is based on the clear-cut classical Aristotelian methodology which is a methodology of closed determinate systems of rules. Western thinking has *not yet problematized* in an essential way the view that *a theory has to be rule-governed.*

A closer look on Western culture however demonstrates that there have always been *single voices* which have recognized the limits of rule-governed theorizing. In his criticism of fixed codes, Roy Harris (1981: 187) has already taken the decisive step towards introducing the concept of indeterminacy which should not be misunderstood as an additional category. It is a basic fact of performance as it is a basic fact of modern physics that 'nothing can ever be measured with perfect accuracy' (Gell-Mann 1994: 26). I would also like to mention Martinet (1975: 10) who focused on the distinction between object and methodology and told us 'not to sacrifice the object's integrity to methodological exigencies'. The language myth confuses object and methodology and is thus the victim of a basic methodological fallacy insofar as it starts with the methodological concept of rules instead of first reflecting on the object. Dascal (1994) emphasizes the concept of open-endedness and introduces presumptions as a methodological technique (cf. also Toolan 1996: 142). Other voices that have recognized the limits of the determinacy view come from holistic models such as Daneš's (forthcoming) or from prototypical approaches such as Rosch's (1978) and Lakoff's (1987), which contradict the classical Aristotelian concept of a category.

The necessity to overcome the determinacy view has already been acknowledged in modern physics with the revolutionary approach of quantum physics and its *principle of uncertainty*. In the year 2000, I think it is time for linguistics, too, to balance the books and to acknowledge an analogous turning point. Theorizing in open systems of principles which allow for indeterminacy, probability and individuality will be the challenge of the new millennium.

2. The language myth of reducing the complex to rules

When characterizing theories of fixed codes as victims of the determinacy fallacy, Harris (1981: 55ff.) maintains that a certain level of indeterminacy is necessary in order to provide the flexibility which communication demands. In this way he distinguishes between orthodox linguistic methodology which considers language as a theoretical artifact and our real object language-in-use which is characterized as a complex integral phenomenon, part of the self-understanding of societies, part of 'everyday experience', a 'type of activity', a 'human faculty', a means for a 'multiplicity of functions' (p. 2ff.). In the year 2000, after three decades of pragmatic thinking, the orthodox linguistic view belongs to the history of science even if it still may simulate some power. Linguists have finally come to recognize that their object of study is indeed the complex phenomenon of language-in-use and that the way of theorizing by means of logistic systems and well-formed formulas cannot be the adequate one.

On the one hand, we are aware of the fact that human beings are in principle always different human beings and that they act and react in dialogue by negotiating their positions even across languages and different cultures. On the other hand, there is this type of orthodox explanation as offered by structural and generative theory which has nothing to do with language-in-use but keeps to the Aristotelian view that complexity has to be traced back to fixed rules. The mythical way of reducing the complex to rules had some attraction for linguists because it offered a simple method of dealing with the complex, namely the method of avoiding it. There is no superior explanatory quality, nothing mythical in the method itself. Only the belief that it solves the problem of the complex seems highly mysterious. Intensive criticism over the last two decades has finally broken down the dogma of language as a sign system. It is now time to reconstruct language as a complex integral phenomenon.

The real problem we are facing at the beginning of the new millennium in my opinion can be expressed with the dichotomy of *'the simple and the complex'*, used in the sub-title of Gell-Mann's well-known book 'The quark and the jaguar' (1994). Finally, after more than two millennia, we feel able to *address the complex.* De Saussure was aware of the fact that 'la parole' has to be considered our real object of study; however he did not see any possibility of addressing it. For the same reason, Bloomfield and the American structuralists excluded meaning from analysis. Abstraction used in theorizing, however, has to fulfil certain criteria which guarantee that the abstract representation remains related to the original. But by abstracting from 'parole' to 'langue' and defining 'langue' as rule-governed system of signs no relation to 'parole' has been left. We are confronted with the thesis that 'langue' is basic to 'parole', a thesis which completely lacks justification. Having in the meantime realized that our hope of one day arriving at 'la parole' will remain an illusion, we are now in a position to address the complex once again without reservation.

If we separate language system and communication, the mythical way turns out to be not only the language myth but also the communication myth. The fixed codes of language system re-appear in the rule-governed well-formed utterances of communicative competence. There are in principle two variants of the communication myth: *the variant of so-called modules and the variant of pattern transference.* The variant of modules starts from the conviction that a complex whole can be divided into parts or modules by abstraction and can be re-constructed as a combination of modules. By using the magic word modules it seems possible to gain sub-areas which are intended to be both independent and interrelated. It should however be clear from the very beginning: only artifacts can be rebuilt from artificial modules.

The other version of pattern transference may refer to complex action patterns which however are reduced to artificial ones by presupposing understanding and in this way considering the hearer to be a doubled speaker. The point of departure is set up by the premise that the object to be described has to be a rule-governed or conventional system. The obvious contradiction with *performance* is rejected by reference to underlying communicative *competence* which is constructed on the basis of pre-established harmony. Doctrines of self-defence are developed which should, as Harris (1981: 152) comments, 'allow any awkward question to be fobbed off with no trouble'. In this way, misunderstandings or difficulties in understanding are excluded. They are reduced to cases of missing information which could have been avoided if only the right information had been given.

3. Addressing the complex:
general methodological reflections

Having learned from the fallacies of the language and communication myth, we are now in a position to outline a *holistic view*, which is the only way of addressing the complex directly and not of evading it. Postulating a holistic view means that it is senseless to isolate components, elements, without knowing the minimal unit in which they function. It was Austin (1962: 147) who told us that it is 'the total speech act in the total speech situation' which 'we are engaged in elucidating'. In the half century since Austin's days, our view of what can count as minimal functioning unit has changed. We have not only left behind the single speech act but also the sequence of action and reaction and have arrived at the *unit of the Dialogic Action Game* (cf. Weigand 1997). It is not acts which could be considered to be the minimal communicatively autonomous units. It is human beings who act and react and are dependent in their interaction on conditions of the cultural unit of the Action Game. Interaction is always performance, and it is 'competence-in-performance' which we are trying to describe (cf. Weigand forthcoming d). In principle, human beings are different individuals. Problems of understanding therefore are constitutive from the very beginning (cf. Weigand 1999a).

What I have called a holistic view is *nothing other than an integral view* stressing the point that the components must not be separated but have to be considered as interrelated. Neither reality nor language can be separated from human beings. There is no independent encyclopaedic knowledge just as there is no independent structure of the world. How could we, in the past, really assume that human beings could separate their abilities of speaking, thinking and perceiving?

How could we assume that they would take account only of general conditions and exclude particular and individual ones?

Addressing the complex means addressing human dialogic interaction as a set of Action Games. The attempt to explain the complex is to be seen as the attempt to explain how the complex functions. There are in my opinion two possibilities: *the evolutionary one* which traces the complex back in time and demonstrates how it evolved and *the analytic one* which identifies components integrally related and demonstrates how the complex works. Both ways can be seen as 'adventures in the simple and the complex' (Gell-Mann 1994). In contrast to the language and communication myth, the simple now is to be *derived* from the complex as an integral part not defined in advance by the premise of rules.

Whereas Gell-Mann, winner of the Nobel Prize for physics, may identify the simple with the quark, the complex with the jaguar, the linguist does not yet immediately know right at the outset what could count as the simple. Nor might it be sufficiently clear how to understand the complex. The comparison with the jaguar, the highly elegant and perfect wildcat suggests that we see the eloquent human being effectively managing dialogic purposes as the complex. It is complex adaptive systems, according to Gell-Mann, which are able to behave in complex surroundings by mediating between order and disorder. They provide the explanation for how it is possible for the jaguar to emerge in the end from quarks. The concept of the complex adaptive system is highly interesting insofar as it combines regularities with chance, general cases with individuality, determinacy with indeterminacy, and allows from the very beginning chaos to be present. Even if we as linguists must be cautious not to lapse back into the old mistake of taking natural science unreflectedly as a model, I think we can learn from the concept of complex adaptive systems insofar as they once again reveal the distinction of different levels, performance and underlying competence, as a myth.

3.1. The evolutionary perspective

Our point of departure, in my opinion, seems to be clear: *the complex* we are trying to explain is represented by the complex human ability of dialogical interaction. Now what is *the simple*? If we try to find something similar to the quark in physics, the candidate would be the minimal element of the brain. Recently, an interesting discovery has been made (Rizzolatti/Arbib 1998). A special type of neuron, called the *mirror neuron*, which is considered to be the starting point of the evolution of language and communication has been experimentally proven in its function of matching observed events to internally generated actions. These mirror neurons discharge if a gesture is made, and surprisingly, they discharge, too, if the gesture is only perceived as having been made by someone else. I am not quite sure how this experimental result should be interpreted. Neurolinguists draw the conclusion that communication evolved from gestures and that the mirror neurons might represent the link between the sender and the receiver of a message. We are reminded of Harris's (1981: 163) conclusion, two decades ago, that 'language evolved behaviourally from the creative adaptation of non-linguistic behavioural patterns'. The mirror neuron thus plays its role as candidate for the simple with regard to the evolution of communication, i.e. with regard to a process in time:

Fig. 1 The simple in an evolutionary perspective

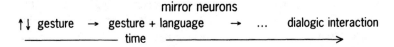

What is revealing, in my opinion, is the fact that the mirror neurons as matching system represent from the very beginning minimal integral complexes firing if a perceptual phenomenon is noticed or carried out. Assigning gestures a communicative function means relating a perceptual phenomenon to a mental ability. Localising this mental ability in the brain means assigning to it a biological basis. Thus the evolutionary process can be described as a succession of integral minimal complexes consisting of a concrete, perceptual event, its mental and its biological basis:

Fig. 2 Evolution of dialogic interaction

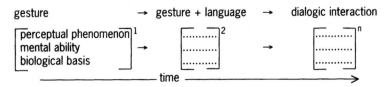

In this way, by and large, evolution might have started from mirror neurons in the brain. The mirror neurons, however, as specific cells with a specific function represent from the very beginning minimal integral complexes. How should the issue of matching the different faces, perceptual, cognitive and biological ones, be tackled? In a highly interesting way, integration of different dimensions seems to exist at the outset. Neurobiological research of recent years seems to confirm that the brain functions in an integral manner with different neuronal systems synergetically interacting (Damasio 1994). But does our question regarding the simple really refer to the evolutionary process?

3.2. The analytic perspective

Gell-Mann asked how the complex could evolve from the simple, and he tried to give an explanation for evolution including the evolution of the universe. What is going on in the universe seems to be determined by evolution, by the consequences of the big bang. What is going on in dialogic interaction, however, cannot be explained by tracing it back to the beginnings of evolution. In trying to explain how human behaviour works, we need a key concept to guide our analysis and this is provided by the question: *why do human beings behave in a certain way?* Human beings interact dialogically because they are social beings and have certain interactive purposes and needs. It is communicative purposes therefore which are the key concept for our analysis. I agree, for instance, with Michael Toolan (2000) that it is inevitable to elaborate what these purposes and needs are and what the means are which are employed. In the end, both explanations, the evolutionary and the analytic one, should converge. We are however still far away from such an overall view. Even if neurolinguistics has made great progress, we still know very little of how the brain functions, too little to begin with the brain. Let us therefore begin with the complex integral whole of dialogic interaction which is only in part an observable phenomenon:

Fig. 3 The complex

perceptual phenomenon
mental ability
biological basis

One might interpret the complex as combining different disciplines, linguistics, psychology, biology, etc. An interesting proposal for the relation between the different disciplines is offered by Gell-Mann (1994: 111) with his staircase model which orders the different disciplines hierarchically 'with the most fundamental at the bottom and the least fundamental at the top':

Fig. 4 Staircase model of the different disciplines

....

↑ psychology, linguistics, etc.

↑ ....

↑ biology

↑ chemistry

↑ physics

If we acknowledge the integration of different dimensions, the problem of the relation between the different disciplines, from physics to psychology, is no longer only a matching problem; it is in the first instance an integral problem of demonstrating how different variables are synergetically interrelated.

The analytical answer to the question of the simple in dialogic interaction has to fulfil the following general criteria:

- it must be a minimal component derived from the complex
- it must be a meaning component
- it must be a meaning component which is quasi-universal

These criteria are justified by the assumption that we have to give priority to meaning concepts. Human beings as complex adaptive systems are guided by meaning concepts such as purposes and needs. Communicative purposes might in the end be shaped by cultural conditions; as fundamental meaning concepts however they are to be thought of as independent of individual languages, i.e. as quasi-universal. Having communicative purposes, human beings are in need of communicative means. They integrally use different abilities resulting in observable non-verbal as well as verbal means and cognitive means.

I would therefore suggest as an *analytic answer*: the *simple* is represented by *minimal quasi-universal meaning positions* which I take as cognitive-social concepts. Cognitive meaning concepts are to be distinguished from cognitive means. Cognitive means are techniques, such as conclusions or suppositions, which are used to express and understand social meanings. A Theory of the Dialogic Action Game has to tackle the question of what are the minimal meaning positions, a question which includes the issue of the basic types of meaning.

4. The Theory of the Dialogic Action Game as an integrational theory

I am now going to outline the Theory of the Dialogic Action Game which addresses the complex directly and demonstrates how it works by elaborating the variables and their interrelation on a cognitive level. The relation to the biological basis is left for future research. True to the basic methodological exigency already mentioned, the theory will be divided into two parts: underlying assumptions regarding the complex object and adequate methodological techniques to be derived from them. There are many aspects I can only briefly point to or even have to presuppose; otherwise this outline of the theory would become a whole book.

Preliminarily to our attempt of understanding the object, it seems necessary to reflect upon the much discussed *issue of access*: should we begin with empirical facts or with theory? In my opinion, there is no empirical evidence as such. It is a modern fallacy to think the empirical text or the corpus itself could tell us the truth. There is no absolute truth to be found in the world. Truth is to be conceived of as a claim by human beings in their attempt to understand the world of which they are part. There might be such a thing as reality as such but it is impossible for us to recognize what it is. Our recognition of reality is always dependent on our abilities. Already at the very outset we find some sort of integration of empiricism and theorizing. We are confronted with a phenomenon which seems to be our object. But how to structure it? As integrationalists know, language-in-use not only represents a sequence of sounds or other empirically registrable means. It manifests itself as a complex integral human ability of speaking, perceiving and thinking. For this very reason, the text corpus, even if representative, can never be considered our whole object of study. It is part of our object, namely the empirically registrable part. To identify our object of study, human dialogic interaction, we have to address language-in-use with specific theoretical questions, among them the first question of what

63

is to be considered the minimal dialogically autonomous unit. It is therefore human cognition orientated towards empirical facts which represents our integral access to the complex.

4.1. Theoretical assumptions about the object of study

Our *object of study* can be characterized by the following assumptions (cf. also Weigand 2000):

- The *Dialogic Action Game* is considered to be the *minimal dialogically autonomous unit* within which the components function. It has to be comprehended as a *cultural unit* with human beings at the centre being engaged in dialogic interaction.
- The verbal *text* cannot be fully understood on its own, it represents only *a component* in the action game.
- The *central reference point are human beings* and their abilities which shape what goes on in the action game. Human beings are socially purposeful beings. It is their communicative purposes and needs which represent the *key concept for analysis*.
- Human beings are, in principle, *different individuals*, with different cognitive backgrounds, different personal experiences. Consequently, meaning and understanding are different for every interlocutor from the outset, *problems of understanding* are therefore *constitutive*. The dialogic action game as a complex cultural unit comprises the different world views of the interlocutors and relates them to each other.
- As a consequence, *meanings are not defined* but depend on the individual users. *Indeterminacy of meaning* thus becomes a basic feature of the action game and this causes meaning and understanding to be *subject to negotiation*. Meaning indeterminacy of everyday language can however be secondarily regulated and reduced in languages for specific purposes.
- The dialogic action game as a cultural unit is determined by and can be delimited by its interactive social purpose. On the basis of negotiating meaning and understanding, the *general interactive purpose* of the action game can be seen as an *attempt to come to an understanding* or to *negotiate and clarify the respective positions*.
- *Negotiation does not mean that there are no rules, no order, no determinacy at all.* For specific purposes meanings can be

defined, for instance, in terminologies, and determinate rules are used, for instance, in morphology.

- In negotiating their respective purposes, the interlocutors are in need of *dialogic means*. Human beings *integrally* use different abilities as communicative means, mainly the abilities of speaking, perceiving, and thinking.
- Dialogical purposes are related to states of affairs. *Concepts of probability* like preferences and habits are an integral part of it.
- Meaning in dialogic interaction is in a way complex that *not everything can be expressed explicitly*. Much is left to cognitive means. Otherwise communication would never end or at least would become clumsy and ineffective. As a consequence, the observer perspective in analysing a foreign text necessarily remains incomplete. Corpus linguistics therefore cannot be considered a fully adequate approach to the object of dialogic interaction even if it gives us valuable support in various respects.

Summarizing these assumptions, the conclusion has to be drawn that our object of study does not represent a closed system of rules presupposing understanding but *an open system integrally combining order and disorder, determinacy and indeterminacy, and interactively accepting problems of understanding.* Human beings as complex adaptive systems address the complex by trying to find regularities but being in principle different human beings and unable to join the other on the level of fixed codes, they have to tackle the problems of individuality, probability, particular situations, and even chance.

4.2. The methodology: principles of probability

The second part of the Theory has to tackle the question of how human beings deal with such an open-ended object. It follows from the conditions of the object that the methodological techniques used cannot be eternal rules. They have to be dependent on the speaker's decision, and they are valid only with a certain degree of probability. I call such techniques *Principles of Probability*. These are principles not in the sense of axioms but in the sense of guidelines and maxims in the process of negotiation which are, according to Michael Toolan (1996: 142), 'provisional and open ended'.

I have treated *meaning indeterminacy* as a *feature of the object* insofar as it does not represent a principle in the sense of a guideline which could be chosen deliberately by the interlocutors. The phenomenon seems to be comparable with what is called the Principle of Indeterminacy (Gell-Mann 1994) or the Principle of Uncertainty (Hawking 1988) in quantum physics. Both terms mean the same in physics, the term principle being used for a 'fundamental, inescapable property of the world' (Hawking 1988: 61). For the dialogic action game, however, I would like to speak of indeterminacy of meaning as a property or feature of the object which causes uncertainty in dealing with it. Indeterminacy therefore is dealt with by means of Uncertainty Principles or Principles of Probability.

From the very beginning, we should be clear in explaining our methodological tools. On the interactional level I assume Principles of Probability as a superordinate methodological technique used by human beings. Otherwise we could not tackle the feature of indeterminacy nor the fact that it is always different human beings who are interacting. These *principles relate to different reference points, among them rules and conventions.* Being principles for dealing with rules, with rational conclusions or suppositions, etc. the rules also become dependent on the speaker's individual decision whether to apply them or not.

Let me briefly comment, for reasons of clarity, on the three major methodological techniques used in linguistics. I take the term *rule* in the sense of a speaker-independent method which enables us to reduce empirical variety by a general feature which should be valid for at least more than half of the cases. The rest count as exceptions. In this sense, morphology is governed by rules. In contrast, the term *convention* is dependent on speaker groups. As I have been told by native speakers of English, there is, for instance, the convention to say *with high seriousness*, in German *mit tiefem Ernst*, literally **with deep seriousness.* Simultaneously, however, there seems to be the convention to say *with great seriousness.* Some native speakers object that the adjective *great* is only used in negative phrases: *with no great seriousness.* These ways of using multi-word lexical phrases demonstrate clearly the difference between rules and conventions. Different speaker groups may use different conventions for the same case. Conventions established for so-called standard use depend on frequency and have to be checked in a representative corpus. It is the *descriptive* feature of frequency which may be correlated to what is called the '*normative* force' of conventions and rules (Taylor 1997: 11). In the end however reference to rules and conventions is dependent on individual human beings interacting in the action game according to *principles of probability*.

4.2.1. The basic principles

Among the principles, we have to distinguish *basic principles and a set of corollary ones*. The basic principles are the *Action Principle, the Dialogic Principle proper, and the Coherence Principle*. The **Action Principle** (AP) derives from the assumption that we are acting when speaking. Such a view needs a clear *concept of action* in general and of dialogic action in particular. Orthodox speech act theory, unfortunately, does not offer a concise general explanation of action insofar as it is not sufficient to explain 'illocution' by what happens 'in-locution'. Illocutionary points are defined only on the level of particular action types.

Action, in general, is based on the *correlation of purposes and means*. For instance, the practical action of washing the car has a specific purpose, the car should be cleaned, and needs specific means. The concept of dialogic action must correspond, on the one hand, to this general concept of action, on the other hand it must specify the particular characteristics of dialogic action. Thus it can be defined as having specific dialogic purposes which are carried out by specific dialogic means.

One of the characteristics of dialogic action is that the *single speech act cannot be considered communicatively autonomous*. This feature of dialogic action will be addressed with the second basic principle: the Dialogic Principle proper. Communicative actions are always dialogically orientated. Aristotle's principle of the autonomy of the single act may relate to practical acts but not to communicative ones.

One might think of another distinction to be made in defining communicative action: the distinction between *an action and an attitude*. The general term behaviour might refer to both, to actions as well as attitudes. To distinguish actions from attitudes is not an easy task because attitudes might also be deliberately shown, for instance, the attitude of being friendly to a person in order to take advantage of that person. However, deliberately demonstrating an attitude, even a dialogically orientated attitude, remains with the speaker whereas dialogic actions make specific claims towards the interlocutor and imply a specific reaction. The intended result of an attitude is mostly left to chance.

In describing dialogic interaction we have to differentiate the general concept of dialogically orientated action insofar as we always carry out specific actions. I am now coming back to the *question of the simple* which I have left without a concrete answer, only indicating that the simple is to be considered as *minimal quasi-universal meaning position*. As we know from Searle (1969), the speech act on its functional level does not consist only of the communicative function F. F refers to specific states of affairs, called proposition p, as represented in the well-known formula F(p) which indicates that F is to be considered a higher level predicate. This formal explanation refers to the simple fact that in speaking we not only carry out a REQUEST or a PROMISE etc., but have to express in the proposition what we are requesting, what we are promising, etc. The propositional function consists of the functions of reference and predicating. Thus we have arrived at *three fundamental meaning types: action function, reference function, and predicating function*:

Fig. 5 The Action Principle

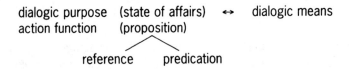

The differentiation of the concept of dialogically orientated action relates to the issue of a speech act typology which I have dealt with in detail in my book 'Sprache als Dialog' (1989) and in a supplementary article of (1991). Dialogic purposes are derived from specific social-pragmatic claims mainly of two types: *a claim to truth and a claim to volition*. These social-pragmatic claims can be considered to be the meaning positions which, in the end, constitute the different types of speech acts. They correspond to the fundamental mental states of *belief and desire*. In this sense we have traced back the 'complex' action function to 'simple' meaning positions and have already indicated how they might be derived from a cognitive base. The same could be done with the referential and predicative function but I cannot dwell on that here.

Instead we have to address the important question of the *means*. Harris (1998: 29) emphasises that the *integration* of activities is a necessary condition of life. There is no basic programme of language to which an optional extra programme of communication is added. Human beings use in an integral way different abilities in order to communicate: speaking, thinking, and perceiving. These abilities have a *double, i.e. dialogic face*: speaking corresponds to understanding, thinking means, among other things, drawing inferences and assuming that the interlocutor will do the same, and perceiving refers not only to perception but also to producing means which can be perceived. We are reminded here of the mirror neurons which fire if a gesture is carried out or observed.

An additional point should be mentioned regarding the means. Normally, there is not only a single utterance to carry out a speech act, for instance:

(1) Could you please fetch Doris?

but an open set of alternatives, for instance,

(1') Would you please fetch Doris?
       Can you please fetch Doris?
       Doris is waiting at the airport.
       etc.

These alternatives might be roughly classified as communicatively equivalent:

Fig. 6 REQUEST (FETCH (sp2, doris)) ↔ {utterances}

They confront us with the difficult problem of indicating the subtle functional differences between the individual alternatives (Weigand 1992).

The term *utterance* does not mean the verbal utterance form only but the complex integrated means by which actions are carried out, i.e., it includes verbal, cognitive, and perceptual means. Utterance forms are represented in correct phonetic transcription only if phonetic details are communicatively relevant. Communicative relevance is defined by reference to the functional structure of the action. American pronunciation, for instance, in contrast to British pronunciation may in particular cases be communicatively relevant but in general and on its own does not necessarily have to be transcribed.

We are now in a position to transform Figure 5 to Figure 7:

Fig. 7 The speech act

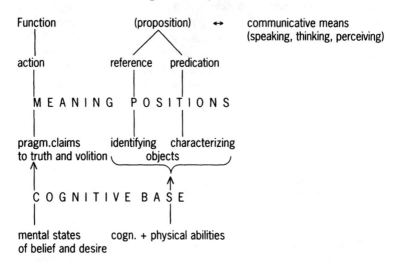

Figure 7 starts from *the complex* phenomenological level of the dialogically orientated speech act, identifies *the simple* with regard to meaning positions, on the one hand, and indicates the integration of means, on the other. Meaning positions are considered to be cognitive-social positions developed from a cognitive base. The mental states and abilities of the cognitive base would have to be traced back to the brain.

The final question to be addressed concerning the Action Principle turns out to be the most important: it is the question of how to read the *arrow*, in figure 7 the horizontal one which correlates functions and means. We do not want to fall back into what Michael Toolan (2000) calls the 'fallibilities of speech act analyses', namely to read the arrow as a codificatory principle. It is simply not the case that utterances are related to speech act functions by a fixed code in relation to specific situations: nor is it the case that the set of roughly communicatively equivalent utterances is closed and could extensionally define the speech act grammatically in a given language as I assumed some time ago (Weigand 1992). On the contrary, speech act functions and propositional meanings are negotiated in the integrational unit of the action game. The arrow symbolizes the methodological technique of negotiation, which is the technique of using probability principles. There might be simple cases, such as

(2) Please, give me the journal.

which seem to be governed by rules. What they actually mean is however dependent on the individual speaker, as in all other cases. Harris (1981) gives an illustrative example:

(3) It's going to be a nice day.

I would like to add another authentic example:

(4) You are playing the Game-boy again.
You are playing the piano again.

It is a declarative sentence which can be used for a representative speech act. However whether it expresses joyful surprise or an angry reproach or just a statement, depends on the particular situation and individual psychological conditions of the speaker. Intonation usually does not clearly express the action function. Even an interlocutor who knows the speaker very well may be uncertain about what the utterance means in the actual situation.

At this point, I would like to make a few comments on the referential and predicative part of the utterance. We are again confronted with the language myth insofar as it is an illusion to think we would refer and predicate using a fixed code of single words such as the article or single lexical words. We refer and predicate with phrases in the context of the utterance (cf. Weigand 1998a). Harris's example (1981), the *newspaper agent,* demonstrates that it is multi-word units or conventional phrases from which the utterance is constructed. Syntax plays its role on different levels – the level of the word, the phrase, and the utterance – as combination of meaningful elements. It is however the meaningful elements to start with, not abstract syntax.

The view of language-in-use as a network of phrases is confirmed by language comparison:

(4') You are playing the piano again.
Du spielst schon wieder Klavier.
Te revoilà à jouer du piano.
Suoni già di nuovo il piano.

It is not a question of whether we refer definitely to 'the piano' or indefinitely to 'Klavier', nor is the function of predicating composed of two units 'play' and 'the piano' but consists of the phrases *play the piano, Klavier spielen, suonare il piano*. Syntactically defined phrases represent the units from which the utterance is built up in a complex process of integrating morphology, syntax, and lexicology (cf. Weigand forthcoming a). The speaker cannot freely construct the phrases but has to know the normative rules and conventions of morphology, syntax, and lexicology if he/she wants to behave as an educated member of society (cf. also Sinclair 1991: 109f.).

Fig. 8 Utterance construction

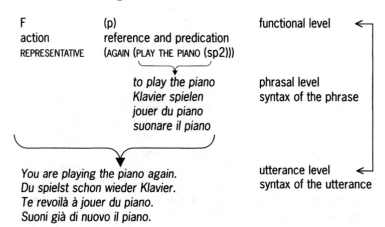

Having characterized the Action Principle as correlation of purposes and means, we now have to tackle the issue that the single speech act is dialogically orientated. Speech acts are different with regard to 'prospection' and 'retrospection' as Michael Toolan (2000) calls it. They are either initiative or reactive in the sequence. It is the second basic principle, the **Dialogic Principle proper** (DP), which explains the interdependence of action and reaction in the 'complementary sequel' (Harris 1996: 71).

The fundamental issue in overcoming the identification of the speech act with illocution refers to the question of what it means to be initiative versus reactive in dialogue. It means not only a formal feature of sequential distribution but functionally different action types. We initiate a dialogic sequence by making a pragmatic claim, and we react by fulfilling this very claim. We fulfil a claim by accepting or rejecting it or only by addressing it. In this way action and reaction are distinguished by their function, not by their position in the sequence. A speech act typology has to start from the complementary sequel of action and reaction, which is the minimal sequence by which the interactive purpose of coming to an understanding can be negotiated:

Fig. 9 The Dialogic Principle

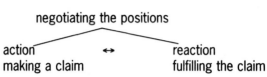

From the complex interactive function of negotiating our positions global speech act types are to be derived by using functional criteria only, namely criteria which differentiate the pragmatic claims. It is the initiative act of making a specific claim which determines the expected specific reaction as fulfilling the claim. If, for instance, the speaker wants the interlocutor to carry out a certain action, it follows from the speaker's claim to volition via rational criteria on the basis of cooperation that a speech act of consent is expected if the action cannot be carried out hic et nunc. In this way, specific minimal dialogues can be derived from the general level of action and reaction and consist of the following global dialogically orientated speech act types:

Fig. 10 Minimal dialogues

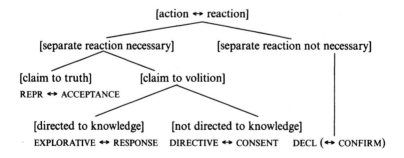

REPR = REPRESENTATIVE, DECL = DECLARATIVE

These global dialogic types are to be further differentiated to a variety of sub-types by modifying the claim. For instance, by modifying the claim to truth, representatives can be sub-divided into assertions, statements, news, and other types, or by modifying the claim to volition, directives are sub-divided into orders, requests, and pleas. By including propositional criteria warnings, advice, threats, predictions can be distinguished to name only a few.

In the ten years since my book on a dialogic speech act typology has been published, I have finally come to the conclusion that a specific type, not yet accounted for in the literature, has to be included as a sub-type of the representatives. I would like to call it the NAME-GIVING type expressed by deictic utterances whose function is to give things a name. Picking up the issue of giving things a name, we are back again in the jungle of the language myth. Word meaning in ordinary language use is not a predefined construct but an individual concept to be negotiated. It is speakers who name things in a specific speech act, for instance,

(5) Such an action I call violence.
I would call this object a cup.

There is however a tendency to define word meaning in languages for specific purposes, for instance, the language of law. This tendency results in terminologies, lists of words which have to a certain degree constructed meanings.

I would like to refer briefly to another type of action because it seems to be strictly related to the issue of the so-called reflexivity of language, which for integrationists manifests a real problem (e.g. Harris 1998: 24ff.). However, I do not see why precisely integrationists should have trouble with it. There is no such thing as reflexivity of language insofar as language cannot be considered an autonomous part in the action game. Toolan (2000) focuses on the right point in asking what we are *doing* when we classify language. It is not language, not the metasign which reflexively classifies language; it is again human beings acting with language in a specific way, for instance:

(6) I classify an utterance expressing a belief as a representative speech act.
I abbreviate Action Principle by AP.

Utterances of this type create a specific part of the world which refers to language. They therefore belong to the type of the DECLAR-ATIVE speech act whose reach is far beyond the simple acts of baptizing and wedding.

Let us now come again to the crucial point of the *arrow* which in the case of the Dialogic Principle proper correlates the initiative and the reactive speech act. Ten years ago, I took the arrow to be a sign for conventional correlation. Suppositions, problems of understanding, open points were then excluded. Having however acknowledged our object of study as an open system, the arrow consequently is to be read as principle of probability. It is the initiative speech act itself which tells us via rational reasoning which reactive speech act is expected. Rationality, however, is not the only thing on which communication is based. Language-in-use, being part of our daily life, refers to life concepts which are performance concepts, i.e. concepts of probability, such as preferences and everyday habits. At the very outset, therefore, open points come in which are dealt with by suppositions and might cause misunderstandings.

Let us once again take example (4) and embed it into an authentic dialogue (in English translation) manifesting a *misunderstanding*. The dialogue takes place within a family where everyone knows the other's preferences, among them the mother's preference for working in silence and the daughter's preference for practising the piano.

(6.1) Mother: You are playing the piano again.
(6.2) Daughter: Shall I stop it?
(6.3) Mother: No, it doesn't matter, I have to work outside.

On the condition that intonation is not definite, the daughter having in mind her mother's usual preference misunderstands utterance (6.1) as a reproach.

From utterances like (6.1), which represent a typical source of misunderstanding, it becomes very clear that it is the open-endedness of the AP which implies that the arrow correlating action and reaction in the DP proper is to be understood as a Principle of Probability. Misunderstanding in this case is caused by a possible emotional evaluation ranging from positive to negative which is not expressed explicitly. Normally, misunderstanding is corrected immediately, the open variable thus being closed, as in our example.

The risk of misunderstanding therefore can be accepted even if in some cases dialogue may degenerate to mis-communication. It has to be accepted because otherwise language-in-use would lack the high efficiency and flexibility which is needed for dealing with the complex.

We still have to introduce the third basic principle, the **Principle of Coherence** (CohP). It is a principle which clearly confirms the integrational view. Having looked for coherence exclusively on the textual level, the phenomenon has always been elusive. It makes no sense to observe that there are zero connectors on the verbal level and to draw the conclusion that everything is connected by the situation. If we take account of the fact that we are always different human beings interacting and that we must 'concede indeterminacy of what is meant' (Harris 1981: 187), coherence has to be understood as the persistent attempt by the interlocutors to combine the means, verbal, cognitive, and perceptual, in a way that understanding can be achieved. Again the open-endedness of the AP implies that this attempt might also fail.

Let us consider two examples.

(7) A There's the doorbell.
    B I'm in the bath.

This example taken from Brown/Yule (1983: 196) clearly illustrates that it is the interlocutors themselves who establish coherence in their minds when trying to understand the utterance of the other. What is meant is not explicitly expressed. Both utterances are indirect speech acts of the directive type. On the literal level a representative speech act is expressed, the primary directive function being left to conclusions. In the end, both utterances are connected by the DP proper making and fulfilling the same claim that someone should open the door.

The other example, an authentic dialogue, is mainly based on perceptual means. The situation is the following: A family – father and mother and two young children, a boy and a girl – are out for a walk around a lake with willows on the bank. The father cuts a willow branch and gives it to the boy:

(8) A Mother: One for her.
    B Father: Eve, too.

The interlocutors see what is going on and interact on the basis of integrated verbal and non-verbal means.

4.2.2. Corollary principles

The basic principles are connected with a set of *corollary principles* applied by the interlocutors in negotiating meaning and understanding. The interlocutors might, for instance, use the **Principle of Rationality** in drawing rational conclusions or they might refer to the **Principle of Convention** using, for instance, politeness conventions such as *How are you?* in small talk. They cannot proceed without the **Principle of Supposition** and, as human beings, they are always bound to emotions and have to know how to treat them in dialogue according to **Principles of Emotion** (Weigand 1998b). There are also **Principles of Rhetoric** which we follow in our attempt to negotiate our positions effectively (Weigand 1999b). Rhetoric in the model of the action game no longer only refers to specific verbal figures presupposing a distinction between rhetorical texts containing these figures and non-rhetorical texts. Rhetoric, like coherence, has to be conceived of as the persistent attempt by the interlocutors, in this case, to negotiate their positions, which implies that they normally try to negotiate effectively. Such a view of rhetoric is congruent with the position that 'meaning is always persuasion' (Burke 1950: 172), a position which I could not understand some time ago but which seems to be a logical conclusion to be drawn from the view of rhetoric as principles of effective action. Effective does not mean that specific verbal elements have to be used. Often it is specific cognitive strategies, for instance, in a positive sense offering something for getting something, or in a negative sense, simulating power which does not exist in order to intimidate the other (cf. Weigand 2001).

I will demonstrate the use of corollary principles with *two authentic examples regarding mainly Principles of Emotion and the Principle of Supposition* (cf. for further examples Weigand forthcoming b and c). These examples require a rather precise description of the situation because language is used as part of our daily life and is dependent on attitudes not explicitly expressed.

The first example consists of a talk between a mother and her 18-year-old daughter who, for some time, has been trying to emphasize her supposed independence.

(in English translation)

(9.1) Mother: When are you coming back?
(9.2) Daughter: *Probably* at 3.
(9.3) Mother: And I am *probably* flying to Madeira on Tuesday.

Inspite of simply telling *I'll come at about 3 o'clock*, the daughter is introducing *probably* not because it would be a case of probability but in order to demonstrate independence and the right of not to be obliged to inform the mother. The mother immediately understands, gets angry and disappointed by the fact that the daughter declines to give reliable information. She applies the same method in announcing a journey which is not at all realistic (9.3) in order to demonstrate what it means when two persons living together only want to emphasize independence. In doing this, the mother does not succeed in controlling her emotions. She neglects the Emotional Principle which tells us not to overreact when we are deluded in our expectations.

This example of a dialogue between two persons living closely together clearly demonstrates that language-use is dependent on life habits and is in itself a form of life. The hope of describing it in a closed model of fixed codes reveals itself to be an illusion. Performance cannot be tackled at the level of competence. We 'must never lose sight of the fact that communication always involves particular individuals acting in particular situations', as Harris (1998: 11) reminds us. There is simply no connection between the complex natural phenomenon performance and the artifact of rule-governed competence.

The next example demonstrates once more that it is individual evaluations, suppositions, and expectations on which interactive meaning is based. What is going on in the action game can be fully understood, if at all, only by the interlocutors themselves not by a neutral third-party observer who simply cannot know what the interlocutors are thinking, feeling, and meaning (cf. also Harris 1998: 23). It is again an example of a dialogue between human beings living closely together. What is meant is not explicitly told. The *basic feature of the indeterminacy* of meaning is demonstrated with regard to the meaning of *words* and the *syntactic construction*.

It is a clear case of 'making and re-making meaning' as Toolan (2000) characterizes 'our dealings with each other' (cf. also Toolan 1996: 146).

(10.1) Y   Come ti sei decisa?
(10.2) Z   Se non c'è più violenza, lo farò.
(10.3) Y   Cosa vuoi dire? Questo lo puoi sempre dire. Significa di no!

(in English translation)

(10.1) Y   How have you decided?
(10.2) Z   If there is no more violence, I'll do it.
(10.3) Y   What does that mean? You can always say that. That means no!

The dynamics of this authentic action game result from a single sign, the word 'violenza'. 'Words have meaning only in the stream of life' (Wittgenstein), and life is different for everybody. The meaning of a sign might be defined as structuralists told us. In language-use however we do not insert signs into an abstract syntactic structure. We use words in order to express meanings which are a 'mere opinion' of the individual and subject to negotiation (Harris 1981: 181). In the example, the interlocutors Y and Z have quite different concepts of 'violence'. What Z calls 'violence' might be called 'rough behaviour' by Y. It is however not only words but also syntactic constructions which do not have a definite meaning in language-use. The conditional construction *se non c'è più/if there is no more* is open to different meanings and understandings. On the one hand, Z apparently understands it in a non-conditional sense: 'if it is as it is', referring to the present, *if* meaning something like *because*: 'because there is no more violence' whereas, on the other hand, Y takes it as conditional referring to the future 'if there will be one day no more violence'. For Z utterance (10.2) may represent an offer. For Y however it is difficult to understand the utterance: *What does that mean?* (10.3). He immediately takes it as massive criticism presupposing that there is still violence. (10.2) therefore cannot count as a positive offer for him but expresses rejection, even extortion. He is deeply disappointed and offended, especially because 'violence' means something brutal for him.

This example, which can be understood only from inside the action game, demonstrates very well the differing worlds of the interlocutors which require meaning to be negotiated and which allow misunderstanding to arise. Dialogues of this type, affected by personal feelings, take place between human beings who have close contacts with each other. The situation is quite different with people who keep a certain distance between themselves. They might cooperate and discuss subject matters in a seemingly neutral atmosphere, concealing their personal evaluations and attempting to control their emotions. However, even in these dialogues meaning and understanding remain in the end open.

5. Linguistics humanised

At the beginning of the new millennium, it is time to finally leave behind us classical Aristotelian methodology as well as orthodox linguistic theorizing and to take a decisive constructive stance in 'redefining linguistics' (Davis/Taylor 1990).

This constructive stance, in my view, has to start from our *complex object of study which is human dialogic interaction*. It is an *integrated* object – integrated in many respects – which cannot be separated from the world nor from human beings. The central reference point is human beings who negotiate their positions and interests within the world, perceiving the world within the limits of their own abilities. There is no clear-cut independent structure of the world by which meanings could be defined. *Indeterminacy of meaning* therefore has to be considered a basic feature of our object of study.

The *methodology* to be derived from the object has to address the complex analogously to the way which human beings use to orientate themselves in the action game. They behave as complex adaptive systems operating between order and disorder, rules and chance, facing indeterminacy from the very beginning. The primary technique of addressing the complex are *Principles of Probability*. In the end everything depends on performance, everything is subject to chance, but human beings nevertheless try to structure the complex by using, among other techniques, *rules and conventions*, even if they know that they might be broken in actual cases.

An essential feature which characterizes human dialogic interaction is the fact that *not everything is explicitly said*. Different means are *integrated*, based on the communicative abilities of speaking, thinking and perceiving. Much is left to cognition, sometimes even the major purposes.

If we accept indeterminacy and probability, language use requires a certain degree of *human creativity* (cf. Harris 1981: 153). It is this aspect of creativity, of playing the game, which is expressed in the term of the *Dialogic Action Game*. Human beings do not play chess in dialogic interaction as was maintained by structural as well as pragmatic linguists who presupposed that human beings would act and react according to rules with equal possibilities for both sides. On the contrary, human beings play the game and make use of the leeway provided by language use for their individual decisions. Linguistics as a natural logistic science is unable to model this type of game. Linguistics must redefine itself as a *human science*, as *some sort of 'quantum' linguistics*, which combines general conclusions with individual assumptions, regularities with suppositions and accepts open points. Integrational linguistics is strong enough to address this complex issue in the new millennium.

References

Austin, J. L. (1962) *How to Do Things with Words. The William James lectures delivered at Harvard University in 1955*, London etc.: Oxford University Press.

Brown, G./Yule, G. (1983) *Discourse Analysis*, Cambridge etc.: Cambridge University Press.

Burke, K. (1950) *A Rhetoric of Motives*, New York: Prentice-Hall.

Damasio, A. R. (1994) *Descartes' Error. Emotion, reason, and the human brain*, New York: Putnam.

Daneš, F. (forthcoming) 'A Retrospect and a Prospect of Dialogue Studies', in: Boudi, M./Stati, S. (eds.) *Dialogue Analysis 2000*, Tübingen: Niemeyer.

Dascal, M. (1994) 'Speech Act Theory and Gricean Pragmatics: Some differences of detail that make a difference', in: Tsohatzidis, S. L. (ed.) *Foundations of Speech Act Theory. Philosophical and linguistic perspectives*, 323–334, London & New York: Routledge.

Davis, H. G./Taylor, T. J. (eds.) (1990) *Redefining Linguistics*, London & New York: Routledge.

Gell-Mann, M. (1994) *The Quark and the Jaguar. Adventures in the simple and the complex*, London: Abacus.

Harris, R. (1981) *The Language Myth*, London: Duckworth.

Harris, R. (1996) *Signs, Language and Communication*, London & New York: Routledge.

Harris, R. (1998) *Introduction to Integrational Linguistics*, Oxford: Pergamon.

Hawking, S. (1988) *A Brief History of Time. From the Big Bang to Black Holes*, Toronto etc.: Bantam Books.

Lakoff, G. (1987) *Women, Fire, and Dangerous Things. What categories reveal about the mind*, Chicago & London: The University of Chicago Press.

Martinet, A. (1975) 'Functional Linguistics. La linguistique fonctionnelle', in: Martinet, A. *Studies in Functional Syntax. Études de syntaxe fonctionnelle*, 9-81, München: Fink.

Rizzolatti, G./Arbib, M. A. (1998) 'Language within our Grasp', in: *Trends in Neurosciences* 21. 5, 188-194.

Rosch, E. (1978) 'Principles of Categorization', in: Rosch, E./Lloyd, B. (eds.) *Cognition and categorization*, 27-48, Hillsdale, N.J.: Erlbaum.

Searle, J. R. (1969) *Speech Acts. An essay in the philosophy of language*, Cambridge: At the University Press.

Sinclair, J. (1991) *Corpus, Concordance, Collocation*, Oxford: Oxford University Press.

Taylor, T. J. (1997) *Theorizing Language. Analysis, normativity, rhetoric, history*, Amsterdam, New York & Oxford: Pergamon.

Toolan, M. (1996) *Total Speech. An integrational linguistic approach to language*, Durham & London: Duke University Press.

Toolan, M. (2000) 'Towards a Simple Schema of Speech Moves', in: Coulthard, M./Cotterill, J./Rock, F. (eds.) *Dialogue Analysis VII. Working with Dialogue. Selected papers from the 7th IADA conference, Birmingham 1999*, 41-52, Tübingen: Niemeyer.

Weigand, E. (1989) *Sprache als Dialog. Sprechakttaxonomie und kommunikative Grammatik*, Tübingen: Niemeyer.

Weigand, E. (1991) 'The Dialogic Principle Revisited: Speech acts and mental states', in: Stati, S./Weigand, E./Hundsnurscher, F. (eds.) *Dialoganalyse III. Referate der 3. Arbeitstagung, Bologna 1990*, Bd. I, 75-104, Tübingen: Niemeyer.

Weigand, E. (1992) 'Grammatik des Sprachgebrauchs', in: *Zeitschrift für germanistische Linguistik* 20, 182-192.

Weigand, E. (1997) 'The Unit beyond the Sentence', in: Weigand, E. (ed.) (in collaboration with Eckhard Hauenherm) *Dialogue Analysis: Units, relations and strategies beyond the sentence. Contributions in honour of Sorin Stati's 65th birthday*, 3-12, Tübingen: Niemeyer.

Weigand, E. (1998a) 'Contrastive Lexical Semantics', in: Weigand, E. (ed.) *Contrastive Lexical Semantics*, 25-44, Amsterdam/Philadelphia: Benjamins.

Weigand, E. (1998b) 'Emotions in Dialogue', in: Čmejrková, S./Hoffmannová, J./Müllerová, O./Svetlá, J. (eds.) *Dialoganalyse VI. Proceedings of the 6th International Congress on Dialogue Analysis, Prague 1996*, Bd. I, 35-48, Tübingen: Niemeyer.

Weigand, E. (1999a) 'Misunderstanding (the standard case', in: *Journal of Pragmatics* 31, 763-785.

Weigand, E. (1999b) 'Rhetoric and Argumentation in a Dialogic Perspective', in: Rigotti, E. (ed.) (in collaboration with Sara Cigada) *Rhetoric and Argumentation*, 53-69, Tübingen: Niemeyer.

Weigand, E. (2000) 'The Dialogic Action Game', in: Coulthard, M./Cotterill, J./Rock, F. (eds.) *Dialogue Analysis VII. Working with*

Dialogue. Selected papers from the 7th IADA conference, Birmingham 1999, 1–18, Tübingen: Niemeyer.

Weigand, E. (2001) 'Games of Power', in: Weigand, E./Dascal, M. (eds.) *Negotiation and Power in Dialogic Interaction*, 63–76, Amsterdam/Philadelphia: Benjamins.

Weigand, E. (forthcoming a) 'Lexical Units and Syntactic Structures: Words, phrases, and utterances considered from a comparative viewpoint', in: Gruaz, C. (ed.) *Quand le mot fait signe*, Publications de l'Université de Rouen.

Weigand, E. (forthcoming b) 'Dialogue Analysis 2000: towards a human linguistics', in: Bondi, M./Stati, S. (eds.) *Dialogue Analysis 2000*, Tübingen: Niemeyer.

Weigand, E. (forthcoming c) 'Constitutive Features of Human Dialogic Interaction. Mirror neurons and what they tell us about human abilities', in: Stamenov, M./Gallese, V. (eds.) *Mirror neurons and the evolution of brain and language*, Amsterdam/Philadelphia: Benjamins.

Weigand, E. (forthcoming d) 'Competenza interazionale plurilingue', in: Cigada, S./Matthey, M. (eds.) *Comunicare in ambiente professionale plurilingue*, special issue of *Studies in Communication Sciences*, Lugano.

5 The Mythical, the Non-mythical and Representation in Linguistics

Philip Carr

Introduction

Integrationists claim that words, syllables and segments are constituted solely as cultural artifacts arising from the fact of literacy; they are said to be 'second-order constructs, belonging not to nature but to culture' (Harris 1997: 270). They also object to the 'fixed code' conception of 'linguistic communication'. These are interesting claims; I examine both here.

I begin, in section 1, by suggesting that the empirical evidence lends support to the view that words, syllables and segments are mentally real objects which exist prior to the advent of literacy in the child, although the evidence also shows that the advent of alphabetic literacy greatly increases the child's capacity for conscious awareness of phonetic/phonological segments. In this section, I also show that the arguments which have been proposed against the mental reality of syllables and phonemes from 'multiple trace' theories of memory are untenable.

I then go on, in section 2, to consider the idea that mind-internal linguistic objects are *encoded* in phonological representations, and are thus externalisable and transmissible to hearers. I argue, in accordance (I believe) with Harris, that this is a deeply mystical, unsustainable notion which is nonetheless widely subscribed to by, among others, generative linguists. The question then arises whether generative linguistics can be sustained in the absence of the 'encoding' conception of the relation between lexical meaning and phonological representations.

In section 3, I suggest that what I will call Chomskian Radical Internalism can be sustained *only if* one abandons the encoding myth. I then provide an outline of the way in which Chomsky's naturalism and Radical Internalism can be squared with the idea of codes as internalisations of socially constituted systems of conventions (a notion of code which Integrationists appear to reject, but which appears perfectly reasonable to me).

1. Words, syllables and segments

1.1. Words, syllables and segments in child acquisition

Integrationists claim that the objects postulated by modern linguists, and mostly given a realist interpretation, such as the word, the syllable and the phonetic/phonological segment, are the products of the emergence of (ideographic, syllabic and alphabetic) writing systems. Such objects are taken by Integrationists to be the second-order cultural constructs of literate societies. The putative myth in question is the idea that such objects have some objective mind-internal existence as something other than (mental representations of) cultural constructs. Put another way, the claim is that such things did not pre-exist the emergence of writing systems.

Unlike many claims in the foundations of linguistics, this claim is empirically testable. It is clear what would count as counter-evidence to it: if it could be established that, during the acquisition process, prior to learning to read and write, children can be shown to access words, syllables or phonetic/phonological segments as units of production and/or perception, that would demonstrate their reality as objects which exist prior to the emergence of knowledge of writing systems.

In what follows I will take a word, *qua* mentally real object, to be constituted a mentally stored phonological representation (see below on multiple traces), a mentally stored lexical meaning and the arbitrary connection betwen them. This Saussurean conception of 'word' is regarded as misguided by Integrationists, but it seems to me that the evidence cited below demonstrates its coherence and validity. I will use the expression 'word tokens' in what follows. This conception of 'word' is a commonly adopted one, but it is one which requires a certain amount of conceptual unpacking. I now offer only a brief sketch of that unpacking here.

Talk of tokens presupposes an appeal to types. It is perfectly coherent to speak of acoustic event types and their tokens (whereby the tokens are spatiotemporally unique acoustic events). I assume that the mind-external acoustic events which constitute 'utterances of' the phonological forms of words (thus conceived) result from attempts to produce acoustic events which correspond to the relevant acoustic images stored in the mind of the speaker. They are thus not tokens of those images (since tokens of image types are presumably images), and the images in question are not types, but for ease of expression, I will follow the tradition of talking of 'word tokens', on the understanding that when I speak of uttering a word token, I mean bringing about acoustic events which correspond to the mentally stored phonological forms of words. I lack the space to discuss the details of the type/token distinction as appealed to here; see Burton-Roberts & Carr (1999) for discussion.

Let us begin with phonological segments. There is clear evidence (Eimas et al 1971) which shows that human beings are born with the capacity to categorise the acoustic events arising from acts of speech on the basis of innately endowed psychoacoustic categories, such as the categories aspirated and unaspirated voiceless stops (indeed, it was this experimental evidence that launched the entire field of research into speech perception by infants). The acquisition of a phonological system builds upon those categories, such that phonemes as mentally real 'super-types' subsume the psychoacoustic types within broader categories. This results in the 'learning by forgetting' phenomenon, whereby a child acquiring acquiring a language in which, say, aspirated and unaspirated voiceless stops is non-contrastive, comes to take them to count as instances of the same thing as early as the second half of the first year of life. A child acquiring a language in which the distinction is contrastive does not undergo the learning by forgetting phenomenon. The point here is that the pre-literate child's mentally real phonology is founded upon perceptual capacities given by nature, not culture, and that language-specific phonemic contrasts are equally mentally real, to the extent that they may occlude, by being overlaid on, those innate capacities. And this happens before the child becomes literate. It is self-evident that the mentally real phonemic categories in the pre-literate child's mind do not emerge as a result of the influence of literacy on the child. Segments are mentally real prior to the advent of literacy.

Now consider the syllable. There is considerable evidence to support the view that the syllable is a mentally real processing unit among adults (e.g. Studdert-Kennedy 1975). But the psycholinguistic evidence from adult speakers need not undermine the Integrationist's position, since (s)he can claim that the mental

The Mythical, the Non-mythical and Representation in Linguistics

objects in question come to be in the minds of speakers precisely because they are literate. What is required is evidence for the reality of the syllable from pre-literate speakers.

Such evidence is available in great abundance. It is widely attested that, around the age of seven months, children enter the babbling period of vocal production. It is equally well attested that the units of babbling are consonant-vowel syllables, often duplicated, as in [baba] and [dada], and that such CV syllables are somehow 'basic', predominating in human languages and often emerging as the first syllable productions among those recovering from loss of speech after a stroke. There is discussion as to whether syllable production is controlled by the supplementary motor area of the brain (Abry *et al*, in press) or not, but it is clear that it is syllables which children are uttering at that stage. The syllable as a unit of production at this stage, and at subsequent stages, of development implies the mental reality of the syllable as a unit of speech perception. As Vihman (1996: 119) puts it: 'a voluntarily accessible link between perceptual and motor processes develops by the second half of the first year of life'. That is, proprioception, one's sense (not fully conscious, perhaps) of what one is doing with one's articulators during vocal production is intimately connected with speech perception. As Vihman & Velleman (2000; henceforth V&V) report, infants develop favoured production patterns through babbling, resulting in both proprioceptive and perceptual familiarity with those patterns. And those favoured patterns exert considerable influence on the child's first word tokens.

There is also clear evidence for the role of the word in child speech perception, and the research in question also demonstrates the mental reality of syllables and phonetic segments in pre-literate children. For instance, it has been shown that, as early as the second half of the first year of life, children can pick out adult utterances of the phonological form of words from the stream of speech, and can even distinguish distinct sorts of phonotactic pattern within those utterances. Work by Friederici & Wessels (1993), reported by Vihman (1996: 93) showed a preference, in 9-month-old Dutch children, for monosyllabic utterances of words which contained permissible consonant clusters over those which contained non-permissible clusters. Similarly, Jusczyk, Luce & Charles-Luce (1994) demonstrated a preference among 9-month-old English-acquiring children for common English phonotactic structures over less common ones.

87

These studies demonstrate that children at this stage already have mind-internal phonological representations. These initial representations are sufficiently detailed as to contain mental representations of syllables and sequences of segments, since phonotactic constraints are constraints on permissible sequences of segments at particular points in syllable structure (i.e. onsets and rhymes). Children at this stage of development also show a preference for familiar word tokens over unfamiliar ones (Jusczyk & Aslin 1995). At this point, the child appears to be storing phonological representations without linking them to fully fledged lexical meanings. This period is then followed, in the second year of life, by a linking between those representations and word meanings. It is at that stage that the child can reasonably be said to have words in the mind in the sense in which adults do, in the form of phonological representations linked to lexical meanings.

The word as a unit of mental representation appears to play a crucial role in the acquisiton of a fully-fledged phonology. The emergence of properly phonological structure can arguably be identified by the end of the single word period, when the (monolingual) child has a productive vocabulary of 50 words or more. It is at this stage that the child begins to latch on to phonemic contrasts. The first evidence of properly phonological organisation comes, according to V&V, when the child begins to exhibit consistent patterning in the production of different adult words. This, according to V&V, has two functions. It supports memory related to the production of a growing repertoire of distinct lexical patterns. It also puts limits on the learning space. The individual child's first word tokens closely resemble the repertoire of babbling patterns which are typical of that child. But, with subsequent development, a more abstract mental representation of 'pronounceable word forms' emerges.

Once the child has reached this stage, (s)he now overgeneralises, disregarding details which stand in the way of a match between the speech input (s)he is exposed to and his/her mentally represented word template. As a result, (s)he now begins to utter some old word tokens less accurately than before ('regressions'), and simultaneously utters tokens of many more newly acquired words. The child's mentally stored word templates are not generally equivalent to adult phonology at this stage. But, crucially, they show that the child is (not necessarily consciously) comparing across the phonological representations for mentally stored types, adding new phonological representations to existing ones.

There is debate in the literature on phonological acquisition as to whether, and to what extent, the child's phonological representations in particular words change during the second year of life, since it is easier to test the child's capacity to produce certain sound types than it is to test their capacity to perceive them, and perception of phonemic differences is widely agreed to be well ahead of production of those differences. It is also debated (Vihman 1996: 67–69) whether the syllable precedes the phonetic segment as a unit of infant mental representation of speech, although it is arguable that the syllable is more easily accessed during development than the segment, and that access to subsyllabic structure (e.g. onsets and rhymes of syllables) acts as a precursor to access to segments. But no-one working on phonological acquisition doubts that, during the acquisition of a phonology, and in his/her perception of speech, the pre-literate child accesses words, syllables and segments as mentally real objects. And the relevance of this for the Integrationist's view is that all of this takes place prior to any knowledge of writing systems.

None of this is to deny that there is an intimate connection between phonological processing and reading skills among literates; what remains controversial is the exact nature of the interaction (Vihman 1996: 174). But it seems clear that literacy appears to have the effect of forcing phonological objects as mental realities closer to the level of conscious awareness. It is interesting that in Liberman *et al's* (1974) tests, only 46 percent of 4-year-olds passed a test requiring conscious manipulation of syllables, while none passed a test requiring them consciously to segment speech into segments. However, at the end of first grade, after beginning reading instruction, 90 percent succeeded in segmenting syllables and 70 percent could now segment into phonetic/phonological segments. It seems clear that both the advent of literacy and purely maturational factors have a role to play in allowing greater ease of access. Strikingly, Japanese children are able to count phonemes without training in an alphabetic script, which, as Vihman (1996: 177) points out, suggests that 'phonological awareness' (the bringing to conscious awareness the existence of syllabic and segmental entitites) 'must have a cognitive component independently of specific reading instruction.'

If it is correct to say that words, syllables and segments are mentally real objects which exist prior to the advent of literacy, it is unsurprising that the writing systems which have been developed have been word-based, syllable-based or alphabetic; such systems tap into pre-existing mental (and mind-external) objects. Anyone

wishing to uphold the claim that these objects are entirely constituted as cutural artifacts will have to show how that view is to be
squared with the empirical evidence on the child's capacities. In
particular, they will have to offer an re-interpretation of the entirety
of the research on pre-literacy phonological acquisition without
making any reference to words, syllables or phonetic segments as
mentally real objects. Or they will have to demonstrate that the
entirety of that research is invalid.

One might argue, against what I have said here, that the
Integrationist need not reject the results of the research on phonological acquisition (I am grateful to Nigel Love for putting this
argument to me). Rather, (s)he need only re-interpret the results,
reconceptualising notions such as 'word', 'syllable' and 'phonetic
segment' as 'confabulation about first order *realia*'. According to
this response, none of the evidence cited here undermines any claims
made by Integrationists, since the researcher on infant phonological
capacities is engaging in such 'confabulation'.

This response will not do. Consider the *realia* in question. In the
first experiments cited above, synthesised tokens of [pa] and [pha] are
played to a 4-month old infant, such that the tokens become
progressively less aspirated. It is observed that the child can discriminate one type from the other, but has poor within-category
discrimination: the child cannot discriminate between physically distinct tokens of unaspirated [p]. The child's perceptual system is set up
in such a way that there is an innately-endowed perceptual threshold
on the physical continuum from completely unaspirated to heavily
aspirated. It is points on either side of that threshold which can be
distinguished by the infant. One can hardly argue that talk of unaspirated and aspirated stops in such cases is mere cultural confabulation.
The degree of aspiration in these experiments is produced syntheti-
cally by a machine. If our talk of degree of aspiration in such cases is
mere confabulation, then *all* of our physical talk is mere cultural confabulation, including talk of the moon, solar systems, the force of
gravity, etc. But the Integrationist wants to deny this, and insist (as
almost anyone would) that the moon and our solar system are first-
order *realia*. So the Integrationist is forced to accept that aspiration is
a non-cultural reality, as is the capacity of infants to perceive it, from
birth, in the way that they do. But a non-contrastive distinction
between aspirated and unaspirated in a language is demonstrably as
mentally real as the innate perceptual capacity (since it overrides it);
talk of such a reality is thus no mere confabulation.

The Mythical, the Non-mythical and Representation in Linguistics

Nigel Love's response is distinct from the more radical (and more interesting) claim made by Integrationists, that the entire modern linguistic enterprise, including the infant speech perception research mentioned above, needs to be replaced by a new, Integrationist linguistics. The weaker, less radical, view (Love's view) is open to the objection that Integrationism has no consequences for the way we do linguistics; it amounts to a kind of Unilateral Declaration of Irrelevance. It is an approach which is surely of little interest, and it is, equally surely, not what Harris intends Integrationism to be.

1.2. Multiple trace models of memory and the reality of syllables and phonemes

Taylor (1997), Docherty & Foulkes, (2000) and Pierrehumbert *et al* (2000) argue that lexical representations are not maximally non-redundant, as is commonly presupposed in generative phonology. They point to evidence which suggests that, for any given word, the speaker/hearer stores multiple memory traces of the tokens of its phonological form, so that variability in the stimulus is directly encoded in mentally stored lexical representations. This is the 'multiple trace' theory of memory (Hintzman 1986) which, they claim, allows them to obviate any appeal to objects such as syllables and phonemes as mentally real objects, the importance for Taylor of multiple trace models of memory being that they appear to him to offer an alternative to the putatively mythical notion of the fixed code.

However, D&F concede a point made by Myers (2000): that the multiple trace approach to lexical representations does not rule out the possibility that language acquirers may also generalise over those multiple representations, abstracting away from them to form more abstract mental categories and generalisations. This concession is fatal to their case and entirely undermines the conceptual work that the multiple trace model is intended to do.

Like Taylor and D&F, Coleman (in press) supports the view that one need not make any reference at all to 'phonological' representations, as distinct from a vast number of individual, richly detailed phonetic representations. But he ends his paper by appealing to Beckman & Pierrehumbert's idea that there is an intermediate level of neural structure, distinct from phonetic representations, and that this can be regarded as the locus of phonological representations. This contradiction entirely undermines Coleman's position.

Additionally, Coleman claims that there is no evidence for syllables (or phonemes) as mentally real objects, but then proceeds to provide a great deal of compelling evidence for their psychological reality, thus undermining his own case. He then switches his line of argument to evidence and argumentation against parsimony of mental representations. But it is hard to see why evidence for non-parsimonious mental representations counts as evidence against such things as syllables and phonemes. Why not allow for non-parsimonious mental representations of syllables-sized and phoneme-sized chunks of material?

In brief, Coleman, Docherty & Foulkes and Taylor have all failed to demonstrate that phonological knowledge consists solely of phonetically rich multiple traces, constituted as memories of (parts of) spatiotemporally unique utterance events. Taylor's attempt to appeal to multiple trace theory in support of Harris's 'language myth' position is therefore unsustainable.

2. Phonological representations and the notion of 'encoding'

The idea of 'encoding' is often appealed to in linguistics. When encoding takes place, one signal is said to be encoded as another. When one speaks into the mouthpiece of a telephone, sound waves are encoded as electrical signals, which are then decoded (converted/transmogrified/transformed/transduced) back into sound waves in an earpiece. On this notion of encoding and decoding, there is an intimate and non-arbitrary relation between the two related signals, and both must be of the same ontic category. This notion of encoding is not appropriate for the description of the relationship between mind-internal word meanings and phonological representations: it makes no sense to say that lexical meanings are encoded in, or converted into, phonological representations, since neither lexical meanings nor phonological representations are themselves signals of any sort. Additionally, lexical meanings are not of the same ontic category as phonological representations. Furthermore, the relation between the two, unlike the relation between the input and the output of a transducer, is arbitrary.

While it makes no sense to say that meanings are literally encoded in (converted into) phonological representations, this is precisely the claim that is made by many linguists. This notion of encoding is often proposed in conjunction with an argument from the non-existence of telepathy. Here is a typical example, from recent work by Chomsky (1995:221): 'UG must provide for a phonological component that *converts* (my emphasis: PC) the object generated by the language L to a form that these "external" systems can use: PF, we assume. If humans could communicate by telepathy, there would be no need for a phonological component.'

The idea that linguistic objects *qua* radically internal mental realities may be realised in speech by being converted into phonological representations, which are then externalised, is, I believe, what Harris calls a telementational conception of linguistic objects. So deep-rooted is this idea that it is very difficult indeed to get any linguist to see what is objectionable about it. But it is nonetheless a deeply mystical idea. It brings with it the notion that the acoustic events we produce in speech somehow possess 'secondary properties', linguistic properties, since the speech sounds in question are conceived of as 'carriers' of linguistic objects. The idea is mystical since it is simply a physical fact that acoustic events possess *only* acoustic properties. There are no other properties of acoustic events to be found. And acoustic properties are clearly not linguistic properties if the linguistic is mind-internal.

The 'conversion' conception of phonological objects as fulfilling an encoding role sits uneasily with the non-telementational conception of linguistic objects assumed elsewhere in Chomsky's writings. It is interesting that Chomsky's radically internalist conception of linguistic knowledge breaks with traditional telementational thinking, but the idea (subscribed to by Chomsky) that such objects may be realised in speech is, it seems to me, a hangover from that tradition. The presence of both notions creates a dilemma for Chomsky: on the one hand, linguistic objects are radically mind-internal (they are not internal*ised*, despite Chomsky's use of this term); on the other, they are externalisable (and thus internalisable). The question then arises whether Chomskian Radical Internalism can be sustained while the idea of the encoding role of phonological representations is abandoned. I suggest in the following section that it can be sustained *only if* the notion of encoding is abandoned. In doing so, I will have recourse to another conception of 'code': codes as sets of conventions governing social behaviour.

Philip Carr

3. Conventional systems of physical representation

3.1 Natural vs conventional facts

In what follows, I will assume that the set of natural facts is a subset of the set of physical facts: not all physical facts are natural facts (tables, and physical artifacts in general, are physical, but not natural, objects). I also assume that there is a valid distinction to be made between facts of nature and conventional facts. In doing so, I will distinguish between two senses of 'natural'. There is a broad sense in which any fact about human beings must be a natural fact. Any species of ant constitutes a part of the natural world, and thus any facts about ants, such as facts about their internal states and social behaviour, are natural facts. By the same token, *homo sapiens* is part of the natural world, and any facts about human beings (such as facts about their internal states and social behaviour) are also natural facts. I will call this species of fact a broadly natural fact. However, there is also a valid distinction to be drawn, with respect to (perhaps only) human beings, between broadly natural and narrowly natural facts. A human being who abides by the conventions of (some version of) vegetarianism is not thereby a member of a herbivore species: the fact of being a vegetarian is a natural fact in the broad sense (it is a fact about the behaviour of a member of a species in the natural world), but not in the narrow sense. Any narrowly natural fact is also a broadly natural fact, but not vice-versa.

This leads us to a distinction between conventional facts and narrowly natural facts. For instance, while it is a natural fact about the present author that his hair is black, it is a conventional fact that his hair has a side parting. By 'conventional fact' here, I mean the following. Firstly, while the presence of a hair parting is a physical fact, it is not a natural fact: hair partings are not naturally occurring objects, and do not emerge in ontogenetic development in the way that, say, hair growth does. Secondly, it is a physical fact which comes into being by adherence to some socially constituted convention (the convention, in the society in which this author lives, being something like: men should either not wear a parting, or should wear a single parting in the middle or on either side of the front of the head; multiple partings or partings solely on the back of the head are not conventional for men). The ontology of any social convention governing hair partings appears distinct from the ontology of the partings *per se*. I will therefore take conventional facts to be

The Mythical, the Non-mythical and Representation in Linguistics

facts which arise from the adherence to conventions of social behaviour. This latter fact about a hair parting is an example of a natural fact in the broad sense, but not in the narrow sense. It also appears necessary to identify natural facts as a subset of the set of physical facts: as we have seen, not all physical facts are natural facts. Conventional facts are therefore part of the natural world in the broad sense, but they are not natural facts in the narrow sense. Henceforth, unless otherwise indicated, I shall be using the word 'natural' in the narrow sense, and contrasting it with 'conventional'.

3.2 The Representational Hypothesis

I now proceed to a necessarily brief sketch of Burton-Roberts' (B-R's) Representational Hypothesis and its implications for the natural/conventional distinction, and thus for the relation between, on the one hand, the linguistic objects said to be generated by Chomskian Universal Grammar (UG: a putatively innately-endowed, species-specific, specifically linguistic state of mind/brain) and, on the other, the acoustic events produced in speech. B-R's view is that relevant acoustic events (the acoustic products of speech events), and the visual events which occur during signing, are produced as implementations of conventions of representation of the (radically internal) objects generated by UG. Here, 'representation' is to be understood in its ordinary sense as a transitive verb (or two-place predicate), rather than in the specialised Chomskian sense, under which linguistic objects as mental representations are constituted as mental representations (not *of* anything, least of all mind-external objects). B-R refers to the latter as C-representations (C for Chomskian or constitutive) and the latter as M-representations (M for Magritte, after the painting 'La Trahison des Images', in which the point is arguably made that a visual representation of a pipe does not constitute an instance of a pipe, does not constitute a token of the type 'pipe'). Appeal to the idea of M-representation in this context is not new, but the conjunction of that notion with Radical Internalism is novel, and has interesting consequences.

One of the main points here is that this conception of the relation between the relevant mind-external acoustic events and the radically internal objects and relations defined by UG is consistent with the gulf between the two that Harris & Lindsay (1995), and indeed Chomsky himself, insist on, whereas the instantiation / implementation / realisation conception does not, since it is a type/token conception, and tokens of types must necessarily belong to the same ontological category as their types. Chomsky himself seems to recognise this when he notes that it is hard to see how UG, a natural object, could be instantiated in a cultural object (an E-language): 'what we call "English", "French", "Spanish", and so on, even under idealizations to idiolects in homogeneous speech communities, reflect the Norman Conquest, proximity to Germanic areas, a Basque substratum, and other factors that cannot seriously be regarded as properties of the language faculty. Pursuing the obvious reasoning, it is hard to imagine that the properties of the language faculty - a real object of the natural world- are instantiated in any observed system.' (Chomsky 1995: 11).

Reserving the term 'linguistic' for UG and the objects and relations it defines, B-R makes the point that neither the relevant mind-external events, nor the relation of representation are themselves linguistic (one must bear in mind here that it is unimportant what terminological distinction one adopts in order distinguish between these two sorts of thing; if 'linguistic' *vs* 'non-linguistic' is objectionable, then some other set of terms will suffice). Radically-internal linguistic objects, on this view, are, as it were, innocent of the fact of being represented, and are not therefore conceived of as instructions to perceptual or articulatory systems, as Chomsky (1995) suggests (see Carr 1997b for further discussion of this point). The main point here is that linguistic objects cannot simultaneously be radically internal while also being instructions to perceptual and/or sensorimotor systems: if they are like such instructions, they must be weakly internal.

3.3 Sociophonetic variation and UG

This brings us to the natural/conventional distinction and to the role of norms (conventions) of social behaviour, and thus the relation between sociophonetic variation and UG as a natural object. For B-R, a specific, mentally-stored, internalised phonological representation is constituted as a representation of a convention (a norm), or set of conventions, specifically a convention governing representational behaviour. But that claim does not exclude the claim that there are internal (inductive) generalisations over those conventions which may interact in complex ways, this interaction being the stock-intrade of the autonomous phonologist. This allows us to accommodate (a) the complex systems of conventions which govern sociophonetic variation with (b) UG as an object in the natural world, and with the object of most generative phonological inquiry. Such conventions are norms of social behaviour, and can have simultaneous, multiple, social and linguistic (representational) functions, as Docherty *et al* (1997) have pointed out. For instance, variation in the pronunciation of the coronal stop in a word such as *better* among speakers of Tyneside English as, among other things, a glottalised stop or a coronal approximant, may involve both representational activity and the signalling of group membership simultaneously.

This approach reconciles the diversity of individual languages (the locus of conventionality) with the uniqueness of UG (a natural, rather than a conventional, state of affairs). Since individual languages (and thus their phonologies) are viewed here as Conventional Systems of Physical Representation, those systems, being conventional, will be subject to diversity and variation. UG, on the other hand, is invariant. The sorts of factor which the variationist is concerned with (age, sex, social class membership, solidarity, formality of discourse, etc) are to be found within such systems of conventions, determining, to some extent, those systems.

Notice that it does not follow from the representational hypothesis in itself that linguistic objects, understood in the radically internalist sense, lack a phonology. But if such objects do have a radically-internalist phonology, then it must be 'phonology without substance', as proposed by Hale & Reiss (2000). For reasons given elsewhere (Carr, 2000, in prep), it seems to me that Hale & Reiss do not succeed in formulating a conception of phonological objects which is genuinely substance-free; crucially, their conception relies on the encoding conception of phonological representations, which I hope to have shown here to be indefensible.

Given this, and the large body of evidence which strongly suggests that the acquisition of phonological knowledge is intimately tied up with a variety of perceptual, general-cognitive, motor-control and social factors, it seems unlikely that linguistic objects, understood in the radically internalist sense, have a phonology. Rather, phonological systems constitute conventional systems of representation. It seems to us (see Burton-Roberts & Carr 1999) that, if phonological systems are regarded this way, this resolves the dilemma, attested throughout the history of twentieth century phonology, whereby phonologists often wish to regard phonological systems as 'purely formal' ('substance-free', to use Hale & Reiss's term), and thus parallel to objects which contract purely syntactic relations, while at the same time allowing (explicitly or implictly) that they have intrinsic phonetic content.

With phonologies regarded, not as devices for encoding mind-internal linguistic objects, but as central parts of Conventional Systems of Physical Representation, Chomsky's Radical Internalism can be sustained. And such systems of conventions are reasonably regarded as codes in the sense of sets of conventions in accordance with which social behaviour is conducted. It seems to me that, if the encoding myth is adhered to, Chomsky's Radical Internalism faces insurmountable conceptual difficulties, difficulties which Chomsky himself alludes to.

References

Abry, C., M. Stefanuto, A, Vilain, R. Laboissière (in press). 'What can the utterance "tan, tan" of Broca's patient Leborgne tell us about the hypothesis of an emergent "babble syllable" downloaded by SMA?' In Durand & Laks (eds.)

Bertoncici, J. & J. Mehler (1981). 'Syllables as units in infant speech perception.' *Infant Behaviour and Development* 4: 247–60.

Burton-Roberts, N, & P, Carr (1999). 'On speech and natural language.' *Language Sciences* 21.4: 371–406.

Burton-Roberts, N., P. Carr & G. Docherty (eds). *Phonological knowledge: conceptual and empirical issues.* Oxford: Oxford University Press.

Carr, P. (1997a). 'Telementation and generative linguistics'. In Wolf & Love (eds): 42–64.

Carr, P. (1997b) Review of N. Chomsky (1993) Language and thought. *Journal of Linguistics* 33.1: 215–217.

Carr, P (2000). 'Innate endowments, sociophonetic variation and scientific realism in phonology.' In Burton-Roberts et al (eds).

Carr, P (in prep) *Phonology, nature and mind.* Oxford: Oxford University Press.

Chomsky, N. (1995). *The Minimalist Programme.* Cambridge, MA: MIT Press.

Coleman, J. (in press). 'Phonetic representations in the mental lexicon.' In Durand & Laks (eds).

Docherty, G. & P. Foulkes (2000). 'Sociophonetic Variation.' In Burton-Roberts et al: 105–129.

Durand, J. & B. Laks (eds) (in press) *Phonetics, phonology and cognition.* Oxford: Oxford University Press.

Eimas, P.D., Siqueland, E.R., Juszyk, P.W. & Vigorito, J. (1971). Speech perception in infants. *Science* 171: 303–6.

Friederici A.D. & Wessels, J.M.I. (1993) 'Phonotactic knowledge of word boundaries and its use in infant speech perception.' *Perception and Psychophysics* 54: 287–95.

Hale, M. & C. Reiss (in press). 'Substance abuse in phonology.' In Burton-Roberts et al. (eds).

Harris, J. & G. Lindsay (1995). 'The elements of phonological representation.' In Durand, J. & F. Katamba (eds) *Frontiers of Phonology*. London: Longman: 34–79.

Harris, R. (1997) 'From an Integrational point of view.' In Wolf & Love (eds): 229–310.

Hintzman, D. J. (1986). "Schema Abstraction' in a Multiple-Trace memory model.' *Psychological Review* 93: 411–428.

Jusczyk, P.W. & R.N. Aslin (1995). 'Infants' detection of the sound patterns of words in fluent speech.' *Cognitive Psychology* 29: 1–23.

Jusczyk, P.W., P.A. Luce & J. Charles-Luce (1994). 'Infants' sensitivity to phonotactic patterns in the native language.' *Journal of Memory and Language* 33: 630–45.

Liberman, I.Y., Shankweiler, D., Fischer, F.W. and Carter, B. (1974). 'Explicit syllable and phoneme segmentation in the young child.' *Journal of Experimental Child Psychology* 18: 201–12.

Love, N. & G. Wolf (1997). 'Epilogue'. In Wolf & Love (eds) 1997:311–318.

Myers, S. (2000). 'Boundary disputes: the relation between phonetics and phonology.' In Burton-Roberts et al (eds): 245–72.

Pierrehumbert, J, M. Beckmann & R. Ladd (2000). 'Conceptual foundations of Phonology as Laboratory Science.' In Burton-Roberts et al (eds): 273–303.

Saussure, F. de (1983) *Course in General Linguistics* (Harris translation). London: Duckworth.

Studdert-Kennedy, M. (1975). 'From continuous signal to discrete message: syllable to phoneme.' In J.F. Kavanagh & J.E. Cutting (eds) *The Role of Speech in Language*. Cambridge, MA: MIT Press.

Taylor, J. (1997). 'Linguistic theory and the multiple trace theory of memory.' In Wolf, G & N. Love (eds): 208–225.

Vihman, M-M. (1996). *Phonological development.* Oxford: Blackwell.

Vihman, M-M. & S. Velleman (2000). 'Phonetics and the origins of phonology.' In Burton-Roberts et al (eds): 305–39.

Wolf, G. & N. Love (eds) (1997). *Linguistics Inside Out: Roy Harris and His Critics*. Amsterdam: Benjamins.

6 Folk Psychology and the Language Myth: What Would the Integrationist Say?

Talbot J. Taylor

Am I conscious? Do you believe that you are reading this sentence? Do you intend to read the whole article? When I say 'Austin Powers', do you know to whom I am referring? Did you understand what I just said?

An intriguing characteristic of 20th-century psychology and the philosophy of mind is the debate whether such questions make any sense. For many psychologists and philosophers claim that such commensense questions are nonsensical, have no determinate meaning, or have only the meanings of myths and primitive superstitions. Such questions, they say, are the product of a folk psychology that has long dominated Western thinking about the mind, the components of which, if the sciences of the mind are ever to progress, need to be eliminated not only from scientific theories of the mind but also from everyday talk. These Eliminativists – including the behaviourist psychologist J.B. Watson and the philosophers Paul Churchland and Stephen Stich – argue that the notions that populate folk psychological discourse – notions such as 'belief', 'wish', 'know', 'desire', 'refer', 'understand' – are 'the heritages of a timid savage past', handed down, generation after generation, at mother's knee (Watson 1924: 3). These notions and the folk reasoning which makes use of them ought to be assigned the same fate as was meted out, following the birth of modern chemistry, to alchemical notions such as 'phlogiston', 'caloric', and 'essences'. As some leading Eliminativists explain:

> Eliminativism ... is the claim that some category of entitites, processes, or properties exploited in a commonsense or scientific account of the world do not exist. (Ramsey, Stich, and Garon 1991: 94)

Folk psychology, they say, is the theory of mind that has dominated Western culture for many centuries. Moreover, as John Searle points out, there are signs of its influence in non-Western culture as well – as the Dalai Lama apparently holds such a theory (Searle 1999: 52).

This paper concerns the opposition between Eliminativists and (what I shall call) Anti-Eliminativists in modern philosophy of mind: i.e., those who claim that terms such as 'belief', 'intend', 'refer', 'mean' and remarks such as 'He believes I'm crazy' should not be banished either from modern cognitive psychology or from lay psychological discourse. But in addition to this explanatory goal, the paper is intended to raise two questions. First, what is the connection between the Language Myth (Harris 1981) and the arguments for and against eliminativism in contemporary philosophy of mind? Second, because it is easy to see the overlap between the concepts of so-called 'folk psychology' and those of what we might call 'folk linguistics', we can ask the following question: What should be the integrational linguist's position on folk psychology and folk linguistics? Specifically, should all, some, or none of the constitutive concepts be retained in the integrational study of language and communication? Should one of the integrationist's goals be to show what meaning, understanding, reference, belief, etc., really are – i.e., properly seen within an integrationist approach that has freed itself from the influence of the Language Myth? Or, should the goal be to replace these conceptual and terminological legacies of the Language Myth (and perhaps other Western cultural myths) with terms and concepts that (a) are motivated directly by the integrational approach and (b) do not 'carry with them' the conceptual baggage of the Language Myth?

To put it bluntly: Should the integrationist aim to explain what it is to mean, to understand, to believe, to refer, to be a sign, etc? Or should this not be one of the integrationist's aims, on the grounds that those terms are too infected by the Language Myth?

Early Eliminativists

What have the Eliminativists got against folk psychology? Some of the earliest Eliminativists were members of the behaviourist school and saw the rejection of 'commonsense' psychological terms and reasoning as a necessary stage in their efforts to make psychology into a proper science. J.B. Watson argued that to become truly scientific, psychology had to purge from its conceptual foundations all 'commonsense' psychological notions and folklore about why people do what they do. These concepts and familiar platitudes of psychological explanation are the cultural legacy of folk traditions, religion, and mythological notions about the mind and its putative contents. Just as progress in other sciences required the purging of commonsense assumptions, concepts, and explanations, the same, Watson argued, is required for psychology to become a true science. And yet, he complained, the introspectionist theories that had hitherto dominated psychological research had done the reverse: they had taken for granted the legitimacy of commonsense psychology. Introspectionist psychology presupposes the existence of genuine psychological phenomena which are the purported referents for such commonsense terms as 'belief', 'consciousness', 'desire', etc. And it assumes that a subject's reports of what he experiences, believes, or desires – or of why he behaved as he did – represent, ceteris paribus, actual mental states – the very mental states that the introspectionist takes to be the objects of psychological investigation.

For instance, in his book *Behaviorism* (Watson 1924: 4), Watson criticizes William James' reliance on 'commonsense' in the definition of the science of psychology. The definition that James gives is 'Psychology is the description and explanation of states of consciousness as such.' But Watson objects that this definition begs the question of the existence of states of consciousness – the question, that is, whether there really are any mental phenomena referred to by the term 'states of consciousness'. Furthermore, Watson accuses James of diverting the reader's attention from this weakness in his definition by rhetorical sleight of hand: namely, by invoking the commonsense, 'everybody-knows' character of the concept of consciousness (Watson 1924: 4). In James' own words

> [When we] look into our own minds and report what we there discover ... [e]veryone agrees that we there discover states of consciousness. So far as I know, the existence of such states has never been doubted by any critic, however sceptical in other respects he may have been .... All people unhesitatingly believe that they feel themselves thinking and that they distinguish the mental state. (...) I regard this belief as the most fundamental of all the postulates of Psychology. (James 1890: 185)

'Consciousness–Oh, yes, everybody must know what this 'consciousness' is' is Watson's sarcastic reply (Watson 1924: 4). And yet, Watson argued:

> [C]onsciousness is neither a definite nor a usable concept. (...) [B]elief in the existence of consciousness goes back to the ancient days of superstition and myth. (...) The great mass of people even today want to believe in magic. (...) As time goes on, all of these critically undigested, innumerable told tales get woven into the folk lore of the people.' (Watson 1924: 2)

Watson saw folk psychology as a form of mythification, religious superstition, and magic. Its familiar patterns of reasoning and explanation he characterized as consisting in nothing but the 'old wives' tales' that each new generation learns and then passes down to the next generation 'as gospel' (Watson 1924: 2). Scientific psychology could never be constructed on such mythical foundations. Its whole ontology, epistemology, and logic had to be rejected in order that a true science of human behaviour could at last be constructed on firm foundations.

Contemporary Eliminativists argue that folk psychology is a theory

Today, proponents of eliminativism take a different tack from Watson while still arguing for the same eliminativist conclusion. In the first place, the central figures in the folk psychology debate today are physicalists. That is, whereas Watson took behaviour to be the explanatory object for the science of psychology, they take physical properties and processes in the brain as the ultimate explanatory objects for scientific psychology. Secondly, whereas Watson described commonsense talk about the mind and its contents as a kind of folklore and mythology, today's Eliminativists argue that commonsense remarks about the mind are theoretical claims or hypotheses. That is, the layperson's remarks about what they believe, what they know, what they refer to or understand, etc, are the 'products' of an underlying theory. 'Folk psychology' is the name given to this theory. A leading Eliminativist, Stephen Stich says:

In our everyday dealings with one another we invoke a variety of commonsense psychological terms including 'belief', 'remember', 'feel', 'think', 'desire', 'prefer', 'imagine', 'fear', and many others. The use of these terms is governed by a loose network of largely tacit principles, platitudes, and paradigms which constitute a sort of folk theory. (Stich 1983: 1)

Stich's point, in other words, is that when the long-suffering Bloggs says that Daniel believes that Neptune is at a mathematically predictable distance from Uranus, Bloggs is uttering a hypothesis. The sense of this hypothesis is a function of the underlying psychological theory, a theory which determines the conceptual content denoted by its component terms (e.g. the term of 'belief'), the logical syntax of the propositions formed with those terms, and the implicational relations between those propositions. Bloggs' utterance thus attributes to Daniel what is sometimes called a 'propositional attitude' or 'intentional state'– namely 'believing that Neptune is at a mathematically predictable distance from Uranus'. As a hypothesis it is true if that propositional attitude is somehow represented in Daniel's brain, false if it is not. Eliminativists such as Stich point out that to take such an utterance to be true is to presuppose an ontology of particular brain states or events – namely, those that must obtain for the sentence to be true.

In other words, Eliminativists (although not only Eliminativists) maintain that in taking ordinary psychological remarks to be true, we make an ontological commitment to the existence of particular neurological states or events – the very ones that must obtain for those remarks to be true.

Eliminativists argue that folk psychology needs replacement

The Eliminativist's central thesis is that not only is folk psychological discourse the 'output' of an underlying theory of the mind, that theory is a bad theory. As another leading Eliminativist puts it:

Folk Psychology is false and its ontology is chimerical. Beliefs and desires are of a piece with phlogiston, caloric, and the alchemical essences. (Churchland 1991: 65)

There are, in other words, no such things as beliefs, meanings, thoughts, fears, desires, and intentions. There is no such neurological state as 'believing TJT is crazy' or 'understanding what I just said'. This at any rate is what the contemporary cognitive neurosciences are discovering: i.e., that no brain states or events are identifiable as corresponding to the folk terms 'intention', 'meaning', 'thought' or to propositional attitudes such as 'believing that Neptune is at a mathematically predictable distance from Uranus'. Furthermore, given what is being discovered about the physical properties of the brain, it is seen as increasingly unlikely that such states or events ever will be identifiable. To put it bluntly: they just aren't there, so we should give up looking for them. From this, the modern Eliminativist concludes that, just as the terms 'phlogiston', 'caloric', and 'alchemical essence' were abandoned as modern chemistry discovered that they had no referents, so folk psychological terms should be dropped – for, like all mythical terms, they refer to nothing at all. The same goes for statements such as 'Henry VIII believed that Pope Clement would allow the annulment of his marriage to Catherine of Aragon'. Stephen Stich put the matter thus:

> Did Henry VIII believe that Pope Clement would allow the annulment of his marriage to Catherine of Aragon? .... [T]he question has no answer. Beliefs are myths, and it is no more sensible to inquire about Henry's beliefs than to investigate whether he had an excess of phlegm or a deficiency of yellow bile. (Stich 1983: 2)

As a bad theory with a chimerical ontology, the Eliminativist Paul Churchland argues that folk psychology should be – and eventually will be – replaced by the much improved psychological theories being developed in contemporary cognitive science.

> 'Folk psychology is a radically inadequate account of our internal activities, too confused and too defective .... It will simply be displaced by a better theory of those activities.' (Churchland 1981: 72)

'Commonsense' resistance to Eliminativism

The Anti-Eliminativist position draws on the rhetorical power of 'commonsense' in resisting Eliminativist arguments. Folk psychology has to be protected from sceptical attack. Of course we believe, fear and desire, are conscious, have intentions, mean things by our words, and understand each other. Of course Daniel believes that Neptune is at a mathematically predictable distance from Uranus.

To get a taste of the rhetorical power of such 'commonsense' defenses of folk psychology, consider the alternative of denying an instance of a folk psychological claim. Suppose we say that Henry VIII believed that the Pope would resist his efforts to divorce Catherine of Aragon. But the Eliminativist says that there are no such intentional states as 'believing such-and-such'. OK, well, if beliefs are no more than myths, then ought we to say that Henry did *not* believe the Pope would resist his efforts to divorce Catherine? Or that he had no such belief? Would it not be absurd to insist that reading this article is not something you are doing intentionally – since there are no such things as intentions? Or that you do not understand any of the words I am using – since there is no such thing as understanding? Or that you are not in fact conscious? After all, if consciousness really is a myth, then how can it be true that you are conscious? But 'commonsense' supposedly tells us that such sceptical claims are absurd, doesn't it? Doubtless anyone who went around asserting that no one believes anything, that no one is conscious, that no one understands anything, that no one means anything would – if her daily behaviour scrupulously accorded with these claims,– end up being sent to a psychiatrist and might well never be seen outside the mental asylum again.

However, it is worth emphasizing that the Anti-Eliminativists agree with the Eliminativists that *if* it is justifiable to assert that Henry believed that the Pope would resist, this is simply because *it is true*: Henry really did believe that. Furthermore, they both agree that the matter whether Henry really did or really didn't believe that is independent of anyone's *assertion* of what Henry believed. In other words, there must be *grounds* for this assertion – some conditions the obtaining of which justify the assertion (*if* it is justified) – and these grounds must be independent of the assertion itself. But it is here where the Anti-Eliminativist school splits into different camps: i.e., on the issue of what conditions must obtain for an assertion such as 'He believes the Pope will resist' to be true. In the following I will identify these two camps of Anti-Eliminativists as the Realists and the Anti-Realists.

Intentional Realism

John Searle strongly resists the sceptical stance of the Eliminativists. He starts from the position that folk psychological discourse *must*, in general, be true 'or we would not have survived' (Searle 1992: 59). Moreover, he accepts that the truth of a folk attribution of a particular mental ('intentional') state, say Henry's belief, depends on the existence in Henry's head of a particular physical state, namely that brain state in which his belief consists. Searle's preferred example concerns not the lusty English monarch of Herman's Hermits fame but a more modern head of state who nevertheless suffers from a similar sort of problem. Searle says:

> Suppose I now believe, as I do, that Clinton is president of the United States. Whatever else that belief might be, it is a state of my brain ... consisting in such things as configurations of neurons and synaptic connections, activated by neurotransmitters. (Searle 1999: 89–90)

Searle accepts that neuroscientists have not yet identified the particular brain states in which beliefs or any other intentional states consist. He even appears to accept that neuroscience may never successfully reduce intentional states to brain states. But this question, he insists, 'is irrelevant to the question of their existence' (Searle 1992: 60). Intentional states, he maintains, have subjective, phenomenological characteristics which may not be identifiable with the tools and techniques currently available in neuroscience.

Another intentional realist, Jerry Fodor, rejects the 'phenomenological' implications of Searle's position, but still resists eliminativist scepticism about propositional attitudes.

> [T]he present interpretation of the relation between neurological and psychological constructs is compatible with very strong claims about the ineliminability of mental language from behavioural theories. (Fodor 1968: 116)

However, Fodor argues that a given belief consists not in a particular brain state but rather in an indefinite set of possibly heterogeneous brain states that are, nonetheless, 'functionally equivalent'. What makes these brain states functionally equivalent is that they enter into the same causal relations – causal relations whose behavioural outcomes are characterized in the same folk psychological terms.

> [I]dentical psychological functions [can] sometimes be ascribed to anatomically heterogeneous neural mechanisms. In that case mental language will be required to state the conditions upon such ascriptions of functional equivalence. (...)
> Every mousetrap can be identified with some mechanism, and being a mousetrap can therefore be identifed with being a member of some (indefinite) set of possible mechanisms. But enumerating the set is not a way of dispensing with the notion of a mousetrap; that notion is required to say what all the members of the set have in common and, in particular, what credentials would be required to certify a putative new member as belonging to the set.' (Fodor 1968: 116–17)

In other words, if we eliminate folk psychological discourse from neuropsychological investigations, we will have no way of classifying any states of the brain as the same or different, at least not in a way with any relevance to explaining human behaviour. Brain states, according to Fodor, simply are categorized by their functional characteristics; and without folk psychological terms to use in characterizing their behavioural outcomes, those categories will not be identifiable.

Searle and Fodor can be seen as protecting folk psychology from the sceptical attacks of the Eliminativists, but it should be clear that this 'protection' is bought at a metaphysical cost. In the first place, they both beg the question of the truth of folk psychological claims. Searle uses a counterfactual conditional in asserting that folk psychological claims 'have to be' true: that is, they have to be true because otherwise we human beings would not have survived. Such a rhetorical maneuver puts the onus on the sceptic to show that, in fact, we *could* have survived even if no folk psychological claim were true. But how is the poor sceptic to do this? Fodor, on the other hand, takes the truth of folk psychological claims for granted and, to provide something that they can be true of, he conjures up the notion of 'functionally equivalent' brain states, which is what intentional claims are really 'about'. Moreover, the functional equivalence of these brain states will only be identifiable if folk psychological terms *remain* a central tool of neuropsychological investigation.

With this argument, Fodor can be seen to push the realist envelope as far as it can conceivably go. To go any further than this is to enter the domain of Anti-Realism, where Daniel Dennett may be found happily residing.

Anti-Realism/Instrumentalism

Dennett has many times made clear his agreement with the Eliminativists' scepticism about the existence of *referents* for folk psychological expressions.

> I believe [it] to be false ... that our ordinary way of picking out putative mental features and entities succeeds in picking out real features and entities. (...) About ... putative mental entities [such as beliefs and desires] I am an eliminative materialist.' (Dennett 1981: xix–xx)

However, it is important to note that Dennett is not suggesting that folk psychological *discourse* ought to be revised or replaced, nor that familiar terms like 'belief' and 'intention' ought to be eliminated. Rather, it is the theorization of such folk psychological terms that is the real culprit. As the following passage illustrates, Dennett thinks that folk psychological terms can lead – and repeatedly have led – theorists to postulate a 'confused ontology' of mental states in the head. It is these putative mental entities, thus 'theorized' into ideological existence, whose elimination he argues for.

> Suppose we find a society that lacks our knowledge of human physiology, and that speaks a language just like English except for one curious family of idioms. When they are tired they talk of being beset by *fatigues*, of having mental fatigues, muscular fatigues, fatigues in the eyes and fatigues of the spirit. Their sports lore contains such maxims as 'too many fatigues spoils your aim' and 'five fatigues in the legs are worth ten in the arms'. When we encounter them and tell them of our science, they want to know *what fatigues are*. They have been puzzling over such questions as whether numerically the same fatigue can come and go and return, whether fatigues have a definite location in matter and space and time, whether fatigues are identical with some particular physical states or processes or events in

their bodies, or are made of some sort of stuff. We can see that they are off to a bad start with these questions, but what should we tell them? One thing we might tell them is that there simply are no such things as fatigues – they have a confused ontology. We can expect some of them to retort: 'You don't think there are fatigues? Run around the block a few times and you'll know better! There are many things your science might teach us, but the non-existence of fatigues isn't one of them!'

We ought to be unmoved by this retort, but if we wanted to acknowledge this society's 'right' to go on talking about fatigues – it's their language, after all – we might try to accommodate by agreeing to call at least some of the claims they make about fatigues true and false, depending on whether the relevant individuals are drowsy, exhausted or feigning, etc. We could then give as best we could the physiological conditions for the truth and falsity of those claims, but refuse to take the apparent ontology of those claims seriously. (...) Fatigues are not good theoretical entitities, however well entrenched the term 'fatigues' is in the habits of thought of the imagined society. The same is true, I hold, of beliefs, desires, pains, mental images, experiences–as all these are *ordinarily* understood. Not only are *beliefs* and *pains* not good theoretical *things* (like electrons or neurons), but the *state-of-believing-that-p* is not a well-defined or definable theoretical *state*. (Dennett 1981: xix–xx)

Given this sceptical conclusion, one might initially be surprised to hear that, all the same, Dennett characterizes the 'intentional stance'– the notion whose virtues he trumpets in all his writings – as 'the view from folk psychology' (Dennett 1996: 27; Dennett 1981: 3). Moreover, it is the intentional stance which, according to Dennett, allows us to recognize our fellow humans (and some other animals) as 'intentional systems', a recognition on which all of our moral thought, cultural behaviour, and self-understanding depend. In other words, it is essential to our understanding of our own and others' behaviour and of the social worlds within which we live and act that we conceive of ourselves as creatures who believe, who desire, who think, who intend, who mean, and who understand. In other words, we cannot give up thinking of ourselves as 'intentional systems'. That is, we cannot give up the view from folk psychology.

An intentional system is a system whose behaviour can be explained and predicted by relying on ascriptions to the system of beliefs and desires and other intentionally characterized features... hopes, fears, intentions, perceptions, expectations, etc.' (Dennett 1981: 271)

Dennett therefore is an ardent defender of folk psychology. In the following extract from one of his published defences, he illustrates the importance of the intentional stance to our understanding of ordinary human abilities, such as the ability to understand a joke.

'A man went to visit his friend the Newfie and found him with both ears bandaged. 'What happened?' he asked, and the Newfie replied, 'I was ironing my shirt, you know, and the telephone rang.' 'That explains one ear, but what about the other?' 'Well, you know, I had to call the doctor!'

If we ... ask what one has to believe in order to get the joke, ... what we get is a long list of different propositions. You must have beliefs about the shape of an iron, the shape of a telephone; the fact that when people are stupid, they often cannot coordinate the left hand with the right hand doing different things; the fact that the hefts of a telephone receiver and an iron are approximately the same; the fact that when telephones ring, people generally answer them; and many more.

What makes my narrative a joke and not just a boring story is that ... it leaves out many facts and counts on your filling them in, but you could fill them in only if you had all those beliefs. (...) Strike off one belief on that list and see what happens. That is, find some people who do not have the belief (but have all the others), and tell them the joke. They will not get it. They cannot get it, because each of the beliefs is necessary for comprehension of the story.' (Dennett 1991: 139–40)

This argument may seem to sit oddly with the Eliminativism that Dennett often advocates. For on those occasions, he is arguing sceptically that an intentional term like 'belief' has no referent. Like the use of the term 'fatigues' in the first passage I quoted, the use of 'beliefs' suggests a 'confused ontology'. Yet in his analysis of what is required to understand the Newfie joke he appears to be arguing that one *must* have beliefs in order to get the joke, and of course the assumption is that we *do* get the joke. So, how can it be that we have beliefs and yet that the term 'belief' has no referent?

The answer to this conundrum lies in Dennett's Anti-Realism. For his point is not that there must be such *things* (mental entities) as beliefs but that it must be legitimate to *claim* that people – e.g., those of his readers who get this joke – have beliefs. Ascriptions of belief, of intentions, of desires, of meanings, and of understanding are essential to our ability to understand ourselves and our behaviour. Belief-claims, for instance, cannot be eliminated from discourse without thereby losing our ability to make sense of what it is to get a joke and what doing so requires. Belief-claims are necessary, but they should not be interpreted on a theoretical model. It is better, Dennett argues, to conceive of folk psychological discourse *not* as the manifestation of a folk theory but rather as a form of 'folk craft' (Dennett 1991: 135). It is a craft – a discursive technique – for predicting and explaining human behaviour. It is the mediating instrument of the intentional stance. And this leads Dennett to affirm its use not only with regard to human behaviour. For he claims to see no objection to using the same folk psychological terms in characterizing the behaviour of computers. Moreover, it is the legitimacy of characterizing computers in such terms that leads to the conclusion that a computer, like a human and some other animals, is an intentional system.

> The computer is an intentional system ... not because it has any particular intrinsic features, and not because it really and truly has beliefs and desires (whatever that would be), but just because it succumbs to a certain *stance* adopted toward it, namely the intentional stance, the stance that proceeds by ascribing intentional predicates under the usual constraints to the computer ... (Dennett 1981: 273)

Folk Psychology and the Language Myth

How are these debates about 'folk psychology' related to the Language Myth? The Language Myth is the assumption that discourse–in this case folk psychological discourse–is understandable because those participating in the discourse know and use a fixed code. This code determines the meanings of the words and sentences used in the discourse. Well, if this is how discourse using words like 'belief', 'intention', 'consciousness', and 'understanding' is understandable, then the question naturally arises: What precisely are the meanings that the code assigns to these words? And what are the meanings of sentences such as 'He believes I'm crazy', 'He intends to resign', and 'I understand what you said'?

Surrogationalism (Harris 1980) is a characteristically Western-cultural corollary to the Language Myth. It is the assumption that the meaning of a word is what it 'stands for' and that the meaning of a sentence is the set of circumstances or state of affairs which the sentence is 'about' – or, according to a common forumulation, those circumstances which must obtain in order for the sentence to be true. In the debates about folk psychology, it seems clear that Realists such as Searle and Fodor take for granted

(i) the legitimacy of folk psychological discourse ('Otherwise how could we have survived?') and
(ii) the surrogationalist explanation of that legitimacy.

In other words, they assume that many of the assertions of folk psychological discourse are true and that this is because the circumstances which their truth requires do in fact obtain. Given this assumption, the Realists naturally conclude that

(a) there *must* be something that mental terms such as 'belief' and 'understand' stand for and
(b) there must be brain states which folk psychological assertions are about and which, in the case of true assertions, do in fact obtain.

Of course, as we have seen, Searle and Fodor differ over the phenomenological or functional identity of these brain states, but the conclusion that they *must* be real is shared by both. Not surprisingly, they conclude that it is these neurological realities that should be the objects of scientific psychology.

The Eliminativist, on the other hand, shares the Realist's surrogationalist premise, although he sceptically refuses to take for granted the legitimacy of folk psychological discourse. So he turns to the empirical findings of scientific research to determine if the brain states required to legitimate folk psychological assertions do in fact obtain. However, neuropsychological research has not succeeded in identifying any plausible neurological candidates *either* for referents of folk psychological terms *or* for truth-conditions for folk psychological assertions. In other words, neuropsychological research has not found anything which the components of folk psychological discourse could plausibly be construed to be 'about'. Therefore, the Eliminativist argues that, *not really being about anything at all*, folk psychological discourse ought to be radically revised – including the elimination of many of its most familiar terms and locutions. If this is not done, argues the Eliminativist, then we will continue to be fooled into retaining the mythological assumption that folk psychological discourse is in fact about something real–that there really are such things as thoughts and intentions–and that people really do believe, mean, understand, and imagine. Worst of all, the onus will remain on the long-suffering neuroscientists to find and explain the properties of these entirely mythical entities and states.

Another characteristically Western corollary to the Language Myth (Harris 1980) is what Harris calls 'instrumentalism'. Instrumentalism offers an alternative to the surrogationalist account of how language means. According to the instrumentalist, meaning inheres in a word or sentence's usefulness for interactional purposes. The Anti-Realist in the debate, such as Dan Dennett, shares the Realist's assumption of the legitimacy of folk psychological discourse; but he rejects the Realist's assumption that that legitimacy inheres in the surrogational qualities of that discourse. On the contrary, he advocates the instrumentalist view that folk psychological discourse is legitimate simply *because it is interactionally useful*. This is Dennett's argument in claiming that folk psychology is a 'calculus' for predicting and explaining the behaviour of others. 'X believes that snow is white iff X can be predictively attributed the belief that snow is white.' (Dennett 1981: xvii). Folk psychological terms and assertions do not mean by representing or 'standing for' neurological entities or states of affairs, but rather as a function of their usefulness in mediating and managing our daily interactional lives with others. The evolutionary advantage of this instrumentalist 'calculus' is assumed by Dennett to be obvious, just as Searle assumes it to be obvious that without folk psychology, humanity would not have survived.

The Anti-Realist therefore concludes that it is mistaken to conclude that folk psychological terms should be eliminated simply because neuroscientists can find no referents for them in the brain. Moreover, it is a surrogationalist mistake. From the Anti-Realist's instrumentalist perspective, it is hardly surprising that neuroscientists cannot find anything for folk psychological terms to stand for. But, so what? As the Anti-Realist sees it, folk psychological discourse can still mean as satisfactorily as other forms of discourse do, as a function of its usefulness in the attainment of human communicational goals.

* * * * *

As integrational linguistics matures in its role as the not-so-loyal opposition to mainstream linguistics, it may find that there is much to be learned from the rhetorical knots into which cognitive psychologists and philosophers have tied themselves over the issue of folk psychology. For it would seem that the same kinds of questions that psychologists and philosophers believe to be raised by folk psychological discourse could also be seen to be posed by folk linguistic discourse. How should the integrationist respond to these questions? (For an extended discussion of how mainstream, or 'orthodox', linguistics has responded to them, see Taylor 1992.) Should the integrationist also adopt an Eliminativist stance on such everyday metadiscursive terms as 'meaning', 'understands', 'refers', 'the English language', etc.? That is, should she argue that there are no such things as meanings or languages, that understanding and referring are not real-world, mental, or any other kind of event, and that it would therefore be better to throw these terms–and language-games concerning them–on the same rubbish heap where have long lain the terms 'phlogiston' and 'caloric'? Or should integrationist be a realist, perhaps arguing that of course there are such things as meanings and languages and that people really do understand each other and mean what they say, albeit not always. The problem, the Realist integrationist could then claim, is neither with the terms themselves or with the ordinary, 'folk' use of them or with the things or events they refer to, but rather with the family of orthodox linguistic theories that have conspicuously failed to say anything sensible about them in over two thousand years of the Western linguistic tradition. The integrationist's task, therefore, would be to say what meaning, understanding, languages, etc., really are–when clearly seen from outside the mystifying confines of orthodox linguistic theorizing. Or, on the other hand, should the integrationist adopt an Anti-Realist position, arguing like Dennett that while reality (mental or phenomenal) does not actually contain such things as meanings and languages or events such as understanding and referring, nevertheless these are essential components of our culture's way of talking about and conceptualizing language; and they should therefore not be eliminated, but just re-thought and re-defined?

Doubtless it would be better to put these questions in more general terms, extracting them from the web of *a priori* assumptions and conceptions that have influenced the strategies adopted in the folk psychology debate – those assumptions and conceptions that have contributed to the absurd character of some of the popular academic positions discussed above. So, to put the matter more generally, we might ask: Should the integrationist's goal be to determine, for instance, what *signs* really are, in contrast to the faulty descriptions given by theorists influenced by the Language Myth? Should the integrationist take it as a goal to give a Language-Myth-free explanation of what it is for an utterance to *mean* something? Or what it is for a speaker to *refer* to something or someone or to *mean* what he says? Or what it is for one person to *understand* what another says? Or what it is to be *a language*? Or what it is for a language to *change*? Or, on the other hand, should the integrationist advocate the elimination of these language-myth-infected terms and concepts from integrational theories of language and communication? My hope is that these questions will enliven the discourse of integrationism in the coming years.

References

Churchland, P. (1981) 'Eliminative materialism and the propositional attitudes'. *Journal of Philosophy*, vol. 78, no. 2
Churchland, P. (1991) 'Folk psychology and the explanation of human behaviour' In Greenwood 1991.
Dennett, D. (1981) *Brainstorms,* Cambridge, Mass.: MIT Press.
Dennett, D. (1991) 'Two contrasts: folk craft versus folk science, and belief versus opinion ' In Greenwood 1991.
Dennett, D. (1996) *Kinds of Minds*, New York: Basic Books.
Fodor, J. (1968) *Psychological Explanation,* New York: Random House.
Greenwood, J.D. (Ed.) (1991) *The Future of Folk Psychology*, Cambridge: Cambridge University Press.
Harris, R. (1980) *The Language-Makers*, London: Duckworth.
Harris, R. (1981) *The Language Myth,* London: Duckworth.

James, W. (1890) *Principles of Psychology,* London: Henry Holt & Co.

Ramsey, W., S. Stich, and J. Garon (1991) 'Connectionism, eliminativism, and the future of folk psychology'. In Greenwood 1991.

Searle, J. (1992) *The Rediscovery of Mind,* Cambridge, Mass.: MIT Press.

Searle, J. (1999) *Mind, Language, and Society,* London: Weidenfield & Nicolson.

Stich, S. (1983) *From Folk Psychology to Cognitive Science*, Cambridge, Mass.: MIT Press.

Taylor, T.J. (1992) *Mutual Misunderstanding: Scepticism and the Theorizing of Language and Interpretation*, Durham, N.C.: Duke University Press and London: Routledge.

Watson, J. (1924) *Behaviorism*, Chicago: University of Chicago Press.

7 The Language Myth and the Race Myth: Evil Twins of Modern Identity Politics?

Christopher Hutton

Introduction

Imagine a conference held on 'The idea of race' around 1930 and a discussion between a race theorist and a sceptical opponent of race theory. In order to bolster the claims of race theory to be a science, the race theorist points to a massive body of work produced by European scholars, studies that use systematic observation, precise measurement and statistical methods involving hundreds of subjects. To this the sceptic replies that there is no need to postulate essences called 'races' in order to explain – if explanation is needed – the physical differences between groups of humans found in different parts of the world. No doubt the retort to this from the race theorist would be: what do you propose to put in the place of the concept of race?

Now imagine a conference in the year 2000 called 'The race myth in Western culture' held by scholars in the humanities. Unless the conference were held under the auspices of an extreme right-ring or neo-fascist organization, all the academics giving papers would be likely to attack the role of the concept of race in Western colonialism, in Nazism and in the politics of contemporary Europe. It would be unlikely that there would be any calls for a new concept to replace the myth of race, let alone questions about how to do race theory without an essentialist concept of race. Why should the existence of a 'race myth' be generally accepted in the humanities, while the claim that there exists a 'language myth' is generally met with scepticism?

But surely, one might object, language and race are not equivalent concepts? The evil consequences of race theory are evident from history, whereas the language myth – if it is a myth – is merely an idealization or a construct that allows linguists to study languages, and societies to have faith in institutions like the law.

In thinking about the role the language myth has played in Western thought, it is instructive to look at the way other comparable 'myths' or intellectual constructs have developed in tandem with or opposition to ideas about language. Race theory (defined as the systematic study of human physical diversity) offers an appealing contrast to linguistics for a number of reasons. Like linguistics, race theory seems to straddle the humanities, the social sciences and the natural sciences. Race theory is taxonomic in a number of different ways, and the categories used in race theory to classify human diversity overlap with and interact with terms and categories used by non-specialists, and with those used by linguists. One key difference from linguistics is that race theory appeals to a very great extent to iconic representation, i.e. the picture and the photograph (though also to statistics), whereas linguistics and the language myth are bolstered primarily by the prestige of writing. As identity myths, i.e. myths about the classification of humans into groups, both rely equally on an abstract set of categories realized, or found through analysis, in the realm of human diversity.

The race myth

There now exists an overwhelming consensus among scholars in the humanities and 'soft' social sciences that the notion that human beings are divided into discrete races is a 'myth'. The politically correct answer to any question about the existence of races is to assert that they are 'constructs' or 'social constructs'. Any discussion of human identity that assumes the existence of races and racial essences is deemed pseudo-scientific. Although race theory as a classificatory system of human diversity and modern eugenics are logically and institutionally distinct, they are both frequently rejected as part of an intellectual package which includes notions of biological superiority, eugenics and genetic determinism. Thus, if the notion of an Aryan race is a myth (for a historical survey, see Poliakov 1974), the assertion of the superiority of the Nordic race must be a myth about a myth. In practice however the term 'race' is often used to mean 'visible human varieties', and assertions are made about racial equality in the context of debates about social and political rights. It seems therefore that we can oppose racism, while insisting that races do not exist.

The situation outside the humanities and 'soft' social sciences is much more complex. For example, anthropometrics plays an important role in archaeology in the study of human remains and in physical anthropology. In the biological sciences and population studies, a whole range of views and practices can be found. For example, Lewontin concludes a study of human variation by affirming that '[h]uman racial classification is of no social value and is positively destructive of social and human relations'. Since the classification of humans into racial groups is 'of virtually no genetic or taxonomic significance [...], no justification can be offered for its continuance' (1997: 397). A sharp contrast is offered by Levin who sums up his defence of the notion of race as follows (1997: 1–2):

> It is strange that race differences should ever have been taboo, since human groups obviously do vary, for instance in skin colour and facial features. [...] Indeed, it is recognized that human groups not only look but act differently. Asians are comparatively restrained; rhythm is a more salient feature of black than European music. These differences are usually attributed to 'society', but to seek to explain them is to admit that they exist. If breeds of dog may differ in intelligence and temperament, there seems no reason evolution could not have differentiated human groups along similar lies.

A middle-ground is occupied by those who would argue that one needs to take into account racial background in treating illness, since human populations vary in their disposition to certain diseases and in their response to particular drugs (Watts 1997).

Within the humanities and social sciences there is comparatively little interest in, or controversy over, the status of the concepts 'language' and 'languages'. Anyone who talks about languages and assumes their existence as discrete essences is unlikely to be denounced on political grounds. Those scholars who hold that the existence of a 'race myth' is self-evident would be unlikely to agree that there is an equivalent 'language myth'. There is also little awareness of the political importance of the 'language myth', whilst discussion of race is so heavily politicized that any generalizations based on the existence of race and races are viewed as politically suspect, even if they are not actually 'racist'. Whilst linguists frequently make comments about the difficulty of defining languages, these comments amount ultimately to a concession designed to deal with a specific philosophical or methodological objection. In practice, linguists are not shy of talking about the grammar of French, the sound system of Italian, etc., since their professional viability depends on statements of this kind.

One does not have to be an advocate of race theory to sense in this academic-political scenario a set of evasions and equivocations. It cannot be the case, for example, that it is a scientific fact that all races are equal, if it is also simultaneously being asserted that races do not exist. The attack on racism as pseudo-science implies an alternative framework of proven facts about races and human variation. Nor can we appeal here to some general, scientifically proven notion of human equality. There is no way within the discourse of science to argue for biological equality, given that when human beings are measured in any of the numerous available ways they show patterns of variation. In our everyday lives we recognize differences in intelligence, health, sexual attractiveness, athleticism, and so on as a matter of course. The denial of biological inequality can only be achieved by appeal to a Christian or post-Christian humanist view of human value and worth.

One basic problem with the liberal consensus on race is that the assertion that races are 'constructs' says very little. For, societies, personalities, texts, tables and dog breeds and just about anything else can be seen as socially constructed. It may well be true that notions such as race are not 'natural', and that '[a]ll constructions of "reality" must be seen as a product of the human capacity for thought and, consequently, are subject to change and variability' (Jackson and Penrose 1993: 2–3). But what then could be 'natural' within such a framework? Leaving to one side this theoretical problem, it does seem evident that race and language are on the same level of 'constructedness'. If we decide that languages exist, then in the same way we would have to say that races exist. If any attempt to classify and characterize different races is unscientific, then any attempt to classify and categorize different languages must similarly be pseudo-science.

It should be noted here that race theorists (including Nazi race theorists), like linguists, readily concede that their classifications are liable to objection, or involve the drawing of arbitrary or problematic distinctions. Both groups of scholars would agree that intermediate cases exist, and that the categories they use are problematic in particular ways. Any attempt to distinguish between the two disciplines by suggesting that linguists are somehow more aware of the problematic nature of the concept of 'a language', whereas race theorists are fanatical essentialists, seems likely to fail.

This paper seeks to explore briefly aspects of the history and politics of the 'race myth' and the 'language myth', suggesting that a comparison between these two myths is instructive in a variety of ways. Its historical focus is on the ideas of Heymann Steinthal and Ferdinand de Saussure, both of whom lived through the rise of academic race theory in the closing decades of the nineteenth century.

Steinthal

In an essay succinctly entitled 'Dialect, language, people, state, race', published in the Festschrift for Adolf Bastian in 1896, Heymann Steinthal (1823–1899) attempted to bring some terminological order into the muddled legacy of nineteenth century political and linguistic theorizing. He began with the conundrum of the dialect-language distinction, making the (to us) familiar observation that attempts to define that distinction by reference to linguistic facts – for example the concept of linguistic distance – could not cope with the inconsistencies with which we applied the term. Thus Dutch is considered a language, though it is no more distant from the Low German dialects and from High German than is Swiss German or the dialects of South Germany. Thus the idea that a language is somehow the aggregation of a set of dialects, that Greek is the sum of Ionic, Attic, etc., and that the difference between two languages is greater than that between two dialects, fails to account for our determination to call the Low German dialect spoken in Holland a language. A traveller, setting out from a point of origin, would, in moving further away from the home village encounter variation in idiom and dialect which could be grouped together in various ways, but never a language. Steinthal comments: 'The concept of *a language* is not to be found at all from the point of view from which we research and classify dialects; that concept lies in a quite different sphere, that is within cultural history, and especially literary history' (1896: 48).

Here Steinthal sets up a familiar opposition between the cultural and the (relatively) natural. Dialects are there on the ground to be experienced by the traveller moving through the landscape; languages are simply not part of that world at all.

But where do languages come from? According to Steinthal, they come from dialects; they are upwardly mobile speech varieties. The Middle High German language was originally the Swabian dialect,

Italian was originally the dialect of Florence, etc. What was for some a tool of domestic communication from earliest childhood gets raised to new functions and levels of expressivity. It distances itself from its 'mother dialect' (*Mutterdialekt*), becomes a vehicle for literature and for the thoughts and feelings of the entire *Volk*, rather than just a part of it. In achieving this higher status, it however ceases to change as rapidly as the dialect; it is fixed in writing and not subject to the constant erosion that the dialect experiences in the 'mouth of the people'. At any event, changes in the language do not affect the development of the dialect. Cultural, political, religious forces operate upon natural relationships, causing one dialect to rise to prominence and separate itself off from its relatives: 'The dialect is the product of the folk; the language is an artificial product, somewhat like our cultivated plants' (1896: 48).

This framework remains familiar to us today, adopted as it was into the basic world view of twentieth century dialectology and, subsequently, sociolinguistics. Figures like Einar Haugen, Heinz Kloss and Joshua Fishman have added little to it. The slogan of engaged sociolinguistics in the British context, that Standard English is just, or essentially, a dialect ('what is now a social dialect was once a regional variety of English', Romaine 1994: 85) obviously has its intermediate origins in nineteenth century discussions of naturalness and artificiality.

What then of race? Race, says Steinthal, cannot have any impact on the standard language (1896: 49). Race has no ethnological significance; it is only anthropologically significant. 'Anthropology' here refers to physical anthropology, the comparative study of human physical types. A language and a people (*Volk*) may however be connected, but a *Volk* is 'always a prehistoric product', formed out of diverse elements which we have difficulty identifying today. However national character (*Volkscharakter*) is both a product of, and a factor in, the development of a language. This, says Steinthal, can be most clearly seen in the languages of the Iberian Peninsula. The pattern of language distribution we find there reflects early population movements and waves of settlement: Portuguese is of Celto-Romance origin; Provençal is Ibero-Romance and Spanish is Celto-Ibero-Romance. The original affinity of the Southern French with the East Spanish is shown by their common love for bull fighting – both groups are Iberians, unlike the Northern French. Nasalization is found in those speech varieties which are Celtic in origin (1896: 49–50).

These somewhat murky reflections lead Steinthal to the key questions: How should we understand the relationship between language and race? Can we infer a correlation between degree of relation linguistically and degree of relation racially? Are peoples whose languages can be traced back to a common source to be seen as a racially one?

The answer is a clear no, and the Romance languages offer the clearest evidence for this. Speakers of Romance languages are Iberians, Celts and Slavs. These are however branches of the same Caucasian race. The Ottomans in Turkey and the Magyars have the same Caucasian racial character, but their language belongs to the Mongolian or Altaic family. The Finns are Caucasian but their language is Uralic, closely related to the language of the Lapps, who are not Caucasian in appearance at all (1896: 50).

That linguistic affinity and anthropological type must be established independently is the consensus of all linguists who have given the matter serious thought, argues Steinthal. But, given the assumption that language and race were originally congruent in each people, which should we look for in seeking origins? The answer would seem to lie with whichever of the two changes shows the greater constancy over time. The linguist would argue that it is language, and apparent counter-examples such as the case of the Romance languages, actually confirm this. For all the high level of development and organizational abilities of the Romans, they would not have transmitted their language without the additional factor of the spread of Christianity. Otherwise the conquerors would have taken on the language of the conquered, as happened with the Normans first in France and then in England. In the Moslem world things worked out differently. There, a more developed religion met up with more developed social organization in the societies they conquered. The Persians remained Caucasian in race and language, even whilst accepting Islam, though they did enrich their vocabulary with borrowings from Arabic. The Turks who adopted Islam retained their Mongolian or Altaic language, again with borrowing. In racial terms they are a geographically defined mixture of Caucasian and Mongolian peoples. But in prehistoric times, when we cannot speak of superior civilizations, we have no reason to assume such processes occurred (1896: 50–51).

Steinthal seems to offer a confused but at least minimally consistent story up to this point, stressing the distinction between racial and linguistic categories, the need to be aware of factors that lead to dramatic language shift, the assertion of a difference between the prehistoric and the historical world. However, in his closing remarks he notes that progress in ethnology leads us to doubt, for example, whether there ever was an original people with an original Indo-European language, whilst the status of the Indo-European languages is a fixed and established fact. According to the latest discoveries, each *Volk* is a composite of many different elements; it is difficult to talk of the race of a *Volk* (1896: 51–52).

In conclusion, Steinthal notes that in all proposed classifications of races the Caucasian race is the highest. But members of this race speak a wide variety of languages, and the same is true for each race (1896: 52):

> Experience shows that racial characteristics disappear and are modified only through racial mixing; but the giving up of one's own language and the taking on of a foreign language may have happened in prehistoric times who knows how often in line with the majority or on account of force, necessity or love.

This conclusion seems to leave us nowhere. Given that we have no basis on which to assume that the identities we discuss today are grounded in historical essences, we have no basis from which to construct any account of how those essences have changed or diverged.

His deconstruction of the notion of a language notwithstanding, Steinthal seems to assume that races, languages, language families and *Völker* exist, but that they are not congruent. The speakers of Semitic languages are not all of Semitic race. But that way of conceptualizing the relationship between language and race only makes sense if we assume that there was once a Semitic race speaking an original Semitic language. Otherwise how could we justify using the label both for a race and a language? The problem for the linguist is that of following through on the deconstruction of the notion of 'a language', since names of languages are a key element of the metadiscourse and a central element in the reconstruction of ethnohistory.

Ferdinand de Saussure (1857–1913)

At first sight the *Cours* seems to take up this same conventional position on the relationship between language and race (in the following exposition, the pagination of the 1922 edition is indicated in square brackets). The statement at the beginning of the *Cours* that linguistics is to be clearly distinguished from (physical) anthropology 'which studies mankind as a species; whereas language is a social phenomenon' (1983: 6 [1922: 20]) seems to settle the case that Saussure clearly distinguished linguistic identity from racial classifications.

The clearest statement on this topic comes towards the close of the published *Cours* (Saussure 1983: 221 [1922: 304–305]):

> It would be a mistake to believe that one can argue from a common language to consanguinity, or equate linguistic families with anthropological families. The facts are more complex. There is, for example, a Germanic race with very distinct anthropological features: fair hair, elongated skull, tall stature, etc. The Scandinavian type exemplifies it perfectly. But it is far from being the case that every population speaking one of the Germanic languages answers this description. The Alemannic people at the foot of the Alps are very different anthropologically from Scandinavians. Could we say at least that a language in principle belongs to given race, and that any others who speak it must have had it imposed on them by conquest?

We could term this the 'original congruence' model of language and race. The *Cours* puts a question-mark against this model, while pointing out that history does offer examples of languages being imposed by conquest, e.g. the Romans in Gaul (Saussure 1983: 221–222 [1922: 305]):

> In the Germanic case, for instance, even granting that they subjugated so many different peoples, they can hardly have absorbed all of those. That would have required a long period of prehistoric domination, and other conditions for which there is no established evidence.

This argument is directed against the idea that languages have easily and routinely been imposed by conquest (incidentally echoing a key point in Steinthal's discussion, with the same example of Gaul used for illustration). But what then follows for the relationship of language and race?

Moving on, the *Cours* asserts that racial unity is far less important than the unity created through social bonds (*ethnisme*) which itself 'tends to bring about community of language, and perhaps gives the common language certain characteristics' (Saussure 1983: 222 [1922: 305–306]). However the *Cours* seems caught in a chicken-and-egg conundrum (1983: 222 [1922: 306]):

> Conversely, it is to some extent community of language which constitutes ethnic unity. Ethnic unity, in general, will always suffice to explain community of language. For example, in the early Middle Ages there was a Romance ethnicity linking peoples of very diverse origins and no political unity

The key question that one might wish to pose to this is whether these Romance peoples had any idea that they were Romance speakers. A second question might concern whether these Romance speakers could all communicate with each other. If the answer to these questions is negative, as it surely would be, then it would appear to involve the anachronistic application of the late nineteenth century notion of linguistic identity as the basis of ethnicity.

On Saussure's model, linguistic unity is created out of social bonds, and this form of identity – unlike racial membership – can be reconstructed historically using linguistic evidence. That it is reconstructable is unsurprising, since the *Cours* here effectively merges ethnic identity and membership of a linguistic community. Thus the best evidence that Etruscans lived alongside the Latins in early Italy is linguistic. The *Cours* allows that linguistic evidence can be used to reconstruct ethnicity, while at the same time attacking Adolphe Pictet and Hermann Hirt's use of linguistic paleontology and their over-reliance on etymology in reconstructing institutions, social structure, material civilization, etc. (1983: 223 [1922: 306–308]).

The denial that race and language are congruent might seem to have threatened the role of linguistic evidence in reconstructing ethnic history; the attack on linguistic paleontology implies scepticism about the tools of linguistic reconstruction. But all is saved when we read back through history a concept of ethnicity based on language.

The Saussure of the *Cours* appears to be a recognizably modern thinker: 'A negro brought to France at birth speaks French as well as any Frenchman', offered in the context of a dismissal of 'the operation of some underlying racial factor' in language change and human affairs in general (1983: 146 [1922: 203]). But the key questions left hanging by the *Cours* have subsequently been little perceived or addressed in linguistic theory. The penultimate paragraph of the *Cours* offers little help in clarifying the muddle (1983: 229–230 [1922: 317]):

> While recognizing that Schleicher distorted reality in treating languages as organic beings with their own intrinsic laws of evolution, we continue – without realizing it – to believe that languages are organic in a different sense, inasmuch as the genius of a race or ethnic group tends constantly to direct its language along certain fixed paths.

This seems to decry the tendency to ascribe personalities to languages based on race or ethnicity, but statements about the relationship of language to civilization and even race in the *Cours* suggest sympathy for this view (or a version of it).

The evidence from the published notebooks does little to resolve the problem of the status of Saussure's concept of ethnicity. (In the following, editorial conventions from the published editions are retained, including underlining, and material in angled brackets represents marginal and interlinear corrections and additions.) If we take first the case of the discussion of the relationship of linguistics to other disciplines, we find in the first Riedlinger notebook (Riedlinger I) the statement that linguistics discovered in its relationship to ethnology that it was not the same as philology (Komatsu and Wolf 1996: 1a):

> It was in its value for ethnology, which it did not suspect, that linguistics saw that it did not coincide with philology. Wilhelm von Humboldt first had the view that people grouped themselves in various races on the scale of their languages. The first question the modern ethnologist asks in order to determine to which race an unknown people belongs is: what is its language? In any event, a single language, for one and the same people, results in the predominance of one race, if not in an absolute homogeneity which also depends on the political history of a country.

This is less than clear. The use of the term 'ethnologist' suggests a contrast with physical anthropology, but why then offer the assertion that speech communities give rise to racial communities? 'Race' cannot here be a term from physical anthropology. In Riedlinger's notes on the second Course (Riedlinger II) the term *anthropologie* occurs in the context of a general assertion about the place of linguistics in relation to neighboring disciplines (Komatsu and Wolf 1997: 7a): 'In order to assign a place to linguistics language must not be taken from all sides; it is clear that if it is, then several sciences, psychology, physiology, anthropology, <grammar, philology,> etc., will be able to claim the language as their object'. In the Patois notebook, external linguistics is defined by connections with ethnology which involves 'civilisations, races'. These connections 'are generally double (are those who speak Slavic all Slavic?)' (Komatsu and Wolf 1997: 123a). Riedlinger II has a similar discussion, linking the definition of the object of study to the question of race and language (Komatsu and Wolf 1997: 25a):

> Thus our definition is completely negative; it [linguistics] is everything which is not relevant to the internal organism: the connections of the different languages with ethnology, the points at which the language becomes involved with the history of different populations, civilisations, races. The relationships <as in general> are here double. Are those who speak a Slavic language all of Slavic race? If it is a wandering race which speaks Slavic, has this not had repercussions on their language?

Constantin's notebook, based on the Third Course, does not include this observation (Komatsu and Harris 1993).

Riedlinger I also contains the observation found in the *Cours* that 'a black man taken to France at birth would there speak the language just as well as the natives' (Komatsu and Wolf 1996: 40a), as well as recording the general observation that comparative anthropology does not support any claims that there are permanent and direct racial factors that determine pronunciation, anymore than we can make a correlation between climate and language type (Komatsu and Wolf 1996 41a–42a). Riedlinger II also discusses the label Indo-European/Indo-Germanic. The notebook records regret that the shorter term of 'Aryans' is not used for the Indo-Europeans (Komatsu and Wolf 1997: 95a):

> This usage has definitively been dropped otherwise than for the completely restricted Indo-Iranian group. It is only here that we find a name of this kind borne by the peoples that it

designates. *Âryas* (old Vedic) opposes the Indo-European race to every population in India which was not Indo-European (*an-âryas*). Only the three highest castes were designated as Aryan (<in> the fourth, that of the *soudras*, the blood <is not> European).

The theme is taken up again in a more general discussion of the relationship of language to race: '<Today> we no longer link these two questions; <it is no longer stated that> the fact that a people speaks an Indo-European language *ipso facto* determines that that people is of Indo-European race or that it is of a homogenous Indo-European race' (Komatsu and Wolf 1997: 107a). This question is much more one for anthropology, which 'determines races by measuring skulls'. If we look at history, we see many complex relationships between the prior question of the relationship of language to people (*peuple*). Thus the language of a conqueror may disappear leaving only its name (Komatsu and Wolf 1997: 107a). Again the conclusion is that '<[t]he immense variety of historical conditions means that the language cannot reveal the race: > thus the language is <only> one of the indices of race' (Komatsu and Wolf 1997: 108a) However, the equivocation implied in the last sentence continues: 'Whitney said that one should not too swiftly abandon the idea that the race corresponds to the language over large expanses. <The opposite case is due only to specific exceptional causes.> The Roman conquest extended Latin <to all of Gaul> only by virtue of the superiority of the civilisation, Islam by virtue of the religious idea' (Komatsu and Wolf 1997: 108a).

The theme of language as useful in historical reconstruction also crops up in the Patois notebook. After noting that French is not a single language, Patois records: 'And there are other radical diversities, for example between Chinese and our Indo-European languages, where the very bases of our expression <of thought> are different; the aptitudes of the race intervene' (Komatsu and Wolf 1997: 111a). Again it is emphasized that linguistic identity is a significant marker of identity: 'The language can be taken as evidence for a civilization' (Komatsu and Wolf 1997: 159a). The Patois notebook ends with a paragraph echoing Riedlinger (Komatsu and Wolf 1997: 167a):

The presence of an Indo-European language with a people indicates that this people is Indo-European, it is moreover said, but to establish this facts quite other than linguistic (anthropology) need to be considered. Before opposing language and race we would need to oppose language and people. <u>The conquering people can absorb a language, or cause its language to be absorbed.</u> Britain is said to have been the victim of a conquest which expelled its language; [but] French was spoken alongside Anglo-Saxon in Britain. What is spoken today in Finland, Finnish, Swedish, or Russian? In a mass of peoples we see that a given branch represents a tribe from elsewhere: the Bulgars are of Tartar race. <u>There is sometimes coincidence, sometimes opposition between language and race. Often there is a coexistence of languages within a single people.</u> We cannot resolve the question, 'Does the language prove the race?', because of the overly great numbers of points to be examined.

If pressed to summarize Saussure's position on language and race, one might arrive at the following. One should not confuse the categories of physical anthropology with those of linguistics; we cannot assume that one domain can be read off the other. We can however speak of a linguistic identity which constructs a collectivity (ethnicity). Saussure believed that this form of identity or ethnicity could be reconstructed as having a history, so that we can tell, for example, that Etruscans lived side by side with Latins.

The key issue is whether it ever made sense to speak of an overlap or correlation between a language and a race. Was there at one time a Semitic race speaking the original Semitic language? If the answer to this question is no, then much of the nineteenth and twentieth century speculations on prehistory by linguists can be rejected as nonsensical. Not only Pictet's assumptions about the Indo-Europeans, but an entire understanding of history and culture is misguided. If the answer is yes, then there are two kinds of relationships between race and language; congruent or non-congruent. On this view, a racially Semitic person speaking a Semitic language as their mother tongue represents an original, prior or natural state; an African speaking French does not.

The language myth

In his discussion of what he terms 'the language myth', Harris (1981: 9) makes two basic points. Firstly that the language myth is 'a cultural product of post-Renaissance Europe' (though with its roots much deeper in the Western tradition) which 'reflects the political psychology of nationalism, and an educational system devoted to standardizing the linguistic behaviour of pupils'. Secondly, the language myth is a product of the telementational fallacy and the determinacy fallacy.

The two aspects of the myth, its external history and internal logic, combine to create a powerful social theory where personal identity (the identity of the individual as a native speaker of language X) is merged into a higher order community, the cohesion of which is guaranteed by a shared linguistic system of fixed form-meaning relations. The idea of a nation or *Volk* as defined by their sharing a common language has been an immensely powerful one in post-Renaissance Europe. But while this is a political idea which has had real political consequences, it also was transformed and internalized within linguistics, becoming the superficially apolitical concept of 'speech community'.

The political ideal of one 'one country – one language' (Harris 1998: 31) was and is of course problematic in a number of ways. This ideal has co-existed with other intersecting loyalties of religion, class, and historical consciousness, not to mention dialectal loyalties associated with political regionalism. Its relationship to racial identity is similarly convoluted. In the case of the modern Germans, few race theorists wished to argue that the Germans constituted a race. Even Nazi race theorists saw the German people as a hybrid, typically arguing that six races were represented in various proportions in the German *Volk* (Günther 1933). However the parallel conclusion was not drawn in the case of language. The fact that the German language could be seen as composed in some sense of dialects was not generally taken as implying that the German people did not speak German, or that there was no German language. For Nazi political theorists, what was out of alignment was the relationship of the state to the language and its speakers, i.e. the fact that large numbers of German speakers were not living in Germany. Of course, these speakers had to be 'true Germans' rather than Jews. (By contrast during WWI even Yiddish speakers in the East had been co-opted as part of a German cultural sphere).

Ironically, it was race, not language, that was problematic in relation to *Volk* in Nazi Germany. The fact that Jews spoke German as 'native speakers' was not used to deconstruct the ideal of one *Volk* – one language; rather, it led to the conclusion that the category of 'racially acceptable as a member of the *Volk*' was incongruent with the category 'speaker of German'.

Language and race: the myth of *Volk*

In Nazi Germany, the term 'Aryan' caused considerable problems for the authorities, who were faced with the problem that their own in-house race theorists saw the term as a linguistic one with no standing as a racial designation. According to these theorists, there was no Aryan race, just as there was no Jewish race. Even works setting out the complexities of Nazi racial policy and intended to give guidelines to ordinary citizens included discussion of the origin and development of the term. For example, Ulmenstein (1941: 11) explained how the term 'Aryan' had been used originally as the designation for the speakers of languages in Northern India, Persia etc., had then come to be used as an equivalent to Indo-Germanic, both as a linguistic and racial term, but was used in the 1933 laws which purified the civil service to mean 'non-Jewish'. The fact that someone speaks a non-Aryan language cannot be used to infer that they are necessarily non-Aryan, as the cases of the Finns and the Hungarians show. Thus 'the oft asked question of whether a particular people [*Volk*] is Aryan or not rested on a confusion of peoplehood [*Volkstum*] and race'. One term subsequently used by the authorities was 'of German blood or of related stock' ('deutschen oder stammesgleichen Blutes') (1941: 12). Ulmenstein concludes by stressing that we should not ask which particular race a people belongs to, but rather to which race an individual belongs (1941: 13).

What underlies this discussion is the assumption that historical change has led to the rift between the Aryan language and the Aryan people. The original unity and congruity of language and race has been lost. The project of Nazism can be understood as that of restoring that link in some form, by Germanizing those of 'of German blood or related stock' and eliminating or enslaving those non-Aryan speakers of German, e.g. German Jews, and others not fit to join the new racial elite.

This however did not in fact give a clear answer to the question of who was fit to join that elite, nor a clear definition of the nature of the German *Volk*. For where should the racial boundary of the *Volk* lie? What particular combination of the six races was required?

Was there a characteristic mix? One answer, given in various forms, was that all true Germans, whatever their physical type, were fundamentally shaped by the Nordic element, present in different proportions in different individuals and sub-groups, but deemed to be the determining element. In the 'Ten Commandments for a choice of spouse', widely disseminated in Nazi Germany, the fifth commandment ran: 'As German choose only a spouse of the same or Nordic blood'. By way of explanation it was asserted that 'the Nordic blood element unites the whole German people. Each German partakes in this to a greater or lesser extent' (see for example the text given in the 'Handbook for the German family', *Hausbuch für die deutsche Familie*, n.d., pp. 12–14).

Who's confusing whom?

A number of crucial issues arise out of this discussion. There is a historical irony in confident assertions of numerous linguists that the Nazi heresy was the confusion of Aryan, a linguistic term, with a racial identity (see Hutton 1999: 260–305). The further irony is that the myth of an original correlation between a language and a race is shared by both Nazis and anti-racist would-be progressives. In an article attacking the ideas of Arthur Jenson (who sought to show a correlation between IQ and race), one seeking to enroll linguistics 'in the war against racism', Baugh opens with the following statement: 'The relationship between language and racial groups has both a biological and a political dimension. The biological dimension first emerged historically as distinct genetic characteristics evolved among various human tribes in relative geographical isolation. Thus, in the typical case, language and race were originally correlated directly' (1988: 64).

One view widely held in the nineteenth and twentieth centuries, represented by the quotation from Baugh above, is therefore that language and race are not congruent now, but were so once, and thus were fused at the point of origin. However, it is very hard to imagine how this congruity could be defined, beyond the obvious fact that an isolated community may have a high density of kin relationships and may communicate linguistically. But we would have to read onto this hypothetical primordial situation categories such as 'a language' and 'a race'. This 'original congruence' view is however implicit in much linguistic theorizing of the nineteenth and twentieth century. One reason for its persistence may be that it allows us to account for the discontinuities of the present (people of African descent who speak French) without giving up on attempts to reconstruct ethnic history, migrations, etc. through linguistic evidence.

The second view suggests that racial categorization, the anthropometric categorization of individuals into racial groups, is either unscientific or irrelevant. It looks rather to the concept of ethnicity, and one version grounds that ethnicity in language. Others notions of ethnicity look to factors such as subjective identity, group consciousness, constructed tradition, etc., as well as language or speech variety (classlect, genderlect, dialect etc.). In Saussure's concept of *ethnisme*, there is effectively a fusion between ethnicity and linguistic identity. This view also ensures that linguistics can play a role in constructing ethnohistory. In this model, race in the subjective sense (ethnicity) is a product of linguistic identity. Ironically, this modern form of identity replicates the fusion of the racial and the linguistic which was the target of such persistent polemics from the end of the nineteenth century onwards.

But who is the scholar or who are the scholars who committed the crime of confusing physical anthropological identity with linguistic identity? The short answer appears to be: Wilhelm von Humboldt. Humboldt, it should be noted, was writing before the rise of Darwinism, neo-Darwinism and modern 'scientific' race theory in the period from 1850 to 1870, i.e. before the availability of an established scientific discourse of distinguishing physical or bodily type from native language spoken. The more complex answer seems to be: non-linguists, political theorists, nationalists and ordinary members of European and colonized societies who began to think in terms of language communities as the most natural political unit, and almost all professional linguists who in practice could not separate the discourse of ethnic or racial identity from linguistic categories. Slavs were Slavic because they spoke a Slavic language – more or less; Celts were Celts because they spoke a Celtic language, or at least their ancestors had.

Conclusion

The crisis that the congruence model encountered in Europe came from two sources: the assimilation of Jews into the language communities of post-emancipation Europe and the rise of empires in which subject peoples took on a wide range of linguistic roles, working for example in administrative tasks using the relevant European language. This posed again the question of race and set a limit to the viability of what can be termed the 'fictive' ethnic unity of modern linguistic nationalism. The very integrative power of the linguistic community and the ability of the African to grow up a native speaker of French posed the question of the biological or racial nature of the speech community. The power of the speech community to absorb racial diversity raised alarm about miscegenation.

For all the complexities of the history of this question over the last two centuries, one could make the argument that a congruence model of linguistic and ethnic/racial identity has remained central to identity theorizing and linguistic theory. The congruence model took different forms, invoking either lost congruent origins or the transformative nature of the linguistic community and its ability to create ethnic identities with reconstructable histories. Its value for ethnic nationalists of various forms is clear, but why did linguistics not offer a clearer account of the complexities and obscurities of this model? One answer must be that the 'language myth' not only sustained political movements throughout the world but also the discipline of linguistics itself. Further, many linguists have played dual roles as academics and nationalists, either on behalf of their own ethnic group or in their support for 'small' or marginalized languages. Half political principle, half methodological postulate, the language myth allowed linguists to maintain a fictive continuity between descriptive linguistics, the more overtly political sub-disciplines of sociolinguistics and critical linguistics, and the linguistic politics of the post-war (post-imperial) world.

The language myth flatters politically, in that it reassures linguistics that it has a 'real' subject matter, and that linguistics matters outside university departments. It also permits the distancing of linguistics from race theory, whilst allowing linguistics to stake a claim to a role in the reconstruction of ethnohistory. Race theory is scorned as 'pseudo-science' and held responsible for colonial oppression and National Socialism. By contrast, linguists tend to see the history of linguistics in the context of the language politics of post-Reformation Europe. Thus the political history of languages involves the vernaculars throwing off the yoke of Latin, oppressed minorities achieving sovereign status in the break up of the Austro-Hungarian empire, and so on. The paradox that these vernaculars had to be created ('constructed') in order to be liberated is lost, as is the contribution of linguistic theory and linguists to the murder and mayhem of twentieth century ethnic politics.

References

Baugh, John (1988) Language and race: some implications for linguistic science, in ed. Frederick J. Newmeyer, *Linguistics: the Cambridge Survey IV; Language: the socio-cultural context*, pp. 64–74, Cambridge: Cambridge University Press.

Jackson, Peter and Jan Penrose (1993) Placing "race" and nation, editors' introduction to *Contructions of race, place and nation*, pp. 1–23, London: University College London Press.

Komatsu, Eisuke and Roy Harris, eds. and trans. (1993) *Saussure's third course of lectures on General Linguistics (1910–1911), From the notebooks of Emile Constantin*, Oxford: Pergamon.

Komatsu, Eisuke and George Wolf, eds. and trans. (1996) *Saussure's first course of lectures on General Linguistics (1907), from the notebooks of Albert Riedlinger*, Oxford: Pergamon.

Komatsu, Eisuke and George Wolf, eds. and trans. (1997) *Saussure's second course on General Linguistics (1908–1909), from the notebooks of Albert Riedlinger and Charles Patois*, Oxford: Pergamon.

Günther, Hans F.K. (1933) *Kleine Rassenkunde des deutschen Volkes*, München: J.F. Lehmann.

Harris, Roy (1981) *The language myth*, London: Duckworth.

Harris, Roy (1998) *Introduction to integrational linguistics,* Oxford: Pergamon.

[Hausbuch] (n.d.) *Hausbuch für die deutsche Familie*, Berlin: Verlag für Standesamtwesen. [< 1935]

Hutton, Christopher (1999) *Linguistics and the Third Reich: mother-tongue fascism, race and the science of language*, London: Routledge.

Levin, Michael (1997) *Why race matters: race differences and what they mean*, Westport Connecticut/London: Praeger.

Lewontin, R.C. (1997) The apportionment of human diversity, in ed. E. Nathanial Gates, *The concept of "race" in natural and social science*, pp. 7–24, New York: Garland.

Poliakov, Leon (1974) *The Aryan myth: a history of racist and nationalist ideas in Europe*, translated by Edmund Howard, London: Heinemann.

Romaine, Suzanne (1994) *Language in society: an introduction to sociolinguistics*, New York: Oxford University Press.

Saussure, Ferdinand de (1983) *Course in General Linguistics,* translated & annotated by Roy Harris, London: Duckworth.

Steinthal, Heymann (1896) Dialekt, Sprache, Volk, Staat, Rasse, in *Festschrift für Adolf Bastian zu seinem 70. Geburtstage, 20 Juni 1896*, pp. 47–51, Berlin: Dietrich Reimer.

Ulmenstein, Freiherr Christian Ulrich (1941) *Der Abstammungsnachweis*, Berlin: Verlag für Standesamtswesen.

Watts, Elizabeth S. (1997) The biological race concept and diseases of modern man, in ed. E. Nathanial Gates, *The concept of "race" in natural and social science*, pp. 147–67. New York: Garland.

8 The Language Myth and Mathematical Notation as a Language of Nature

Daniel R. Davis

The language myth is the set of ideas and cultural practices that shape our understanding of language. Harris (1980) says of the cultural embeddedness of the concept of a language:

> The concept of a language may find expression in various ways and at various levels. It may take the form of myth, legend, or folklore. It may also in certain circumstances become the focal point of an explicit body of knowledge, doctrines, practices and methods of inquiry, tending towards the establishment of what is nowadays usually called a 'study', or 'discipline', or 'science', overtly concerned with linguistic matters. (Harris 1980: 31).

In other words, our understanding of language appears in a range of cultural settings, from myth to doctrine to science. Harris's point in the first instance is to demonstrate the cultural context in which our ideas about language arise, as well as that in which these ideas are formalized as a science. He later comes to characterize this entire complex of ideas about language as a myth:

> ... it is important for people to understand that a great deal of impressively authoritative modern theorizing about language is founded upon a myth.

> ... Like other myths, it has ancient origins in the Western tradition. Like all important myths, it flatters and reflects the type of culture which sponsors it. It has many contemporary ramifications. (Harris 1981: Preface)

That is to say, he claims that the elaboration of our concept of language into the science of linguistics is founded on, and itself constitutes part of, a myth. The mythic status of our concept of language does not merely account for the nature of modern linguistics. It connects linguistics to other cultural practices involving our concept or concepts of language.

In this paper I wish to trace the effect that this myth of language has had on the conceptualization of mathematics and mathematical notation in the Western philosophical tradition. This undertaking is part of intellectual history, but, given that we are dealing with a myth, its implications are relevant to the history and philosophy of mathematics, and the philosophy of science, but also, and more importantly, to mathematical behaviour in general. Harris's point is not merely that the myth shapes the science of language for better or worse. It is also that the myth shapes other areas of intellectual endeavour (science, scientific method, philosophy, and the popular understanding of these) and the behaviour based on them. This observation redefines intellectual history. We integrationists are not just telling the story of certain ideas. We are promoting awareness of a vision which shapes our vision; we are responding to an ideology with a counter-ideology. In this way we can escape the ghetto-ization of intellectual history, despite the ignorance of linguists, the aloofness of mathematicians, and the compartmentalization of philosophers (with apologies to free-thinkers in each of these categories).

Harris has discussed the language myth in terms of the notion of pattern transference (see Harris's paper in this volume). In the Western philosophical and grammatical traditions, as well as in modern orthodox linguistics, language is theorized as having the following function. It enables an idea to be copied from one mind into an external medium and then into another mind, preserving enough of a pattern that the idea can be recognized as 'the same'. This pattern transference model is used not only to explain language, but also sense perception. Thus the language myth expands into a communication myth. It purports to explain how an individual receives information from the external world, but also how individuals may share information and constitute a community. The myth reconciles the inconsistencies of somatic particularism (the individuality of sense experience) versus shared experiences within the Western tradition.

Mathematics takes this a step further. It not just that mathematics is frequently compared to or seen as a language (see, for example, Devlin 1998). It is a language with an extremely important function, that of expressing patterns which correspond to an objective or external scientific reality. At least some of the patterns transferred are seen to exist, not only in social reality, but in the physical world:

> Mathematics originated as a quantitative description of the external world, but it has become abstract and now concerns itself with conceptual operations upon symbols. The scientist can sometimes find or invent sets of mathematical symbols and operations that correspond to measurements obtained from the external world; he can then construct a mathematical model and make predictions. (Walker 1963: 50)

Mathematics is seen, not simply as a means of capturing and reflecting patterns, and transferring these patterns from individual to individual, but as a means of organizing them, transforming them, and predicting what new patterns will be encountered. By construing mathematics as a pattern-transferral language, the western philosophical tradition bridges the gap between individual reports of sensory data, and the ordered reality from which they may be said to derive. This incorporation of mathematics into the language myth immensely increases the prestige of the latter, not only because it gives an account of mathematics coherent with that of language and sensory perception, but more importantly, because it makes a statement about both epistemology and the philosophy of science. Reality is knowable through the language of mathematics. Science can be conducted through the formulation of patterns in mathematical language, and the testing (by observation) of the predictions made by these patterns. Mathematics is the language in which the laws of nature are written.

By saying that mathematics is a language, what is the western tradition saying? That is it systematic. That it is symbolic. Neither of these properties would trouble most mathematicians or linguists. Systematicity gives the basis for the formulation of patterns, and the relation of one pattern to another. The symbolic property of mathematics and language, on first spec the least contentious thing that anyone could claim about either mathematics or language, is where the above account runs into trouble. What sort of patterns are being copied and transferred? Where does mathematics exist? The cost of seeing mathematics as a language has forced this question on philosophers, and they have busied themselves coming up with answers to it.

Before launching into a consideration of these answers, we might consider what possibilities are offered by the language myth. As characterized by Harris (1980), the myth adopts specific approaches to the symbolic nature of language. Harris terms these surrogationalism, instrumentalism, and contractualism. These terms identify modes of justification used frequently by both linguists and the lay public in linguistic analysis and cultural discussions of language. A surrogationalist approach to language treats language as a set of signs for things in the physical world (in which case it is 'reocentric' in Harris's terminology), or a set of signs for ideas (themselves standing as surrogates for things in the physical world, termed 'psychocentric' by Harris). Within an instrumentalist approach, linguistic signs must be seen in terms of their function as tools. Correlation between signifier and signified, if achieved at all, must be related to the effect or utility of a sign upon an audience. Note that instrumentalism can subsume surrogationalism (Harris 1980: 87), as 'standing for' can be seen as a kind of function, although an instrumentalist approach would question whether surrogacy confers on language its primary utility. A contractualist approach emphasizes the role of social contract or one might say convention in the symbolic function of signs; a sign 'has meaning' only in so far as it relates to the other signs in a system.

One might summarize Harris's work in *The Language-Makers* (1980) as a discussion of how these different approaches to the symbolic aspect of language have been deployed by different theorists within the western philosophical tradition; further, *The Language Myth* (1981) analyzes the specific character of the compromise adopted by orthodox linguistics in the twentieth century. Reocentrically surrogationalist approaches, after a strong start in early texts such as *Genesis* and *Cratylus*, are overtaken quickly by psychocentric surrogationalism (most prominently in Aristotle). Instrumentalism comes into its own during the Renaissance, but through its development of institutions such as the monolingual dictionary, leaves an opening for contractualist approaches, most notably Saussurean structuralism, to fill. In the twentieth century psychocentric surrogationalism and contractualism are neck and neck, the former dominating philosophy and the latter dominating linguistics, but in the final stretch psychocentric surrogationalism lunges ahead to win by a nose. In his paper for this volume Harris quotes the octopus passage in Pinker (1994: 15), 'Asking you to surrender your imagination to my words for a few moments, I can cause you to think some very specific thoughts ...', in which it is clear that orthodox linguistics has settled on an uneasy compromise between contractualism and psychocentric surrogationalism. The contractualism accounts for certain superficial aspects of language, such as the existence of thousands of 'languages' on the face of the earth. The psychocentric surrogationalism justifies linguistics as a cognitive science, and more importantly, allows linguists as cognitive scientists to identify the transfer of ideas as an evolutionary adaptation and advantage. Thus language can be said to be an instinct, and the science of linguistics has not only a mental basis, but a physical/neurological basis in the evolution of the species.

I present this hasty run through the history of language studies to point up the difference between the symbolic aspect of language as seen by linguists, and the symbolic aspect of mathematics when treated as language by philosophers and scientists. Reocentric surrogationalism has been declining steadily within language studies. Words in general cannot be made to refer directly to things; the counter-examples are too immediate, too accessible. The existence of 'different' languages emphasizes the arbitrary nature of the relationship between signifier and signified. The messiness of external reality begs for an intermediary to secure the relationship. Imaginary beasts such as Pegasus need to be housed as ideas in men's minds. Harris (1980) traces the struggle that philosophers have had with these problems. It is quite clear that, in the course of the twentieth century, psychocentric surrogationalism has won out over reocentric surrogationalism as far as language is concerned. In comparison, the symbolic character of the 'language' of mathematics is much more open to interpretation.

I recently had occasion to spend a rainy weekend with a physicist, an applied mathematician, and an optical engineer in Wales. Between the roast and the pudding, I asked them if, in their view, mathematics might be called 'the language of nature'. The physicist agreed, saying that laws discovered exist in nature, or, one might say, that ultimately the mathematically-expressed laws constitute nature. The mathematician disagreed, saying that mathematics is a way of thinking not tied to nature (or even language) in any necessary way. The engineer proposed a compromise, that mathematics provided a language for modelling nature for specific purposes. (I would like to thank P. Dauncey, J.T. Sheridan, and A. Skeldon for taking part in this discussion, while taking full responsibility for this liberal characterization of the views expressed).

This anecdote goes some way toward illustrating the possible positions that practicing scientists in the present day may take: Mathematics can be said, in all seriousness, to express reality directly, a position which lines up with that of reocentric surrogationalism in language. This approach is more usually termed platonist or realist, and can be seen in the work of Frege. Nominalism can also be said to be a reocentric surrogationalist approach. Taking a different tack, mathematics can be said to operate logically in the construction of systems which do not refer to anything outside themselves. This formalist position in some respects resembles contractualist approaches in language. Finally, mathematics can be said to provide a language which accurately models certain patterns occurring in nature, for certain purposes. This position has a lot in common with the sort of pattern-transference embodied in the psychocentric surrogationalist position, although it is kept in check by the instrumentalism inherent in the utility of scientific descriptions. Within mathematics the conceptualism espoused by Brouwer is an example of psychocentric surrogationalism (see Barker 1967: 528–530; I am grateful to Roy Harris for drawing my attention to this article and for commenting on its relevance to integrationist views of language and mathematics).

Reocentric surrogationalist positions on mathematics and number are found in Pythagorean thought. I quote from the Neo-Platonist, Iamblichus:

> Pythagoras adds that the survey of the whole heaven, and of the stars that revolve therein, is indeed beautiful, when we consider their order, which is derived from the first and intelligible essence. But that first essence is the nature of Number and 'reasons' (*logoi*) which pervades everything, and according to which all those [celestial] bodies are arranged elegantly, and adorned fittingly. (Iamblichus, *The Life of Pythagoras*, in Guthrie 1987: 70)

Iamblichus has Pythagoras profess that the function of a philosopher is to know beauty. Hence the aesthetic of the passage. But the striking point is that the order of the stars in the heavens is derived from number, which is yoked to the logos and which imbues everything. Mathematical notation, in this case, refers directly to the number on which existence is based. Later in *The Life of Pythagoras*, Iamblichus gives the following lecture topic in his description of the Pythagorean School: 'What is the wisest thing? Number. The next wisest thing is the naming power' (Iamblichus, in Guthrie 1987: 77). Again, the number and the word are linked together, although number is given priority. Without reading too much into a lecture question, one might say that number enjoys this priority because it is reality, whereas the naming power is secondary because it is standing for reality. Support for this interpretation may be drawn from other authors concerned with Pythagoras, such as Porphyry:

> ... the Pythagoreans specialized in the study of numbers to explain their teachings symbolically, as do geometricians, inasmuch as the primary forms and principles are hard to understand and express otherwise in plain discourse. A similar case is the representation of sounds by letters, which are known by marks, which are called the first elements of learning; later, they inform us these are not the true elements, which they only signify. (Porphyry, *The Life of Pythagoras*, in Guthrie 1987: 133)

In this quotation we see an explicit comparison between numerical notation and written marks, both of which allow the learner to gain access to learning, but which nevertheless are merely signs or surrogates for reality. The quotation also indicates the abstraction of the 'true elements', which will play an increasingly important role in defending reocentric surrogationalism. If the objects for which the surrogate symbols stand are not directly accessible to the senses, then (unless reocentric surrogationalism is misconceived) one is led toward supposing an abstract world of referents which makes itself known only obliquely within the world of the senses. In the case of language this abstract world of referents finds expression in the Platonic world of ideal forms (Harris 1980: 52). It is yet another illustration of the linking power of the language myth that mathematics is so well served by a reocentrically surrogationalist theory. A theory of ideal forms serves a double purpose, accounting for the referents of problematic words, and also for the referents of mathematical notation.

One aspect of the link between numbers, numerals, and letters as symbols may escape a modern readership. It must not be forgotten that, for Greek mathematics, there was no special set of characters earmarked solely for the purpose of representing numbers. Arabic numerals in a sense have become 'real' for us, at least for those of us with 'school' mathematics (Dantzig 1930: 259).

Introductory histories of mathematics emphasize two points about numeral systems: First, that systems which, like the Roman, are derived from tally systems (thus embodying a token-iterative aspect, see Harris 1995: 137), lack the zero or cipher, and are therefore somewhat cumbersome for calculations (Ifrah 1985: 431). A calculation such as the following in Arabic numerals is relatively simple:

$9 \times 12 = (9 \times 10) + (9 \times 2) = 90 + 18 = 108$
(two multiplications and an addition, with zeroes holding the empty ones and tens places)

This is made possible by the use of the zero as a place holder. The same calculation performed in Roman numerals would be:

ix × xii = (x × x) + (x × ii) − ((i × x) + (i x ii)) = xxxxxxxxxx + xx − (iiiiiiiiii + ii)
= cxx − xii = cx − ii = cviii
(four multiplications, two additions, and one subtraction)

The alternative would be to look up the ninth row and the twelfth column in a multiplication table. This problem is aggravated in systems such as the later Greek alphabetic numeral system, which did away with the token-iterative aspect of the system but still did not introduce a place holder (such as zero). Introductory histories make the point that the saving in paper made by scribal substitution of alphabetic characters for tallies (as in v for iiiii in the Roman numeral system) ultimately prevented mathematicians from developing a simple set of rules for arithmetic, and even blocked the development of alphabetic characters used as algebraic variables. What many of these accounts miss is that the substitution is not just a matter of conserving the writing material, but also essential for calculations performed by tally (see Ifrah 1985: 141). These must make use of grouping as soon as the calculations leave one or two hands; it is a short step to the use of symbols representing these groupings. When I tally the number of mugs obtained from a quarter pound of coffee at \$7.99/lb., I write something very like the following on the coffee bag:

||||
||||
||

(Four verticals with a crossbar, new line, four verticals with a crossbar, new line, two verticals.) No space or ink saving here, but the grouping makes it very easy to check the tally and to convert into Arabic numerals. Compare:

|| || || || || || (Twelve verticals in a row).

(Incidentally, one can get twelve decently-strong mugs of coffee from a quarter pound, working out to 22 cents per mug when the cost of filtres is added in. Fortunately this allows for 190,909 mugs per year at my salary.)

The second point made by historians of mathematics is that the use of alphabetic characters to represent number made possible the practice of gematria, or the interpretation of words according to their specific numbers, assigned by virtue of the numerical value of their component letters. Dantzig (1930: 39) introduces it as 'one of the most absurd yet widely spread forms which numerology took'. Hogben (1937: 170) defines gematria as, 'the name for the quaint superstitions which arose in connection with the use of alphabetic letters for the numbers of the Hebrews and Greeks'. Both of these texts treat gematria as a distraction for the mathematically naive, an error of judgement brought on by semiotic accident. This is to misunderstand the cultural context of these symbols. If number is the essence of reality, as for the Pythagoreans, and if, by means of the dual function of alphabetic symbols each word may be assigned a number, then it would be foolish not to take this into account in the interpretation of texts. Gematria is a means for identifying not only the referent of a surrogate sign, but also the equivalences or relationships between the referents of surrogate signs.

Within the branch of Jewish mysticism known as the Cabbala these two points are made explicitly. First, knowledge of the mystic significance of words, in particular divine names, gives access to the nature of reality:

> For so it is when a man's thoughts are bound to the Creator, blessed be He, then he has the capacity to discover the unification of His name, blessed be He, in all matters, and he will know the origins of every thing in the root of the qualities and the channels of the supernal flow of grace. (Eichenstein 1832/1995: 111)

Although this passage is concerned with knowledge of origins, that is, the relationship between reality and the Creator, nevertheless it is the decoding of names which gives access to this particular aspect of reality.

In the following quotation the point is made that the connection between the alphabetic and numerical function of the letters is not accidental, but given:

> For the kabbalists, the letters of the Hebrew alphabet are not mere ciphers; because of their source on high, they are the divine entities that provide cosmic energy ... (Eichenstein 1832/1995: xix)

This strengthens the significance of gematria as an interpretative technique, since it is not founded on accident, but ordained by the Creator. Furthermore, it points to the reason for our inability to accept gematria: Our commitment to the arbitrariness of the linguistic sign, and to the arbitrariness of the sequence of our writing system, but at the same time to the non-arbitrary sequencing of numbers, requires us (us meaning 'most academics') to see a connection between linguistic signs founded on the union of word, letter, and number as nonsense or madness. Nor does this say that arbitrariness rules out gematria. Cabbalistic writings are quite clear on this point:

> In every word that comes from your mouth, you can find, if you so wish and if you recall the days of your life, some unification of His Name, blessed be He, whether in the initial letters or the end letters or through the numerical value, or

through an alphabet in code. The intelligent will find good sense and good taste even in any language spoken. (Eichenstein 1832/1995: 111)

For those working within this tradition, a connection can be found and then given significance in an interpretation. The specific language spoken is not important (although the writing system is, at least in the case of gematria). Our inability to take gematria seriously is a result of our assumption that linguistic signs are arbitrary, and that numbers are not. My calculation of the cost of a mug of home-brewed coffee (see above) is not likely to shock, though it may not be run-of-the-mill academic writing. That behaviour may be eccentric, but it is not beyond the pale. Within our mathematical and economic behaviours we are allowed room for saying that a mug of coffee costs 22 cents, and that this is less expensive than the $1.25 that one might pay in a coffee-house. We may even compute how many mugs of coffee could be purchased per annum at this price given a certain annual income. But we are not allowed to connect or compare this number to a Roman numeral value assigned to a proper noun (such as that of the author, DanIeL DaVIs, DIL DVI = 1,057) or even one assigned to a type of coffee (SVMatran ManDheLIng, VM MDLI = 2,556). I am not denying that these are all culturally based forms of behaviour. But I am saying that we treat the former by reocentrically surrogationalist assumptions which we do not make about proper or common nouns. Within a reocentric surrogationalist approach, the sign need not be arbitrary, and even apparent arbitrariness may conceal a deeper insight into the structure of reality. We exempt mathematics from the current dominance of psychocentric surrogationalist and contractualist approaches to language.

Nevertheless, in the history and philosophy of mathematics, one witnesses a struggle to work out the implications of the specific nature of 'mathematical language'. In the case of a reocentric approach, one encounters the problem of a law of nature. The problem would seem to be that a 'law of nature' is described directly by a reocentric mathematics. One would say that the law of nature actually has the form of the equation which states it. Where does this law exist? Or, maybe, what is its shape in physical reality? The question of right and wrong comes in: If the law as put in mathematics is a direct reflection of the shape of 'reality', then how can it be wrong (see Eddington 1939: 67 for an attempt to address this problem)? And yet the history of science is replete with examples in which a natural law, formerly taken to be 'true' and therefore a correct depiction of reality, is unable to account for certain observations, and is superseded by a new formulation. Einstein's physics overtaking Newton's physics is perhaps the best example. This occurred simultaneously with a crisis of foundations in mathematics, brought on by the development of non-Euclidean geometry (Tiles 1996: 339).

A step toward abstraction is necessary, and can be found in two places. Rationalism, operating deductively, holds that reason is sufficient in and of itself to enable human beings to grasp the true structure of reality. It accounts for grounding of mathematical discoveries but does not account for their usefulness. How did this come about, that my reasoning capabilities as a human being enable me to determine the nature of reality? Empiricism, operating inductively, holds that we absorb data through our senses and arrive at generalizations about the nature of reality. It thus manages to explain the usefulness of mathematical discoveries, but cannot maintain them as descriptive truths (see Tiles 1996: 326; Hahn 1959: 148–151).

Wittgenstein addresses this problem in the *Tractatus*. Here he adopts a reocentric surrogationalist (or realist) position (see Shanker, 1988). The characteristics of this position with regard to logic in general and mathematics in particular are made clear by the following long quotation:

2.1 We make to ourselves pictures of facts.

2.11 The picture presents the facts in logical space, the existence and non-existence of atomic facts.

2.12 The picture is a model of reality.

2.13 To the objects correspond in the picture the elements of the picture.

2.131 The elements of the picture stand, in the picture, for the objects.

2.14 The picture consists in the fact that its elements are combined with one another in definite way.

2.141 The picture is a fact.

2.15 That the elements of the picture are combined with one another in a definite way, represents that the things are so combined with one another.

This connexion of the elements of the picture is called its structure, and the possibility of this structure is called the form of representation of the picture.

2.151 The form of representation is the possibility that the things are combined with one another as are the elements of the picture.

2.1511 Thus the picture is linked with reality; it reaches up to it.

2.1512 It is like a scale applied to reality. (Wittgenstein 1922)

The 'picture' theory of meaning is of course familiar, but it is worth examining the text to elucidate what this involves: First, the picture exists in logical space. Second, it is a model of reality. This would require a one-to-one correspondence of the elements of the picture to the objects of reality, a surrogate relationship. In addition, the structure of the picture (the combination of its elements) mirrors (at least potentially) the combination of objects in reality. It turns out to be the case that this is necessary in the definition of a picture:

2.16 In order to be a picture a fact must have something in common with what it pictures. ...

2.173 The picture represents its object from without (its standpoint is its form of representation), therefore the picture represents its object rightly or falsely. ...

2.18 What every picture, of whatever form, must have in common with reality in order to be able to represent it at all – rightly or falsely – is the logical form, that is, the form of reality. (Wittgenstein 1922)

By adopting the picture theory of meaning, the author of the *Tractatus* takes on certain necessary problems of surrogationalism. These are, first, the correspondence of surrogate to object requires consideration of truth or falsity, that is, correctness or incorrectness of the picture as a depiction of reality. Second, some resemblance must exist between picture and reality, this being a resemblance of form. A pattern is reproduced in the picture. One might suppose that, logic being the province of the mind, that this pattern is manifest as ideas, and one would be concerned with an instance of an psychocentric surrogationalist approach to logic and mathematics. But this interpretation does not fit with the following statements:

6.13 Logic is not a theory but a reflexion of the world.

Logic is transcendental.

6.2 Mathematics is a logical method.

The propositions of mathematics are equations, and therefore pseudo-propositions.

6.21 Mathematical propositions express no thoughts.

6.211 In life it is never a mathematical proposition which we need, but we use mathematical propositions only in order to infer from propositions which do not belong to mathematics to others which equally do not belong to mathematics.

(In philosophy the question 'Why do we really use that word, that proposition?' constantly leads to valuable results.) (Wittgenstein 1922)

In this passage we have it that logic reflects, it does not suppose or discuss. In the case of logic we are dealing with reocentric surrogationalism, that part of a picture which is a direct reflection of reality. Mathematics is situated within logic, as a logical method. Following this, its propositions do not express thoughts, but link non-mathematical propositions. This is possible because, unlike those non-mathematical propositions, mathematical propositions as a form of logic are a direct reflection of what is 'out there' in the composition of external reality. This accounts for their utility. Now the problem is to explain how they are known to us. Wittgenstein here turns to language:

6.233 To the question whether we need intuition for the solution of mathematical problems it must be answered that language itself here supplies the necessary intuition.

6.2331 The process of calculation brings about just this intuition. (Wittgenstein 1922)

This solution to the problem is quite striking, considering that this is the realist early Wittgenstein. Mathematics is a reflection of reality pure and simple, but we have understanding of it through intuition developed on the basis of our language practices, such as calculation. This move illustrates the importance of language in the conception of mathematics in two ways. First, logic and mathematics are a kind of language (pseudo-propositions, perhaps, but nonetheless of the same form as language by Wittgenstein's own criteria), differing from ordinary language in that they directly reflect reality (and therefore are reocentric in character). Second, it is ordinary language behaviour which enables us to understand how to operate within the language of mathematics.

Mathematics in this sense is doubly structured on the basis of language, in that language permits the early Wittgenstein to solve the two problems associated with the nature of mathematics, the rationalist versus empiricist divide in attempting to explain mathematical utility and mathematical discovery. Mathematics, as a logical method, is ultimately derived from the composition of the external world. It is therefore a reocentric surrogate for the relations of the external world. This explains its utility in relating propositions which model the external world (and which make predictions about what observations one will find). Mathematics, as a kind of language, is propositional. It enables the relation of one non-mathematic proposition to another, and can be intuitively grasped through our more properly linguistic mathematical behaviour. Thus the 'discovery' of mathematics may involve intuitive leaps without privileging the human intellect or adopting some form of mysticism.

The important point in the context of this paper is that, for the early Wittgenstein, the character of logic (and mathematics) is reocentrically surrogationist. Intuition is essentially experience of language, and therefore open to interpretation according to other approaches to language. As Wittgenstein moves toward a contractualist (be this normativity- or games-based) interpretation of language, he adapts his views on mathematics, but, unlike his views on language, it is clear that he does not entirely revise his position. In *Remarks on the Foundations of Mathematics*, we see a linguistic foundation to logic (as opposed to the mirror-image of reality given in the *Tractatus*):

> *So* much is true when it's said that mathematics is logic: its moves are from rules of our language to other rules of our language. And this gives it its peculiar solidarity, its unassailable position, set apart. (Wittgenstein 1983: I–165)

Mathematics, like logic, is the transformation of one rule to another. This abstractness sets it off. One might read this as saying that logic and mathematics are meta-linguistic in character. But certainly, they are not of necessity a direct reflection of the structure of reality. Wittgenstein warns of the following:

The dangerous, deceptive thing about the idea: 'The real numbers cannot be arranged in a series', or again, 'The set ... is not denumerable' is that it makes the determination of a concept – concept formation – look like a fact of nature. (Wittgenstein 1983: II–19)

This would appear to be an abandonment of the reocentric surrogationalist position on mathematics advanced in the *Tractatus*. This opens up the possibilities for interpreting mathematics:

What does mathematics need a foundation for? It no more needs one, I believe, than propositions about physical objects – or about sense impressions, need an *analysis*. What mathematical propositions do stand in need of is a clarification of their grammar, just as do those other propositions.

The *mathematical* problems of what is called foundations are no more the foundation of mathematics for us than the painted rock is the support of a painted tower. (Wittgenstein 1983: VII–16)

The term *grammar* may be misleading in this context, as it is not mathematics in particular which is conceived of as having grammar in common with language. Rather the use of this term is symptomatic of the more general linguistic turn in Wittgenstein's work. More significant is the image of the painted rock, with its suggestion that we are looking in the wrong place for an understanding of mathematics. Even careful grammatical determination is not the aim of Wittgenstein's inquiry:

But, you say, this is just what the logical calculus of Frege and Russell does: in it every word that is spoken in mathematics has exact significance, is an element of the calculus. Thus in this calculus we can really prove that 'multiplying is possible'. Very well, now it is a mathematical proposition; but who says that anything can be done with this proposition? Who says *what* use it can be? For its sounding interesting is not enough. (Wittgenstein 1983: II–56)

Even admitting that the logical calculus is sound as a foundation for mathematics, Wittgenstein is concerned with the role that it could play in mathematical language games. The interpretation which we are moving towards is one in which mathematics, like language, is to be seen in terms of its game-context:

> Mathematics – I want to say – teaches you, not just the answer to a question, but a whole language-game with questions and answers. (Wittgenstein 1983: VII–18)
> I want to say that what we call mathematics, the mathematical conception of the proposition 13 × 14 = 182, hangs together with the special position that we assign to the activity of calculating. Or the special position that the calculation ... has in our life, in the rest of our activities. The language-game in which it is found. (Wittgenstein 1983: VII–24)

The 'language-game' approach is here being applied to mathematics. But mathematics is intractable. It can be constructed in terms of a language game, but part of that language game must be that it is not played out entirely on the surface of social interaction, nor are the rules of the game entirely arbitrary:

> We say: 'If you really follow the rule in multiplying, you must all get the same result.' Now if this is only the somewhat hysterical way of putting things that you get in university talk, it need not interest us overmuch.
> It is however the expression of an attitude towards the technique of calculation, which comes out of everywhere in our life. The emphasis of the *must* corresponds only to the inexorableness of this attitude both to the technique of calculating and to a host of related techniques.
> The mathematical Must is only another expression of the fact that mathematics forms concepts.
> And concepts help us to comprehend things. They correspond to a particular way of dealing with situations.
> Mathematics forms a network of norms. (Wittgenstein 1983: VII–67)
> It is not in every language-game that there occurs something that one would call a concept.
> Concept [sic] is something like a picture with which one compares objects. (Wittgenstein 1983: VII–71)

Wittgenstein's position on the foundations of mathematics comes to resemble his position on language, in its concern for the rules of language-games, and in their normative character. However, if it is one of the language-games which we play, it is distinguished from those other language-games in that it has a representational character. It forms and denotes concepts. These in turn exist as functional entities, as responses to particular problems and situations. Thus the resulting view or understanding of mathematics is ultimately instrumentalist, with a strong psychocentric surrogational character.

In conclusion, one might make the following points. First, in our language games, we treat mathematics as different from other communal behaviours in that it can be seen as surrogationist, and specifically as reocentrically surrogationist. Second, even a philosopher with a strong commitment to breaking with surrogationalism, such as the later Wittgenstein, cannot escape entirely from surrogationalism in his arguments on mathematics. These two points taken together indicate that the adoption of the language myth in Western culture provides a means, an almost irresistible means, of rationalizing mathematics. This rationalization forms the structure underpinning or linking consistent experiential observation with the utility of mathematical statements.

It is likely that any position seriously questioning this (such as an instrumentalist position) is going to get short shrift from many (though not all) mathematicians, logicians, and scientists. This is the case because the act of questioning surrogationalism threatens the modus operandi and epistemology of these fields, if not their ontology. Broadly speaking, the philosophy of science has inherited the problems created by the adoption of the communication myth, and many of its arguments attempt to address these problems.

Integrationism, by recognizing these problems, has the following threefold task: First, to identify the grounding of mathematics in our experience (cultural, economic, etc.). Second, to state how these scientific or mathematical arguments rely on the plausibility of the language/communication myth (for example, in pattern transference). Third, in some sense to propose an alternative (not an 'equivalent' or even a 'translation') but at least an alternative way of seeing things. And this, integrationism can do. It can meet this challenge. How? Through its cultural contextualization of the mathematical act or acts; through its reflexivity and reciprocity in meta-mathematic terminology, and through its recognition of different modes of meaning (surrogationalist, instrumentalist, and contractualist) as well as different integrational scales (biophysical, macrosocial, and circumstantial). Integrationism makes room for a surrogationalist mathematics in the appropriate instrumental context by means of these modes and scales, without determining one mode or one scale or even mathematics itself as a set of fixed practices having priority over our understanding of mathematical or other communicational events.

If we as integrationists cannot meet the challenge of interpreting mathematics we are in trouble, not in the least because we will have no position upon which to fall back. Mathematics has been appropriated by orthodox linguistics in order to fabricate an account of language (see Devlin 1994: 65–71). If mathematics is seen to elude an integrationist grounding, then linguistic orthodoxy will similarly escape the integrationist critique.

References

Barker, S.F. (1967) 'Number'. *The Encyclopedia of Philosophy*. Paul Edwards, ed. NY and London: Macmillan. Vol. 5: 526–530.

Dantzig, T. (1930) *Number: The Language of Science*. NY: Macmillan.

Devlin, K. (1994) *Mathematics, the Science of Patterns: the Search for Order in Life, Mind, and the Universe*. NY: Scientific American Library.

Devlin, K. (1998) *The Language of Mathematics: Making the Invisible Visible*. NY: W.H. Freeman.

Eddington, A. (1939) *The Philosophy of Physical Science*. NY: Macmillan. Cambridge: Cambridge University Press.

Eichenstein, Z. H. (1832/1995) *Turn Aside from Evil and Do Good: An Introduction and a Way to the Tree of Life*. Louis Jacobs, trans. London and Washington: Littman Library of Jewish Civilization.

Guthrie, K. S., ed. (1987) *The Pythagorean Sourcebook*, Grand Rapids, MI: Phanes Press.

Hahn, H. (1959) 'Logic, Mathematics, and Knowledge of Nature'. Arthur Pap, trans. In *Logical Positivism*. A.J. Ayer, ed. NY: The Free Press. 147–161.

Harris, R. (1980) *The Language-Makers*. Ithaca, NY: Cornell University Press.

Harris, R. (1981) *The Language Myth*. London: Duckworth.

Harris, R. (1995) *Signs of Writing*. London and New York: Routledge.

Hogben, L. (1937) *Mathematics for the Million: How to Master the Magic of Numbers*. NY and London: W.W. Norton.

Ifrah, G. (1985) *From One to Zero: A Universal History of Numbers*. Lowell Blair, trans. NY: Viking Penguin.

Pinker, S. (1994) *The Language Instinct*. London: Penguin.

Shanker, S.G. (1988) *Wittgenstein and the Turning-Point in the Philosophy of Mathematics*. State University of New York Press.

Tiles, M. (1996) 'Philosophy of Mathematics'. *The Blackwell Companion to Philosophy*. Nicholas Bunnin and E.P. Tsui-James, eds. Oxford: Blackwell. 325–357.

Walker, M. (1963) *The Nature of Scientific Thought*. Englewood Cliffs, NJ: Prentice-Hall.

Wittgenstein, L. (1922) *Tractatus Logico-Philosophicus*. C.K. Ogden, trans. London and NY: Routledge.

Wittgenstein, L. (1983) *Remarks on the Foundations of Mathematics*. G.H. von Wright, R. Rhees, and G.E.M. Anscombe, eds. Cambridge, MA and London: MIT Press.

9 The Language Myth and the Law

Michael Toolan

1. Integrationists on the law

In the short history of integrational linguistics, there have been a number of discussions of aspects of legal reasoning and jurisprudential practice. One is that of Roy Harris, in *The Language Myth*, concerning the situated grounds on which judges may have to decide upon meanings or descriptions in particular cases: whether a drunkard wheeling a bicycle is 'in charge of a carriage', whether to sell a Bugs Bunny T-shirt in particular circumstances amounts to selling a souvenir, and whether for the purposes of an insurance claim, the accidental scorching of trousers by an electric iron is justifiably described as a fire. In all these cases, Harris's comments chime with the view of Hart, in *The Concept of Law*, who famously observed that legal rules are necessarily, at best, open in texture. To quote a part of just one sentence from Hart, on legal rules and their non-automatic application:

> It is ... important to appreciate why, apart from [law's] dependence on language as it actually is, with its characteristics of open texture, we should not cherish, even as an ideal, the conception of a rule so detailed that the question whether it applied or not to a particular case was always settled in advance, and never involved, at the point of actual application, a fresh choice between alternatives. (Hart, 1961: 127–8)

More recently Christopher Hutton, reviewing contributions to a conference on Law and Linguistics at Washington University, has found not proven the claim made by some linguists, that linguistics, in its scientificity, has important things to say to lawyers. Why so? Essentially, because the legal profession is of the world, and applies

159

its expertise on a case by case basis, so that there is far more common ground between the literary critic who, as it were, enters a plea or makes a judgement on a particular unique poem, than with the orthodox linguist, who purports hypothetico-deductively to elaborate a maximally generalized and abstract system underlying performance in one or all natural languages. Literary critics, legal judges, and linguists are all 'judges' of a kind, in what they do. But it is the orthodox linguist, among these three professions, who would most resist being thus characterized.

As good a place as any to enter upon a discussion of the continuing influence of language-mythological assumptions upon the law is with *obiter dicta* in Harris's judgement on Saussure's *Cours*, delivered towards the close of his *Reading Saussure*. Harris has been discussing the economic analogy to language behaviour, where the buying of, say, a loaf of bread for a certain sum of money – a transaction entailing a setting of values – is compared with the set values of signs in *la langue*. He suggests that for all the brilliance of Saussure's theoretical account, it nevertheless starts 'from the wrong end':

> Saussurean linguistics begins by focussing upon the properties of the individual sign in the abstract, and hoping that somehow at the social end, where signs are put to everyday use, everything will work out satisfactorily in terms of communicational corollaries. Unfortunately, it does not work out at all. But it could have worked out if only Saussure had grasped the full implications of the economic analogy and seen that values are subordinate to transactions, and not the other way round. (1987: 230–231)

In economics, actual transactions are not subordinate to values: it is not the case that values come first, before transactions arise. In a parallel way, we might suggest, metalinguistics must be subordinate to communication. Harris goes on to suggest that Saussure's failure to give priority to transactions led him to the theoretical impasse of attempting to reconcile the implicit synchronic fixity and uniformity across a speech community of *la langue*, with the inherent fluidity and variability of values. But these forces are utterly incompatible: 'Just as in the economic case, it is only if we postulate that the economy is a closed system that it makes sense to speak of fixed currency values and equivalences' (234). Overwhelmingly, human experience

The Language Myth and the Law

suggests that in both our economic and linguistic practices, dynamism and change, in signal, signification, and value, are permanent potentials. Hence a vase bought for £5 yesterday can entirely reasonably be sold for a higher sum next week, even though, relatively independently, the general purchasing power of the pound may have increased, and even though the bought object may by then have been re-classified as a bowl rather than a vase. Here Harris makes the crucial point that it is not simply that with the new transaction, and contingent upon it, a revision of multiple values may occur; in addition, as a corollary of this, it makes no sense to privilege any one price paid, or purchasing power of the currency, or naming of the object traded, as *the correct* price, *the correct* currency value, or *the correct* name. Correctness is so confined of application, to each self-same transaction, as to be hardly worth invoking. (See also Harris's rejection of the notion of context-neutral correct translation, and contrasting emphasis on communicationally-relevant efficacy of reformulation, in *The Language Myth* (1981: 148–9)). Rather different checks on 'utter fluidity of revaluation' are (a) biomechanical errors where, e.g., a price of £500 is agreed but the purchaser writes a cheque for £900: here it is not so much that in writing '£900' the purchaser has failed to write the correct price, rather they have failed to write the agreed price; and (b) deceptions and unconscionable dealings, where a seller knowing an item is worth £500 induces an 'unequal' contractual partner to pay, say, £5,000 for it – see especially the observations of Lord Denning, on economic duress and 'inequality of bargaining power', in *Lloyds Bank Ltd v Bundy* [1975] QB 326. Again we find that the law might protect the victim here not on the grounds that they have paid an *incorrect* sum, but on the grounds that they have been lured into paying a wholly *unreasonable* and *unconscionable* sum. So even in these extreme cases, it seems, economics and contract law have no time for doctrines of 'correctness' of values. Nor, in ordinary circumstances, should linguistics.

We are approaching the question of the language myth and the law by way of the principle of correctness, then, notwithstanding the fact that in theory there is no place for a system of values or local correctnesses that is not contingent upon particular transactions.

Michael Toolan

2. The literal rule in statutory interpretation and the fixed-code theory of language

The most directly pertinent of previous integrationist discussions of legal activity, for my purposes, is Nigel Love's commentary on customary procedures in the interpretation of statutes. For, Love suggests, these 'enshrine the fixed-code theory in a number of respects' (1998: 57), which he proceeds to itemize. They include the assumption that legislators' communicational intentions can be precisely captured, without delimitation of the ruling or provision to a single situation, provided a sufficiently careful and general wording is adopted; this reflects a faith in words as carriers of meanings, and of meanings as stable and detachable from those words.

In that same spirit, as Love notes, where doubts arise as to a statute's intent and as to whether a particular set of circumstances was intended to be 'caught' by the statute or not, English legal procedure has traditionally firmly disbarred direct consultation of Parliament. Thus appellate judges, grappling with a hard case, and notwithstanding the constitutional sovereignty of Parliament, have not traditionally been allowed to ask Parliament what its members, or the government, or the relevant secretary of state, intended by the statute they may have only recently enacted. Among the arguments against such 'secondary' consultation is the prospect of endless second thoughts and revisionism, to say nothing of the complications if a new Parliament dominated by Party A is called on to explain legislation passed by a previous Parliament dominated by Party B. Besides, how would one arbitrate as a judge, with constitutional probity, between an ambiguous statutory instrument at time$_i$, and its unambiguously radical reinterpretation, by the present secretary of state, at time$_{ii}$? In all such concessions to assumed lack of fixity and autonomy the legal system has traditionally seen intolerable affronts to that most cherished of principles, certainty. The lawyer complains that without certainty, or without a pretty close approximation to it, no-one knows where they stand, whether she be lawyer, judge, claimant, defendant, or police officer, and the law's vital roots in open and fair dealing are severed. Far better, then, if a new Parliament wishes to revise the laws of an older Parliament, that new laws (revisions, repeals, amendments) be passed, creating a new, different, free-standing, meaning-encapsulating, statute or provision. In that way, it is argued, a new certainty abruptly replaces an old certainty, like the handing on of kingship, and uncertainty is minimized.

162

The Language Myth and the Law

Besides, it might be countered, should there really be a need for secondary and tertiary interpretations of statutes? Insofar as such a practice concedes that texts, even immensely carefully crafted texts, cannot stand alone and make autonomous communicative sense without benefit of supporting documentation, it may raise questions about the ethical and logical justification for *ever* resorting to the enactment of free-standing Acts. And at that point you may find, in addition to the big guns of the legal profession trained on you, the little guns of the world of literature, literary criticism and publishing. It has therefore traditionally been held to be better, and more congruent with other prevailing assumptions about the place of the written law in relation to society, Parliament, and the judiciary, for statutes to have their autonomous meaningfulness reaffirmed rather than put in doubt.

Even where the reasonable meanings of the words of a statute clash with legislators' declared intentions, the meaning 'in the Act' will prevail, because, it is implicitly assumed, the meaning in the wording of the Act is the meaning of the Act. It is particularly interesting to note that the traditional qualification to this principle states that, where the literal meaning 'in the Act' would result in absurdity, then the golden rule can be invoked, which allows an alternative but still possible interpretation of the words, overriding the 'ordinary signification' of the words, to be applied: that is, a less proper signification which the Court thinks the words will bear (as per Lord Blackburn in *River Wear Commissioners*). What is most striking in that manoeuvre is the way that this preserves the principle that the meaning is still 'in' the words, and proper to them, even if less proper than their ordinary or literal meaning. We may be tempted to conclude that, in light of other declared jurisprudential desiderata such as certainty, consistency, and equal protection, subscription to a fixed-code picture of language is implicit in the very idea of resorting to written statute.

At this point I should disclose that I myself am almost as convinced by these arguments as traditionalist adherents of the literal rule seem to be. There is an immensely powerful pragmatic attraction in the idea of devising a form of words that will encapsulate a rule or provision authoritatively and definitively, that stands the test of time, is proof against the picker of loopholes, the sceptic and the revisionist latecomer. In short, transcendental sentences. Are such things so unthinkable, or so unreasonable an aspiration? Do not the memorable texts of religions of the book, and of great literature,

163

aspire to this condition? Why should such fixed and permanent meaningfulness be looked for or projected onto literature and not onto legal statute also? Conversely, how can one question the very idea of determinate meaning instantiated in a determinate text, fully accessible by every fluent speaker-reader of a language by means of fixed-code telementation, without also questioning the validity of religious and literary texts?

For all such reasons, a fixed-code telementational approach remains immensely attractive, so that if it is set aside as ultimately unworkable, it is not without a sense of loss, and a sense of clarity and the promise of perdurable insight being superseded by complexity and only passing illumination.

In the more complex integrationist picture that only with effort displaces myth-based thinking, fixed-code literalist telementation must not be allowed to dictate all the terms within which written statutes, or common law precepts, are viewed. That is the mistake made in suggesting that resort to and reliance upon written codification necessarily entails subscription to a myth-based picture of language: we need to distinguish different kinds of resort and reliance. The appearance of permanence, certainty, fixity of meaning, of meaning 'in' the sentences and fully replicated in the head of one competent legal practicioner after another, may be no more than appearances, and not tenets uncritically subscribed to by the entire legal profession. It is perfectly possible that lawyers regard statutes and case law as a network of signposts, pointing out broad general categories and principles even in the most specific-seeming of domains, so that the potential for new and revised meanings is what chiefly adheres to the wordings of the texts and judgements consulted if anything does. If that is the situation, instead of fixed meaning subsisting 'in' the words of the statute, it is rather a matter of variable meanings, in one situation or the next, *accruing to* the words of the statute, on a necessarily temporary basis.

If one looks for a tension, in the legal system, between autonomous literalist assumptions and contextualist or integrationist assumptions, one soon encounters it. To begin with, we can set beside the statute, and its intimations of dispensing with the services of common law judging, the appellate recourse to judges, always in the plural: a telling supplement, a frank acknowledgement that the nominally shared and invariant code, like a fragile plumbing system, is prone to breakdowns. It is not a system that runs on its own, without constant maintenance.

The standard recent history of statutory interpretation is that the mischief or purposive approach was for many decades displaced by the literal rule, this bolstered by a 'golden' rule allowing application of a possible but secondary meaning where the literal interpretation would result in absurdity. Thus, through much of the twentieth century, the literal rule has reigned supreme. And that assumption in turn seems to put great trust in the principle of stable, invariant forms and meanings, generally known and shared. As Love remarks, 'it is hard to see how such procedures could become established in a society which did not take it for granted that what a language basically has to offer its users is a context-neutral code for the expression and extraction of determinate meanings.' (58) On the other hand for anyone who believes that a language's forms and meanings are generally stable and invariant, it must be a wonder why that stability is not used as a resource to stabilize the *remainder* of the language, where indeterminacy and difference seem to lurk; conversely, how is it that those indeterminacies do not spread like a virus, rendering the entire system open or fluid? Is it really possible for a language to be fixed in parts, motile in other parts, and how can you tell the parts apart? However one answers those questions, there is a large body of practice that we have to set beside the fixed-code assumptions that are arguably still powerfully at work in everyday statutory drafting and interpretation: this body of practice is all the work of the appellate courts, that is, the Court of Appeal and the House of Lords. For in the very idea or countenancing of an appeal on a question of legal interpretation, which is what the appeal judges routinely hear, there seems to be an acknowledgement that fixed-codeism is fallible if not fallacious.

As has often been noted the demise of the purposive or mischief approach coincided with the firm establishment of the sovereignty of Parliament and, one might suggest, the growing democratic legitimacy of Parliament. Insofar as the mischief approach is oriented towards the framers' presumed intentions, rather than the sense of their words, it affords judges an enlarged scope, actively to postulate and interpret propositions – the legislators' intentions – which are rather less in the public domain than the words of the statute. But as Parliament grew to predominate in lawmaking, this brand of judicial activism declined and out of the shift in the balance of power from judges to legislators a paradox emerges: where previously judges might have claimed to be 'empowering' legislators by attending to the latters' intentions rather than merely their potentially imprecise statutory expression, a transfer of some judicial power to Parliamentarians carried with it an injunction on judges to cease contemplating legislators' purposes and to look no further than the statutory text to uncover meaning.

3. Telementation and legal process

More will be said in support of the contention that a significant part of legal culture adopts a fixed-code view of language, but in relation to the language myth, code-fixity is only one of the two founding assumptions that needs to be considered; the other assumption is that linguistic communication is telementational, an iterative transfer of one language user's thoughts to another language user, such that ideational identity is preserved: in linguistic communication, what you get are ideas, and the ideas you get are the very same that your interlocutors have formulated and sent to you. So linguistic communication is, essentially, ideational replication without change or deterioration. As Harris's account of the language myth emphasizes, code-fixity and telementation are distinct but mutually enabling. Each, in its own domain, entails a ruthless and near-absolute act of reduction or exclusion, so as to bring our picture (and thus our theory) of language close to a 'degree-zero' point of variability: code-fixity asserts or promises an absolute and mono-semic matching of forms and meanings, without variation or exception, uncertainty or lacuna, to the point where to know the form is to know, absolutely, the meaning, with the related requirement that linguistic forms or expressions are to be understood as linked of necessity only to well-formed thoughts. Telementation similarly reduces speculations about all the things you might 'get', or 'conceive', or come to appreciate differently in the course of an interaction involving language; it reduces this range of creative possibility to a virtual zero, a scenario in which you get only what you are given, so that you are the most passive and subordinate of interactional partners.

So, is the law's working picture of language telementational as well as fixed-code-assuming? This is perhaps harder to demonstrate directly, in a cultural practice which involves language but does not often explicitly theorize about language. But perhaps one small reflex of telementationism is the way judges talk about statutes–as when, near the beginning of his controversial Court of Appeal judgement in *Davis v Johnston*, Lord Denning declares 'To my mind the Act is perfectly clear.' And telementation is arguably implicit in the law at every turn, for without assuming something akin to it, it would be hard for a society to justify imposing the same penalties and sanctions on the diversity of people that come before it. Rather it is assumed that, excluding minors and the mentally impaired, everyone is effectively equal, equally free, equally cognizant, and–it is reasonable and necessary to assume–equally able to understand 'the same injunctions' in the same way, whatever their circumstances. All people can thus be judged by the standard to be expected of 'the reasonable person'.

Another way in which one might suggest that telementationism is so much the commonsense background of judicial proceedings as to be imperceptible would be to point to the broad assumption that 'anyone who is English-speaking' ought to be able to stand up in court, answer questions, understand the charges, and so on, in an English court – and that a speaker who claimed to know and speak a kind of English quite removed from that of the court would be unlikely to receive a sympathetic hearing. That is, the basic right to a fair hearing in practice also carries the assumption that the language heard in court will approximate educated Standard English in pronunciation and lexicogrammar; the courts proceed as if defendants and claimants and their representatives approximate that norm, and are disinclined to consider the extent that prosecution and defendant might not share one and the same language.

Telementationism is also fairly directly apparent in the matter of *mens rea*, the so-called 'mental element' which is required in most serious crime prosecutions, but that underlies a great many legal proceedings. The *mens rea* requirement in serious crimes means, for example, that the prosecution must establish that the defendant acted intentionally, or at least recklessly. At the same time a version of telementationism extends to at least one category of civil law cases, namely defamation cases. As far as the twin pillars of the language myth are concerned, fixed-codeism and telementation, there seems a tendency for statute-controlled law to lean particularly heavily on the fixed-code notion, while common-law-controlled law leans more heavily on telementation–that is, on the assumption that, for prosecution or claimant to succeed, it *must* be the case, or is beyond a reasonable doubt the case, that the meanings that judicial participants (judges, barristers, jury) derive from defendant X's utterances are identical to the meanings that X attached to them.

But both elements of the myth are woven into practice in both branches of the law.

To highlight the telementational thread running through the legal system, it is important to emphasize the fact that quite systematically the law reduces situated acts to propositions–and in doing so is proceeding in a way that is perhaps analogous to Saussure's privileging of values over transactions at the opening of this paper. In legal proceedings, a complex and often desperate or tragic nexus of situated acts – like those of Mrs Ahluwalia and her husband culminating in his death – are reduced to propositional form, to an idea cast as an assertion or a question. In the case of Ahluwalia, the proposition that was formulated was roughly the following: In using the defence to a murder charge of provocation, must the defendant show that their sudden and temporary loss of control followed immediately upon the provocation itself? Juries and sometimes judges must decide on the facts of the case before them, but as any law student learns, legal training and practice is ultimately ill-disposed towards mere facts, and would prefer them reduced to the bare and strictly relevant minimum, when making an argument. Because in all the higher courts, cases ultimately turn on single propositions, questions and their answers, purporting to allow of general application and application to the instant case on the balance of probabilities or beyond a reasonable doubt. Those probabilistic caveats might appear to be an overt qualification of the telementational assumption, but they are a qualification that only arises at the point of referential application. Thus the entire apparatus of the law is predicated upon all parties accepting – as common ground – that the crime of theft is the dishonest appropriation of property belonging to another with intention to permanently deprive, and is equally predicated upon all parties sharing a common idea of what dishonest means here, what appropriation means here, and so on. So like the heads in Saussure's speech circuit, lawyers, judge, jury – even defendant – are assumed to have a shared ideational matching of the word 'appropriation' and a particular meaning, just as each of Saussure's individuals has the same sign for tree as their partner has. And just as in Saussure the chief area of uncertainty is whether the sign should apply to a particular tree-like object in the world, heterogeneity and interactional difference is treated as emerging only at the stage of application of agreed ideas to a particular contested or variously-represented act or omission. I am thus suggesting that telementationism is more germane and assumed in the higher circles of the law, where complex problems are reduced to propositional ideation. By contrast in the everyday law of Citizens' Advice Centres, Magistrates' Courts and high-street solicitors, where advice and warnings and settlements predominate, telementation is far less prominent. This to some extent alters the pattern of influence of the two elements of the language myth, since it is in everyday legal practice that code-fixity is presumed while in the 'higher' reaches of the law – in the two English courts of appeal, in the work of leading Queen's Counsels, and in academic legal circles – it is distrusted. To support the latter contention I need to return to the principles of statutory interpretation, and comment on some important changes that these have undergone since Nigel Love's 1985 paper.

4. From the literal back to the purposive

From a language-mythological perspective, the literal rule must appear unequivocally as the default option, akin to Lawrence's injunction 'never trust the teller, trust the tale'. For the literal rule trusts that, giving the words of a statute their ordinary and reasonable meanings, a coherent account of the Act can be derived. Zander (1994: 110) suggests that the 'most rigorous' expression of the literal approach came in Lord Halsbury's remarks in *Hilder v Dexter* [1902] A.C. 474, where he argued that the draftsman of a statute was the worst person to interpret it, since he would be the most powerfully influenced by what he meant rather than what he had said. On those grounds, because he had himself drafted the statute relevant to the case, Lord Halsbury refused to give judgement. While this ingenious line of reasoning invokes the familiar contrast between 'what was meant' and 'what was said', it is worth emphasizing that it really entails the postulation of two potentially distinct meanings: 'the meaning of what was meant' and 'the meaning of what was said'. It then asserts that the meaning of what was said is there, in the literal objective wording of the statute, autonomous and fixed, but that a clear view of that meaning is vulnerable to obscuring or contamination by parti-pris interpreters, especially the author with his exceptional stake in affairs. To proceed otherwise–according to this line of reasoning – that is, to seek to lay bare the meaning of what was *meant*, is clearly to seek to be guided by intentions – the draftsman's intentions, or the

169

government's intentions, or Parliament's. And to do so, particularly in the spirit of Lord Denning in *Magor and St Mellens*, might involve 'filling in the gaps and making sense of the enactment' in ways which are then criticized as an *ultra vires* enlargement of the judicial function, where 'making sense of a law' may appear to be not very different from roundly 'making law'. So Lord Simonds, reasserting the norm, censures Denning and reminds that 'the duty of the court is to interpret the words that the legislature has used'. Similarly Denning was in the dissenting minority in the notorious will case, *Re Rowland* [1963] 1 Ch. 1 (CA), where everything hinged on the meaning of *coinciding* as applied to the deaths of the testator and his spouse. Speaking for the majority, Lord Russell argued that two contrasting interpretations or definitions of *coinciding* were at stake, rather like alternative dictionary senses: (i) was 'simultaneous' and (ii) was 'on the same occasion and by the same cause'. There being no evidence that the deaths coincided in what Lord Russell declared – without argument – was 'the natural sense of simultaneous' in the mind of the ordinary man, he held that the deaths could not be deemed to have coincided.

Lord Denning complained that such a construal proceeded from fallaciously assuming that in construing a will 'It is not what the testator meant, but what is the meaning of his words' that matters, and he disapproved of this as a nineteenth-century view. But that view, that 'the meaning of the words' was sovereign, prevailed in that 1963 case. By contrast, there is little fixed-codeism – or at least, a heavily qualified if not locally contradicted fixed-codeism – in Lord Denning's dissenting judgement:

> You must put on [the testator's] words the meaning which they bore to him. If his words are capable of more than one meaning, or of a wide meaning and a narrow meaning, as they often are, then you must put on them the meaning which he intended them to convey, and not the meaning which the philologist would put on them. In order to discover the meaning which he intended, you will not get much help from a dictionary. It is very unlikely that he used a dictionary, and even less likely that he used the same one as you. What you should do is place yourself as far as possible in his position, taking note of the facts and circumstances known to him at the time, and then say what he meant by his words ... I decline, therefore, to ask myself: what do the words mean to a grammarian? I prefer to

ask: What did Dr Rowland and his wife mean by the word 'coincide' in their wills?

Lord Denning proceeds to a vivid dramatisation of the Rowlands' communicational situation at the time of making their wills; 'it is not difficult to piece together the thoughts that ran through their minds', he avers, before proposing a conjugal dialogue, in the course of which the wife says 'Yes, but what if we both die together?'. This helps Lord Denning to conclude that 'coinciding with' means here 'on the same occasion and by the same cause' – although as Lord Scarman noted, there was no evidence either way concerning a range of possible intervening acts; by the Denning standard, it is unclear whether or not, on the evidence available to those who found their bodies, the deaths of Romeo and Juliet would be judged to have coincided.

Lord Denning, then, long before most of his fellow judges, was sometimes prepared to favour a purposive approach over a literalist one; very often, however, as in *Rowland*, he was outvoted by his fellow judges. Accordingly we can say that the literal rule has in the recent past remained predominant, as is only confirmed by the traditional judicial disbarring from consulting Parliamentary debates and the like. This was very much the situation when Love published his article fifteen years ago.

But it is of great interest that this is no longer quite the case, particularly at the appellate level where law is not merely dispensed, but made or revised. The literal rule has lost some of its former dominance, under pressure from the purposive approach which has taken hold over the last quarter-century. And following *Pepper v Hart*, there is no longer the absolute exclusion of reference to Hansard and similar Parliamentary records, as there formerly was. The ruling in *Pepper v Hart* is only one of many indications that, in the last couple of decades, English law has qualified its preference for statutory interpretation to be literalist and its treatment of the text of a statute as free-standing. Other indicators include Lord Scarman's two Interpretation of Legislation Bills of 1979–1981, both unsuccessful, but indicative of a growing willingness to contemplate a degree of intercourse between the courts and Parliament that would have been hitherto unthinkable, least of all from a leading law lord. Yet another, of profound importance, has been the growing enmeshment of English law within European Union law, the latter characteristically drafted so as to be applied by means of a purposive rather than a literal interpretation (see Denning in *Bulmer v Bollinger*, and again in *Buchanan v Babco Forwarding*). It should be no surprise that the judicial activism of the European Court of Justice was congenial to Lord Denning:

> The judges do not go by the literal meaning of the words or by the grammatical structure of the sentence. They go by the design or purpose which lies behind it. When they come upon a situation which is to their minds within the spirit–but not the letter–of the legislation, they solve the problem by looking at the design and purpose of the legislature–at the effect which it was sought to achieve. They then interpret the legislation so as to produce the desired effect. This means that they fill in gaps, quite unashamedly, without hesitation. They ask simply: what is the sensible way of dealing with this situation so as to give effect to the presumed purpose of the legislation? They lay down the law accordingly. If you study the decisions of the European Court, you will see that they do it every day. To our eyes–shortsighted by tradition–it is legislation, pure and simple. But, to their eyes, it is fulfilling the true role of the courts. (Denning in *Buchanan v Babco*, [1977] 2 WLR 107)

Once condemned for advocating such an approach in much earlier domestic cases (Lord Simonds, in *Magor and St Mellons RDC ;* a House of Lords case, called it a 'naked usurpation of the legislative power'), Lord Denning evidently embraced this changed judicial role with satisfaction.

But as noted, most influential of all has been the ruling in *Pepper v Hart* (1993), where in his leading judgement Lord Browne-Wilkinson proposed that in questions of statutory interpretation, reference to parliamentary materials is permissible where the legislation was ambiguous or obscure or threatening absurdity, the material to be referred to came from the relevant minister or promoter of the Bill, and the material itself was unambiguous. Despite this limited relaxation, subsequent cases suggest that references to parliamentary documents for clarification or contestation of legislative intent may become quite extensive.

5. A racial group is a group of persons defined by reference to ethnic origins

The bulk of Love's 1985 article is taken up with close scrutiny of the appellate court judgements in the important racial discrimination case of *Mandla v Dowell Lee*. The case involved the exclusion of a Sikh boy from a school on the grounds that his turban and long hair violated the school dress and appearance code. On behalf of the boy's father, the Commission for Racial Equality claimed that the private school's rejection of the boy was a discriminatory contravention of the 1976 Race Relations Act, a crucial part of the claim asserting that the Sikhs constituted, within the meaning of the act, a racial group; this argument was controversially dismissed by the Court of Appeal (as it had been by Birmingham Crown Court), and not uncontroversially upheld on appeal by the House of Lords.

How, Love asks, did the two appeal courts go about scrutinizing and interpreting the language of the Act, especially s.3(1), so as to determine whether Sikhs were or were not, in the Act's terms, a racial group? His premise is straightforward: by the way in which judges scrutinize the words of an act shall be disclosed their implicit theory of language: what it is, what it does, and how it relates to people and the world.

Love demonstrates the lack of cogency of both the CA and HL attempts to pin down whether the Sikhs are a racial group, where the Act provides, as the grounds for defining a group as a racial group, that it is a group of persons 'defined by reference to colour, race, nationality, or ethnic or national origins'. He shows the incoherencies that the judges fell into in pursuing the hare of *ethnic origins*, and the clear dissonance between declaring that Sikhs were a racial group by virtue of being 'defined by reference to ethnic origins' when it was also common ground that some people, of disparate ethnicities, become Sikhs by conversion. Since no particular ethnic origin is, in fact, an essential criterion of being a Sikh, Sikhs evidently are not defined by reference to ethnic origins. The law lords did not distinguish defining characteristics from typical characteristics; or, to put things more positively, chose to interpret 'defined by reference to' as meaning 'typically recognizable by distinctiveness of' rather than 'necessarily having a distinctiveness of'. In this they might be said to have taken a purposive rather than literalist approach to the statute. It is important to note that s.3(1) of the Act also implies that a person can belong to more than one racial group.

On this occasion, the earlier judgement of the Court of Appeal and of Lord Denning in particular, was not signally more perspicuous. For while Denning was prepared to categorize the Jews 'as a whole' as a racial group sharing a common characteristic, even though particular Jews may be converts, he with little explanation declines to apply the same reasoning to Sikhs.

More careful was the literalist point made by Oliver LJ in the Court of Appeal: that s.3(1) does not require simply that a protected racial group be an ethnic group but specifically a group defined by reference to ethnic origins. Even if every member of a group, without exception, shared an exclusive ethnicity, it would not be–in the act's terms–a racial group unless it was *defined* by reference to those ethnic origins. Similarly an Irish chess club is not a racial group even if all its members enjoy a long shared ancestry, if club membership is defined by interest in chess, payment of dues, and so on, and not by ethnic origins. Having an attribute is not the same thing as being defined by reference to that attribute.

Love contends that if their lordships had dwelt upon the term *Sikh*, and had decided what characteristics or conditions were the necessary ones for someone to be defined as a Sikh, then a degree of clarity would have been established. Whatever things *Sikhs* were deemed to be defined by (and not merely 'ordinarily associated with'), if those things included reference to ethnic origins then the case for saying Sikhs are a racial group would be made; if not, not. That way of putting things allows that Sikhhood might be defined by multiple criteria, whereas Love asks for a single decisive criterion, and even offers one, namely 'adherence to the tenets of Sikhism'.

If Parliament had intended Sikhs to be covered by the Act, it is hard not to conclude that the wording of the Act is inadequate to the purposes aimed at. The leading judgement of Lord Fraser, as Love notes, simply ignores the wording 'defined by reference to', while the concurring judgement of Lord Templeman interprets it very liberally. If Parliament meant what those words mean, Love says, then the judgement of the House of Lords in *Mandla* seems scarcely tenable.

Indeed as soon as one begins delving into this episode of near-contemporary socio-legal incident, the sense of mixed motives and social friction is pervasive. The bare bones of the interpretive issues outlined above does not alert us to the fact that the private school involved had a significant number of pupils from ethnic minorities attending, and that five Sikh boys were already in the school, wearing their hair short; that the school had a distinctly Christian ethos,

The Language Myth and the Law

including Christian religious classes, and that on that basis Mr Mandla Singh would not have subsequently sent his son to the school even if the headmaster had allowed the boy to wear his turban; that the headmaster lacked funds to hire lawyers to make his defence for him, and therefore defended himself in the Crown court, and thereafter in both appeal courts; that the father of the plaintiff was a solicitor practising in Birmingham, and that the case was pursued out of the public purse by the recently formed Commission for Racial Equality, whose attorneys on the case included Geoffrey Bindman; that Lord Denning's Court of Appeal judgement came on his penultimate day in office as Master of the Rolls before retirement, and that in saluting him the second leader in *The Times* commented 'he was in fine clear form yesterday ... on the subject of the ethnicity of Sikhs'; that in reaching their decision the Court of Appeal were not overly mindful of two recent industrial tribunal decisions, which had decided that Sikhs were an ethnic group; that the Jewish Employment Action Group responded rapidly to the Court of Appeal ruling, well before the Lords' appeal was heard, warning that if Lord Denning's actual criteria were embraced, then even the Jews that he believed to be protected by the Act might on closer scrutiny be held not to be; that both Lord Denning and Lord Oliver roundly criticized the CRE for relentless pursuit of the headmaster, suggesting that it had fanned the flames of racial conflict, Lord Oliver going so far as to call the Commission 'an agent of oppression'; that the law lords equally sharply rebuked the appeal court judges for this unwarranted attack on a recently created statutory body and further intimated that such remarks bordered on interference with the sovereignty of the legislature; that in response to disquiet in and out of the House following the Court of Appeal decision, on November 18 the Home Office minister reported that leave to appeal to the House of Lords had been granted (notwithstanding the Court of Appeal's earlier denial of this), and he went on to say 'The Government ... will be able to consider whether legislative action is necessary in the light of the Lords' decision.'; that the White paper on racial discrimination which preceded the 1976 Act specifically mentioned the wearing of turbans as an area which would be covered by the legislation; that in the *Birmingham Post* reporting of the original crown court hearing the plaintiff was consistently misnamed as Mangla; and so on.

Where should their lordships have gone to discover what Sikhs are defined by? Their knowledge of the world, a good encyclopedia, a dictionary aimed at furnishing definitions? Love objected to Lord

175

Templeman looking up *ethnic* in a dictionary, on the grounds that whether the word *ethnic* applies to Sikhs would be a matter of the word's extension (while the dictionary would only supply its intension). Arguably, had Lord Templeman looked up *Sikhs* in a dictionary, he would have been less misguided; whether a dictionary would say enough to give grounds for resolving the question is, however, doubtful, since dictionaries tend to deal in standard or established usage and definitions, rather than contentious, border-line or emergent ones that become critical in legal actions. Love's integrationist-minded conclusion was that both the glosses 'typically recognizable by' and 'necessarily having' are competing interpreta-tions of *defined by reference to*, and that an argument in support of the latter, over that preferred by the law lords, is an opinion rather than a definitive account. The meaning of *defined by reference to* is not fixed, so that Lord Templeman's opinion that it means 'recog-nizable by' is at best rebuttable rather than refutable. Interestingly, in more recent cases appeal judges have moved from 'recognizable by' to 'referable to': in the *Dawkins* Court of Appeal case – 1993, IRLR, 284 – it was held that Rastafarians 'do not have a separate identity referable to ethnic origins'. It is chiefly on grounds of coherence and consistency with other interpretations of statutes that the second, criterial approach is preferable (that *defined by reference to* should be interpreted as meaning 'necessarily having'). For, Love says, in truth there is nothing 'on the face' of the actual wording of the Race Relations Act that can unambiguously guide us to an answer to the question whether Sikhs are supposed to count as a racial group:

> Those who want to know whether Parliament would like the Sikhs to enjoy the protection of the 1976 Act will have to look elsewhere (for example, to Parliament) for an answer. (66).

If judges do that, one line of resistance counters, why should they – or Members of Parliament–strive unduly for definitive accuracy in the drafting (or even the passing) of Acts at all? That rejoinder how-ever is more recalcitrant than reasonable: is it raised so as to protect certainty, or simply to minimize inconvenience? And if the chief objection to supplementing the interpretation of ambiguous statu-tory language by making reference to disambiguating Parliamentary explanation is simply that it is time-consuming, should this be given any more respect than one might extend to a complaint that a particular search was 'too thorough'?

But perhaps the House of Lords have 'violated the rules of the legal language-game' (Love, 1985: 65), and in particular the rule that says literal interpretation of statutory language, where it does not yield absurd results, can and should be relied upon to determine correct interpretation. At the same time Love points out that the law lords' 'going through the motions' of interpreting by means of fixed-code literalism is important for anyone who wishes to displace the language myth. For it means that the fixed-code thinking 'cannot simply be dismissed as a sort of naïve, empirically refutable mistake made by linguists' about language: rather, fixed-codeism, and telementationism, are tacit assumptions in the thinking of ordinary people, the mythical reasonable man, legislators and judges.

To re-cap, when the law lords hand down a ruling that Sikhs are, or are not, 'a racial group' within the terms of the 1976 Race Relations Act, as in countless other legal 'hard cases' that hinge on a nomenclatural issue (what *is* 'loose soil', or 'provocation', or 'torture', or 'member of the family', or 'mental capacity', or 'direct professional reliance', or 'dishonesty', etc. and do the circumstances of the present case involve an instance of this?), a codificatory and classificatory act entailing both inclusion and exclusion is required from the court. Sikhs must be determined either to be, or not to be, a racial group. And so on. There lies the reflection of a 'fixed-code' view of language with, in light of the principle of equality before the law, the related assumption that the fixed code is the same fixed code for all citizens within the jurisdiction. The law equally, via binding precedent and the hierarchy of the courts, seeks to enforce a homogeneity, in principle, across the entire judicial system, from magistrates up: what the law lords have fixed as code prevails for an indefinite period, until such time as the lords overrule themselves (itself a relatively new notion, only explicitly declared in 1966). This is surely a Saussurean solution to the difficulty of subscribing to homogeneous code-fixity while recognizing that at another time, an equally fixed code – not intrinsically open to 'development' or change – may apply.

The Race Relations Act s.3(1), to recapitulate, characterizes 'racial group' as follows:

'racial group' means a group of persons defined by reference to colour, race, nationality, or ethnic or national origins, and references to a person's racial group refer to any racial group into which he falls.

The difficulties that arise in interpreting and applying this section relate not merely to the fact that *race* is here supplemented, *inter alia*, by the idea of *ethnicity*: in addition, reference is made to ethnic origins, requiring some clarification of what can be meant by 'origins'. It has been argued that concerning the conjoint phrase, 'national origins', what needed ascertaining were 'identifiable, historical and geographical elements, which at least at some time revealed the existence of a nation' (*NJPB v Power*, 1997); but this still leaves unclear the precise basis on which, given the acknowledged existence of a nation in those terms – e.g., the Breton nation – an individual can be determined to be a member of a group defined by that nationhood: must the individual have been born in Britanny, or speak Breton, or have at least one Breton grandparent, or simply claim to be Breton? *Origins* would appear to have something to do with 'status of the individual through or at birth', but what precisely? What are these kinds of origins, that implicitly apply equally to national and to ethnic characteristics? A host of judges and academics have argued that the wording of s.3 confirms that Parliament wanted 'racial group' to apply on bases quite other than contentious biological or genetic grounds, and that the Act is robust in its treatment of race as a sociocultural category. That being so, is reference to 'origins' misleading, or a compromise with science and genetics? Caught somewhere along the continuum that ranges from nature to culture, those drafting the race relations legislation knew that the discrimination they wished to catch was directed at other than biologically distinct races (even assuming those could be established), but were evidently directed not to characterize racial group so loosely that it might include uninherited cultural group affiliations, including religious affiliation. One of the reasons sometimes given for not replacing the problematic Race Relations Act by a more comprehensive Cultural Discrimination Act, including religions, is that such an Act would have made immense difficulties for the position of England's Established Church, a constitutionally-privileged group. As things stand, religious discrimination in itself is not currently unlawful in England and Wales (unlike Northern Ireland), but the position is likely to shift with the coming into force of the Human Rights Act (from October, 2000): article 9 protects freedom of religion, while article 14 disallows, *inter alia*, discrimination on grounds of religion. Thus new balances will likely need to be struck, reconciling these entitlements.

In the mean time, since *Mandla*, there have been a few important cases that have claimed to apply that ruling. Perhaps most notable has been *Dawkins*, which hinged on whether Rastafarians were a racial group defined by reference to ethnic origins, for the purposes of the act. (The plaintiff, refused a job as a van-driver because he refused to cut off his dreadlocks, claimed racial discrimination.) In this case counsel for the plaintiff sought to highlight the inconsistencies and uncertainties that arise in any attempt to reconcile Lord Fraser's nomination of two essential characteristics (long shared history, and culture and customs) with Lord Templeman's three criteria (group descent, shared geography, group history). Giving the leading judgement, Lord Neil suggested that counsel had fallen into 'the error of equating the language used in speeches and judgements with that of a statute' and besides, he confessed he was unable to detect 'any real difference in substance' between what the two law lords had said. Interestingly, the prosecution also attempted to make reference to the comments of the Home Secretary at the time of the passage of the Race Relations Bill, on the new *Pepper v Hart* grounds that the statutory term 'ethnic origins' remained obscure and ambiguous. But Lord Neil rejected this proposal also, on the grounds that the law lords had effectively disambiguated the contentious term. As Parpworth has noted (Parpworth, 1993: 612), it will be interesting to see if the courts will always favour prior judicial interpretations – generally felt to be inconclusive – of ambiguous terms. Applying the guidelines of Lords Fraser and Templeman as constructively as possible, it might be concluded that definition of a group defined by ethnic origins, further delimited so as to require more than group religious identity, reduces essentially to the following:

A self-identified and other-recognized group with a long and distinct culture, where that culture entails significantly more than purely religious observances.

On this basis, for the purposes of the act, Jews would be a group of ethnic origin while Catholics are not (but what about Polish Catholics, or Irish Catholics?). Whether Rastafarians or Brummies or Woodcraft folk are ethnic groups becomes a matter of largely subjective determination. Lord Neil decided that the sixty years since the founding of Rastafarianism was not 'long enough' to count as a long history, and this alone seems to have been the basis on which the appeal failed.

6. Hard cases, decisions, and results

Essentially, the law would *like* 'theft', 'capacity', 'dishonesty', 'a building', 'in control of', 'entry without permission or licence', 'a member of the family', etc. etc. to carry, indefinitely, context-neutral invariant meanings: if they were truly context-neutral invariants, why ever – or how ever – would a need to change their meanings arise? But the evident reality is that meanings, applications, and rulings turn out to be extensively non-identical, and responsive to change and innovation.

One of the things that can be said about the *Mandla* case is that it is incontestably an example of what lawyers call a hard case. And, as is well known, to a great extent the important reported cases heard by the two Appeal courts are hard cases. But these do have to be decided – even if, thereafter, practising lawyers, legal academics, and fellow judges continue to dispute over quite what the *ratio decidendi* of the decision was. In the circumstances it might be better to say that, even in hard cases, judgements finally get delivered. Whether that judgement is to be followed, or is an Appeal Court decision promptly reversed by the Law Lords, or whether there are special circumstances that make its general applicability suspect, or whether the legislature is provoked by the ruling rapidly to enact corrective legislation, are all open questions. And a related impression that disputes and crimes are dealt with on a case by case basis is thus affirmed.

But that impression has to be set beside the reality that the law works in a rather different way: in the vast majority of instances, the specificities of cases and the context-sensitive distinctivenesses of meaning are elided and framed, by literally summary means (Atiyah, 1993: 216–7, for example, reports that no more than 1.5% of the 300,000 tort claims that arise in one year actually reach judges). Most civil disputes do not go to court, or if they do so, are not heard *in extenso*; and most criminal cases are dealt with summarily, or upon indictment by means of a guilty plea, so that most situations are concluded without anything remotely resembling a full hearing, but rather by means of a standardizing assigning of situations – as tokens – to established types. In composing this book of the law – the law as an already-completed book – the role of compositor is taken by lawyers, magistrates, and judges of the crown and county courts. By contrast the hard cases project the law as a text some parts of which are only available in draft form and subject to revision. Hard cases are decided in an active unscripted improvisatory process by means of which competing and conflicting interactionally-relevant considerations are weighed up and a balance is struck. The balance may be fair and just, or we may feel that, for example, the thumb of policy or public outrage is tilting it to one side, but decisions are made and handed down, and here much more important than 'correctness of decision' is the fact that a decision, a situated ending, has been reached. Similarly, even in a World Cup Final, more important than the fact that team A's solitary winning goal is clearly adjudged offside by everyone in the stadium save the referee is the fact that by that goal team A win and team B lose. Sports contests, like disputes, must come to an end, even if this is not 'the end', otherwise we could impose no episodic structure on experience at all. In short, hard cases are often decided in a quite integrationist spirit, but most cases are not – indeed they may not travel far enough into the legal system to become cases at all, but are summarily determined, very much along lines laid down by our native language myth, in accordance with which it is thought reasonable to detach a particular act or omission from as many of its surrounding circumstances as possible, and assign it to a collectively agreed determinate category and impose a relatively fixed penalty.

I began this essay with Roy Harris's important observation about how Saussure subordinates transactions to values, when the latter is nearer the truth – namely, that our everyday experience involves transactions and dependent values. My conclusions are that different strata of the legal system embrace or resist the language myth to different degrees: high street law is fixed-codeist and underlyingly telementational, while academic and appeal court law is implicitly telementational but, perhaps increasingly, resistant to code-fixity. That is to say, the most authoritative legal circles, the appeal courts and the law commissions, are the ones where – as reflected by *Pepper v Hart*, European interpretive purposeness, and so on – the law seems most receptive to the business of re-setting values in the light of a new transaction, which is close – perhaps indistinguishable – from the integrationist principle that values may be re-set *in* each new transaction. But if the law is approaching language differently and in a more integrational spirit, and if this gradually filters down to everyday practice at the high-street or magistrate court level, then we should expect a number of equally interesting developments: more improvisatory judicial activism, more 'politicised' jurisprudence, less certainty, and more anxiety about the survival of the rule of law.

Cases

Lloyds Bank Ltd v Bundy [1975] Q.B. 326
Mandla (Sewa Singh) v. Dowell Lee [1983] C.L.Y. 1163
Pepper v Hart [1993] 1 All E.R. 42
Dawkins v Crown Suppliers (PSA) [1993] I.R.L.R. 284
R v Ahluwalia [1992] 4 All E.R. 889
Re Rowland [1963] 1 Ch. 1

References

Atiyah, P.S. 1993. *Accidents, Compensation, and the Law.* Ed. P. Cane. London: Butterworths.
Bell, J. and G. Engle QC. 1995. *Cross on Statutory Interpretation.* London: Butterworths.
Beynon, H. and N. Love. 1984. *Mandla* and the meaning of racial group. *The Law Quarterly Review*, 100, 120–136.
Bix, B. 1995. *Law, Language and Legal Determinacy.* OUP
Evans, J. 1989. *Statutory Interpretation: Problems of Interpretation.* Oxford: OUP
Goodrich, P. *Legal Discourse.* London: Macmillan.
Harris, R. 1981. *The Language Myth.* London: Duckworth
Harris, R. 1987. *Reading Saussure.* London: Duckworth.
Hart, H. L. 1961. *The Concept of Law.* Oxford: Clarendon Press.
Hurst, D. J. 1983. The problem of the elderly statute. *Legal Studies.* 3:1.
Hutton, C. 1998. Law lessons for linguists? Accountability and acts of professional classification. *Language & Communication*, 16:3, 205–214. Reprinted in *Integrational Linguistics: A First Reader*, eds. R. Harris and G. Wolf, Oxford: Pergamon, 1998, 294–304.
Love, N. 1985. The fixed-code theory. *Language & Communication*, 5:1, 1–17. Reprinted in *Integrational Linguistics: A First Reader*, eds. R. Harris and G. Wolf, Oxford: Pergamon, 1998, 49–67.
McKenna, I.B. 1983. Racial discrimination. *Modern Law Review*, vol.46, 759–770.
Parpworth, N. Defining ethnic origins. *New Law Journal*, vol.143 (30.4.1993), 610–612.
Twining and Miers. 1999. *How to do things with rules.* London: Butterworths.
Zander, M. 1994. *The Law-Making Process.* 4th edn. London: Butterworths.

10 The Language Myth and Western Art

Anna Tietze

'It is possible, though controversial, to see the *whole intellectual development of Western culture* as an adoption of, or adaption to, the two essential components of the 'language myth': (i) the doctrine of telementation and (ii) the doctrine of the fixed code.'

The above statement, from Roy Harris's brief conference synopsis 'The Language Myth in Western Culture', usefully introduces some of the central notions of Integrationism and gives a good idea of the ambitiousness of its scope. It makes clear, as do many other similar claims, that for Harris, visual art is just one facet of a communicational megastructure badly in need of redescription by the Integrationist. In his paper in this collection, he notes his sense of the seriousness of the situation; while our 'language myth' assumptions 'promote certain values and practices that Western culture would be the poorer without', they also 'victimise' us, Harris believes, 'inasmuch as the myth inculcates certain attitudes and prejudices that prevent Western culture from realizing its full human and humane potential' (this volume: 1–2). Harris does not elaborate on exactly how our human potential might be being cramped by the language myth, but he does make clear, here and elsewhere, how a more modest enemy, the traditional academic linguist, is stifling creative debate about language acquisition and linguistic communication. Any attempt to trace instances of 'language myth' thinking in the visual arts should perhaps, then, proceed from a careful if brief study of what exactly are Harris's objections to traditional linguistics.

His objections seem to revolve around two perceived errors in traditional thinking. The 'fixed code' is central to the first. For Harris, it is notable that most of us go about our daily lives believing that there is a one-to-one correspondence between words and meanings such that, in entertaining a thought or making a statement about the world, we are verbally capturing or reflecting fixed meanings that rest outside them. Words, we believe, merely serve to give them concrete life, in that bizarre form of grunted sounds or squiggles on a page that we call 'language'. The second error, for Harris, is the view that, in sharing our experiences with others – in communicating successfully with them – what we do is to use language, spoken or written, to transfer a copy of private mental events from our own head to that of our listener – a phenomenon Harris wryly characterises as 'telementation'.

The two questions that immediately arise are: why should these be described as myths, and why particularly *language* myths? Harris's answer to the first has been elaborated at length over the past thirty years and constitutes the theory of Integrationism. It is a theory which pits itself against the 'segregational' tendency of traditional thinking in linguistics, the tendency to visualise words and their meanings as two separate arenas which are nevertheless connected in enduring and predictable ways (the most favoured, although not the only posited connection being a 'surrogational' one in which words gain meaning by itemising objects; compare the 'structuralist' model in which they gain meaning by their difference from each other). Basic to any form of segregational linguistics is, Harris believes, a misguided assumption that, in cases of verbal communication, *all* that we receive from the communicator comes to us embedded in the words that they use. For Harris, this is far too reductive a view of spoken communication in that it leaves out of account entirely the many, non-verbal elements of a communicational situation which will inevitably comprise a rich variety of contextual signifiers. Put simply, the gripe here is with an academic discipline which adopts so narrow a view of 'linguistic communication' that it has nothing *on principle* to say about all the non-verbal features of human interchanges which colour, or lend significance to, or give a necessary slant to our linguistic utterances. The same words can mean very different things in different contexts. Only the Integrational linguist, Harris argues, is prepared to take this central truth theoretically on board.

The second question – why is this myth a *language* myth – seems to me, as an outsider to Integrationism, less squarely tackled. It appears to arise from Harris's assumption – hardly an unusual one – that linguistic experience is *the* central form in which the inner lives of human beings manifest themselves. Now on this question, Harris is, however, rather ambivalent, for while he seems to *allow* for the notion of 'pre-linguistic' or 'extra-linguistic' mental experience, his working view appears to be that, because it is non-linguistic, we cannot talk about it and so had better not try. I sense that something of this kind is going on in Harris's paper in this collection where, in discussing Saussure, he regrets the 'crudeness' of Saussure's 'denial of pre-linguistic ideas' (this volume: 18), but ultimately praises him for his recognition that 'at least for purposes of the theorist of human communication – (i) the only mental items worth considering are those which are communicable, and (ii) to be communicable is to be expressible by means of signs, of which the most important are linguistic signs'. Which, as a starting point for tackling the phenomenon of human communication, is perhaps limiting.

In *Signs, Language and Communication* of 1996, Harris appears to take a more critical view of the tendency to regard language as central to human experience. Noting that this happens particularly in those societies which place heavy emphasis upon written texts, he dubs it the '*fallacy* of verbalism' (Harris 1996: 25. My italics). It is described as the 'assumption that signs in all forms of communication must somehow operate like words; that is, they must be units with a form and a meaning. (A frown means this; a nudge means that; a certain style of dress means something else.) The fallacy of verbalism is even embodied in certain uses of the term *language* itself, as when we speak of *body language*, the *language of gestures*, the *language of architecture* ... etc.' (ibid.) We might doubt whether our tendency to find nudges meaningful has anything particularly to do with the centrality of words to our lives (isn't the meaning of a nudge often, precisely, ineffable?), but Harris's assumption of a connection is very important and marks one of the many points in this book (and elsewhere in similar discussions) where he seems rather to prejudge the issue of mental experience and human communication. Specifically, the impression gained from his writing on communication – and, tacitly, private mental experience – is that for Harris they are so fundamentally and so obviously bound up with the exercise of language that there is little impact to be made by someone wishing to argue for extending the bounds of the 'extra-linguistic'.

I concluded an earlier version of this paper by objecting that Harris's theory of communication 'tends to assimilate aesthetic experience to the business of getting through our daily lives'. His response was to the effect that this was to draw an absurd distinction where none really exists. Understanding artworks just is another example of making sense of pieces of human communication such that we do not trip up, that we remain within the human flow, and are free to move on in our conquest of our society's multifarious and constantly mutating signs. But my point remains, and it is that where a theory of communication does not attend carefully to the aspects of human experience and communication that are *not* language-like, it is going to offer a theory of human activities such as the creation of visual art that is more impoverished than it might be. This said, it has to be noted that Harris is ostensibly pitting himself *against* those who assimilate visual communication too closely to the verbal. But the Integrational answer, it might be felt, does not solve the problem in quite the way that is required for a deeper and more nuanced awareness of the specifically visual to emerge.

One of the very important things Harris does, in his brief studies of visual imagery in *Signs, Language and Communication* and elsewhere, is remind us of the extent to which artists over time have had to take a stand on the question of how their form of communication relates to the verbal. In societies where the possession of superior linguistic skills has been one of the key indicators of intelligence and therefore status, the visual artist has found himself with one of two options: he has either had to struggle to change prejudice against the visual by making claims for its own special insights, or accept the status quo and argue for the senses in which his communicational medium might be seen as analogous to the verbal. Both types of artist have generally crudely overstated their case, and the ways in which they have done so are very interesting. An impartial study of this history is long overdue, and the seeds of it lurk behind what Harris has to say about pictures. But the Integrationist project, we might feel, gets somewhat in the way of the telling of this history. What Harris tends to do often is use examples of visual art to illustrate popular segregationalist notions of how signs relate to meanings and how these meanings get carried from communicator to audience. In the process, he sometimes hits on key assumptions made by one or other of the apologists for the visual noted above. But often, to repeat, exploration of the latter gets blurred by the larger Integrationist argument.

It is important to outline exactly how the main principles of the Integrationist argument are applied by Harris to the case of visual art. One way is by equating the linguistic surrogationalist's assumption that words match up with things with the figurative realist's assumption that images faithfully reflect the appearances of objects.

The latter is dubbed a kind of 'fixed-codism', and it is noted that it has had a very long and vigorous history, being particularly strongly championed by schools like that of the Dutch seventeenth-century Little Masters or the nineteenth-century French *juste milieu*, or the High Victorians. Painters of such schools, and many among their public, seem to have attached particular value to the artist's capacity to generate a likeness, such that appreciation of their works becomes a matter of gasps of wonder at just how much information has been recorded and just how accurately it has been transcribed into paint. This has not been only a lay response, as is revealed by the work of Ernst Gombrich. In his seminal study, *Art and Illusion* (Gombrich 1960), Gombrich based notions of artistic sophistication and progress around the question of the conquest of appearances. For Gombrich, it was Western artists' curiosity about the look of the world, and their increasing capacity to produce detailed pictorial equivalents for it that made this kind of art so impressive.

Where Harris stands on this issue of pictorial mimesis I confess to finding rather unclear. At times, he seems to regard the whole project of mimesis as another example of misguided thinking, based on the mythical notion that pictures of objects could ever be regarded as picking out isolable objects in the world and 'meaning' them. This is, I presume, what motivates the criticism of 'Aristotelian surrogationalism which survives as the basis for much of the theorising about artistic representation in the later European tradition' (Harris 1996: 131). And yet, more recently, he has suggested that 'the theory of natural mimesis is the only serious competitor the theory of a fixed code has ever had in Western aesthetics' (this volume: 22), suggesting in preceding comments that he might himself support the 'theory of natural mimesis' by posing questions such as, 'does the Venus de Milo in the Louvre require us to understand any convention at all? Does it not suffice to recognize the resemblance between certain shapes in carved marble and certain features of the human body?' (ibid). All of which somewhat narrows one's earlier understanding of the notion of a 'fixed code', since initially it did not seem to be restricted to signs which had only a conventional relationship to their signifiers.

However, the whole search for the visual analogy for the linguistic 'fixed code' is perhaps obscuring more interesting issues. For while the human delight at and faith in pictorial mimesis is a fascinating issue, we should surely not overlook the enormous *differences* in motivation for and understanding of picture-making that lie behind some of the realist cultures gathered together by Harris. It is risky, to say the least, to argue that artists of 'the Italian Renaissance' (15th century? 16th century? *All* the artists of Italy?) and 'Northern Europe in the 17th century' were engaged in fundamentally the same project, fuelled by a 'pragmatic rationality' that assumed the world could be known and measured by constructing 'public sign systems' that were believed to reflect it faithfully in all its detail (Harris 1998). Such an account will do, at a general level, but it fails to explain why these versions of pictorial mimesis are so very different. Analysis of Raphael-realism and Terborch-realism, to take just one comparative case, suggests that these artists were conceiving of the way pictures reflect reality so differently that to focus on their shared enjoyment of mimesis is perhaps not very useful. Indeed, given their vast differences (one could speculate that architectural diagrams and mathematical problems are central to the visual life of the one, maps and manufactured goods to the other), it becomes unclear why Harris should distinguish particularly between these 'realist' schools and what he dubs 'non-realist' artistic periods such as the Middle Ages or the Baroque (ibid).The subtle characteristics of different kinds of pictorial imagery seem to be lost sight of, in these discussions of mimesis, under the pressure of a theory of communication simultaneously ambitious in scope and slanted towards the linguistic.

Any theory of human communication that bases its critique of visual art upon the realist tradition finds itself with a problem; either it has to concede that the mimetic experiment was relatively localised and shortlived (peculiar to the West, and only active for certain, if prolonged, periods), and that the errors it embodied are now a thing of the past, or it needs to claim that the misunderstandings made conspicuous by realism lurk in other forms of visual art also, but are simply more hidden. The Integrationist seems to keep both these options open, sometimes suggesting that the realist pictorial tradition provides the classic analogy with language myth assumptions, while other times suggesting that just about *any* kind of visual art embodies the segregationalist error. The latter of these two is the path taken by Harris in *Signs, Language and Communication.* Here he implies that, from the Integrationist perspective, there is ultimately little point in distinguishing between realist and non-realist or abstract art since both alike demand, naively, that we search within them, via their visual signs, for elements of meaning. In the case of, for example, a Mondrian, this involves a good deal of guesswork not demanded by the recognisably realist picture, but the basic assumption is the same – that there will be a correspondence between elements of the picture and discrete items of meaning, and that our coming to understand the work will be a process of successfully matching up the two. What we will probably need, in the case of abstract art, is some schematic dictionary of visual elements of the kind provided by artists like Mondrian or Kandinsky – that straight lines and perpendicular angles mean purity, that primary colours mean rationality, that blue means spirituality, or whatever.

Harris suggests that the world of art and art theory is rife with this kind of reductive search for matches between visual elements and meaning. Whether one starts out with a recognisable image or not is really rather irrelevant. One is going to need more textual help in the one case, but in the other, one's interpretations stand to be just as crude. In *Signs, Language and Communication*, he cites the case of Damien Hirst's recent installation, *Away from the Flock* (a dead sheep inside a tank of formaldehyde), and the artist's suggestion that we should 'think about our mortality' when we gaze at this work (Harris 1996: 239). Harris ponders wryly on whether 'thinking about one's own mortality could stand as the communicational *content* of a dead sheep' (Harris 1996: 240) and decides that the very notion is an absurdity. For him, it makes no sense to suggest that our awareness of Hirst's work is made up of such interpretive procedures.

One understands the impatience with crude interpretations of artworks. Such interpretations are sometimes offered by art critics, and are embarrassingly common, also, among artists. But they are not as unavoidable as Harris implies, and do not in themselves illustrate the need for an Integrationist alternative. What they illustrate, perhaps, is nothing more than the difficulty of approximating in words the extra-linguistic complexities of pictures. Where our experience of pictures has to be communicated, we grapple to give repeatable, conventional Language something of the specificity and flavour of visual experience. It is interesting and important, however, to highlight the problem and to analyse the more flagrant cases of it in action. Two influential groups of recent art writers have demonstrated the dilemma particularly acutely. They are the popular 'social historians' of art (who reigned almost unopposed in some research areas from the early 1970s to the late 80s) and the now more fashionable 'post-structuralist semiologists' of visual art.

In a recent study of late nineteenth-century French painting entitled *Art and the French Commune: Imagining Paris after War and*

Revolution (Boime 1995), social art historian Albert Boime has re-analysed many well-known pictures of the period with a view to showing that, contrary to fondly-held popular opinion, Impressionist art was not an art of pure aesthetic experimentation, but a body of work produced by very solidly middle-class artists concerned to celebrate and preserve the social position they held in their ordinary lives. His argument is that the Paris Commune of 1871 posed a dangerous threat to middle class privilege, and that many of the 'Impressionist' works painted just after this event offer symbolic pictorial recuperations of the socio-political status quo – they reassure us, and the artist, that social order has been re-established. Thus, when Caillebotte, the associate of artists such as Monet and Renoir, opted to paint a scene of floor-scrapers in 1875, he was trying to represent 'artisans ... regimented for the sake of work in an affluent bourgeois milieu. The peculiar viewpoint and upraised horizon subordinates them not only to the exigencies of the architectural space but to the gaze of the viewer who owns it' (Boime 1995: 81). Their 'regimentation' has already been accounted for, by Boime, in the following way: 'the three workers are totally absorbed in their labor and function as a team moving in tandem with each other's rhythm. This sense of mechanical movement is reinforced by the frontal symmetries of the two closest workers and the right-angle position of the third which align them with the geometry of the composition ... In effect, their bodily movements are conditioned by the environment ... ' (ibid, 80).

Elsewhere in Caillebotte's oeuvre, Boime sees further evidence of what he calls 'a class-based modernism that secures the prerogatives of the bourgeoisie while conveying the illusion of a shared public space' (ibid, 82). Caillebotte's 1876 *Le Pont de l'Europe* in turn falls victim to this analysis: 'In the painting we are looking down the rue de Vienne, with the place de l'Europe at the left and the railroad yard at the lower right. Gazing contemplatively into the yard below is a young worker in a smock, who casually leans on the iron parapet of the recently constructed Pont de l'Europe. Moving towards the spectator at a brisk pace along the sidewalk is a bourgeois couple, conversing and strolling in a spacious ambience that suggests freedom of action. Although the perspective lines converge on the couple, the worker is positioned so prominently in the foreground that he sets up a visual opposition to them. As Herbert suggests, this opposition between bourgeois and worker is seen in the other figures as well, with the labourers on the inside of the walkway captivated by the metal trusswork – a metonym for industrial practice – and the upper-class types on the outside distanced from this realm and uninhibitedly engaging in a flirtatious exchange. Thus although present in the same space as the bourgeoisie, the potentially unruly classes are shown as totally absorbed in their own world of industry and work and allow their social superiors to go about their business free from disturbance' (Boime 1995: 84).

This sort of writing about pictures is not at all uncommon in studies, particularly of mid to late nineteenth-century French art, by self-consciously 'revisionist' art historians. What it typically does is to approach the pictures only *after* a coherent purpose or communicational aim on the artist's part has been staked out (this without obvious reference to the evidence of the works) – in this case, the artist's aim, we are to believe, is to reassure the middle-class viewer that Paris has returned to a state of order. This communicational aim is generally, as here, conceived as a narrowly political one – some social group's interests are advanced by the picture, to the exclusion of another's. These political messages are then traced in the work by an ersatz formal analysis which does such things as equating gaps between painted figures as signs of 'antagonism', high or low viewpoints as signs of position in a social hierarchy, repetition of shape as a sign of 'dehumanising loss of individuality', size of figure as a sign of dominance or social importance, and so on. The artist is, in effect, conceived as approaching the blank canvas with a ready-prepared set of opinions about the world formulated in his mind, and with a neat sense of which images in juxtaposition would make his 'position' clear.

Clearly, a very odd notion of pictorial content is operating in analyses of this sort. For, to return to our previous examples, although one would not want to deny that Caillebotte's *Floor Scrapers* or his *Pont de l'Europe* have a narrative aim, the narrative complexity or specificity that Boime ascribes to the works seems to outstrip the pictorial evidence to an outrageous degree. And although this kind of writing is encountered most often in nineteenth-century studies, and in texts of the last thirty years or so, one is reminded here of Freud's notorious account of Michelangelo's *Moses*, which makes basically the same mistake. I cite this earlier example of bad artwriting because it is used by Harris, in *Signs, Language and Communication*, to question the wisdom of ascribing anything at all called 'content' to an artwork ('much of what traditional artistic and literary criticism talks about in terms of content and intentions ... boils down to identifying a plausible pattern of integration: the 'content' and the 'intention' are no more than psychological frills to the integrational question') (Harris, 1996: 241). I would want to claim, far less radically, that there is plenty of point to retaining the notion of content, but that the particular nature of pictorial content needs to be understood. Sometimes it isn't.

Another kind of writing about art that is currently enjoying great favour but that arguably goes about connecting language with art in the wrong way is the semiological visual analysis of writers like Norman Bryson, Mieke Bal, and many others. This has arisen as a reform, in turn, of social art history, which it accuses of a naïve belief in the permanence of pictorial meaning and in the knowability of the social structures that pictures might comment on. The accusation, then, is of a naïve assumption of something like a Harrisian fixed code. In place of it, semiologists of art want to posit a conception of meaning as fluid, and as independent of authorial intention. They envisage it as arising out of encounters between viewer and work, and as having a playfully experimentalist character unburdened by concerns about Truth.

This might look, finally, like Integrationism, except that the semiologists in question would still want to claim that certain observable features of any picture in question might be regarded as signs, which could be equated, in a one-to-one relationship, with meanings. And, as I understand it, this is, for the Integrationist, already to go too far down the road towards talk of pictures *containing* meaning. My objections to this kind of writing, however, are rather different, although they still have to do with how language is conceived as relating to pictorial communication. They are best brought out through a very brief analysis of how an actual piece of semiological visual analysis proceeds. I choose Norman Bryson's essay, 'Géricault and "Masculinity"' (Bryson, Holly and Moxey 1994: 228–59).

The semiologist of art, unlike the social art-historian, proceeds on the assumption that pictures are best conceived as, metaphorically, 'texts'. Right out on the table from the outset, then, is the intention to subsume all forms of human consciousness and creativity under the model of talking, reading, and writing. In practice, 'text' seems to be fairly minimally conceived, as a succinct body of ideas about self or others, or Life. The writer typically outlines it for us in the opening pages of the analysis. In the case of the Géricault essay, the text might be summarised as the claim that the Géricault work under analysis shows the artist exercised by problems of how men assert and maintain respectable degrees of manliness in the face of powerful male hierarchies which oppress the young and weak, and in the face of social pressures – he considers war and military service – which demand too much of human nature. Bryson illustrates this interesting view concerning the difficulties of being male by a consideration of a range of pictures by Géricault, of men straining to hold on to riderless horses (the celebrated riderless horse races of Rome are the subject of the works), of men in military uniform on the back of volatile horses, of men returned, wounded, from war, and of men shipwrecked and dying. He prepares us pictorially for the way he is going to approach the works by opening with an image of a contemporary body builder; he prepares us textually by quoting Woody Allen's self-inquiry, in one of his films, as to why only *women* should have been allowed by Freudian theory to suffer penis envy.

I am crudely summarising an interesting piece of writing and one that can have a lasting effect on the way in which one sees these pictures. But I am critical of it, despite its interest, because of the way, again, that it envisages language connecting with art. Let me try to get at this issue by asking a question that Bryson would rule out, immediately, as illegitimate, but which I'll ask anyway – and it is 'do the pictures illustrated really strongly suggest that Géricault the artist might have been preoccupied about the question of masculinity, and if they don't, is there something deeper, or more nameless that they might be said to embody?' The question is illegitimate for Bryson because it is based on an assumption that it is possible and that it matters to retrieve authorial intention. For Bryson, 'Géricault' is rather more like a shifting construct of viewers' minds, and we are free to impute to our own 'Géricault' whatever reading the pictures sensibly suggest to us. So, the question might be reformulated as, 'if a visual artist were preoccupied by the questions that form Bryson's "text", would they translate in this way into pictures?' And my feeling is that conceiving of a 'text' like the masculinity one as even a possible theme of pictures is to get the notion of pictorial theme, or meaning, or content wrong from the outset. There is *no* picture or set of pictures that could embody quite such an intellectually-elaborated set of ideas about life as is contained in the Bryson-Géricault 'text'.

To sum up, what I'm suggesting that these offending pieces of visual interpretation ('sociological' or 'semiological') are doing is projecting onto pictures forms of consciousness and conceptions of communication that belong outside the world of visual art. In the case of the social art historians, there is some recognition of art's peculiarness, in the efforts made to include formal characteristics of pictures as evidence for interpretive claims. High viewpoints mean 'we dominate', brightly-lit motifs mean 'this is important', and so on. The interpretations are not always sophisticated, but they represent some acknowledgement of medium and structure. In semiological analyses, this is sometimes pared down even further, so that one feels that no efforts at all have been made to imagine what it is like to be someone whose consciousness is naturally biased towards the visual rather than, say, the numerical or the musical or towards speech or writing. But what I want to suggest is that the sort of interpretive inappropriateness that I am discussing is bound to arise if one starts out from the position that visual artworks are 'semiological systems' – and that while only one of these two schools opts to use this term, what both of them are in effect doing is aligning crudely-conceived 'meanings' with (crudely-conceived) 'pictorial motifs' or pictorial signs.

In *Signs, Language and Communication*, Harris seems to be, unsurprisingly, unhappy with some of the heavy-handed pieces of visual interpretation that go by the name of art history or art criticism. His proposed solution is to replace them with an Integrationist account of artworks, with all of its radical scepticism regarding the notion of 'content'. But he does not want to question the wisdom of regarding artworks as systems of signs. By contrast, I suggest that the notion of 'content' is a fairly blameless and useful one, understood properly, but that the concept of 'the sign' has to be treated with caution – and its limited usefulness acknowledged – in discussion of paintings, sculptures, drawings that we find aesthetically interesting.

We might take as an example two paintings by roughly contemporary, and professionally related, artists, Giovanni Bellini and Titian. Their paintings are *Portrait of Doge Leonardo Loredan* (fig. i) and *Portrait of Doge Andrea Gritti* (fig. ii) respectively. What sense does it make to speak of these pictures as semiological systems, and what would be an alternative way of conceiving of them as meaningful? Both are commissioned portraits, designed to advertise the status of their sitter, give him a life beyond the grave and generally flatter him. Both show him in official dress, and the dress has not changed in the thirty-year interval between the production of the two works. On one level, both works bristle with signs, of middle-aged manliness, of dignity and status, of professional position. But how much further does the notion of sign take us? In what sense are the

fig i: Giovanni Bellini *Doge Leonardo Loredan* c. 1502, Panel. National Gallery, London

shiny buttons of Loredan's garb a sign, when viewed in visual contrast with the heavy, speckled fruit-like ones of Andrea Gritti? Or the brilliant, ornately-patterned cloth of Loredan's mantle, when compared to Gritti's smudged fabric? Or the dangling strings of

fig ii: Titian *Doge Andrea Gritti* c. 1535–40, Canvas. National Gallery of Art, Washington, D.C. Samuel H. Kress Collection

Loredan's supportive headwear when compared to the minimal equivalent in the other? Buttons, fabric, headwear signify 'dogehood', in both cases, but what a comparison between two very different doge portraits does is to alert us to the 'much more' that remains to be accounted for, after basic signifying work has been got out of the way.

The Language Myth and Western Art

It may be objected that this does not throw into the doubt the use-fulness of 'sign' talk at all, and that we merely need to acknowledge a realm of 'deep signifying': Gritti's buttons go beyond signifying 'button', 'items of doge's costume' and begin to signify 'abundance', Loredan's 'austerity and rectitude'. But then what of the passages in these works which defy verbal categorisation in the first place – what, for instance, of the passage of paint marks from highlighted, folded-back overgarment, to deeply-shadowed sleeve and folds of under-garment, to highlighted deep fold to vertical streak of white towards right of picture? It hardly seems sensible to say that, as our eye travels across the picture in this way, it is scanning the work for signs, search-ing the work for meaning. Something like a culinary metaphor seems more in order – feasting on sticky paint, tasting seductive colour, or whatever. And to return to buttons or headdress strings or any other painted feature of the work that corresponds to an isolable object in the world – isn't our experience of these most akin to the feeling of pleasure we have when we feel a shiny conker (in Loredan's case) or over-ripe peach (in Gritti's) – that is to say, only minimally an 'under-standing' of them and largely a physical response to them? Even this, though, is perhaps too oppositional. What one want to clear a space for is the 'non-verbal' experience which exercises both animal senses and language, but which is too complex, diffuse, and private to be described. It characterises, surely, most of our daily inner lives. Bryan Magee has noted, in a long passage of introspection, the visual nature of most of our primary experience and the resulting difficulty we have in capturing it in words: 'for most of my waking day my conscious awareness is a predominantly visual experience [but] *whenever* I see, all that language can do is to indicate with the utmost generality and in the broadest and crudest of terms what it is that I see' (Magee 1998: 96). This is the type of consciousness that most visual art is galvanising.

Let me try to sum my feeling about Integrationist theory in rela-tion to visual art by considering a short passage from *Signs, Language and Communication*, from the chapter entitled 'Communication and Content'. It crops up in a section in the chapter where Harris is arguing for words being regarded as basically *func-tional*, as being essentially tools that facilitate our passage through life in the way that useful objects do. Both words and objects do com-municational work, and to privilege words as our only communica-tional tools is, Harris argues, to make a naïve mistake. An 'Enter' sign at a door is quite as much simply a *tool* as is the doorknob; while a doorknob is as much a communicational sign as is the word

197

'Enter': 'the well-wrought doorknob, appositely placed, inviting the grasp of the outstretched hand, is no less communicationally relevant to the visitor than the notice on the door which says 'Enter'. Only a theorist brainwashed in verbalism would suppose otherwise' (Harris 1996: 241). So words are entered into the swim of things, as just one type of sign among many of which our lives are filled.

There follows the Integrationist argument that, since doorknobs and other useful objects cannot be said to have 'content' (we do not say, 'Aha, this means "door-opening tool"' – we just use it), then it would also seem unnecessary to ascribe 'content' to the word 'Enter' on the door. By contrast, Harris notes, a verbalist theory of communication that wants to privilege language, and wants to visualise us understanding language by a constant process of translating words into their meanings is going to have a lot to say about the meaning of the word 'enter', but is not going to have a place in its scheme of things for discussion of doorknobs etc. For, to quote Harris, '[a] doorknob has no "content". It simply has an integrational function ... That is why a segregationalist semiology [that is to say, a semiology which treats signs as having an autonomous existence outside their communicational contexts] ignores its existence.' At this point, Harris brings in the case of visual art. He adds, ' It is also why a semiology which requires aesthetic messages to have content is hard put to it to explain how signification can be generated simply by producing a utilitarian object of which the form contradicts the expected integrational function. The most celebrated example in art history is perhaps Man Ray's flat iron with a row of sharp tacks protruding from the ironing surface. (As separate utilitarian objects, neither the iron nor the tacks have any 'content'. So how can their combination produce any?) The work stands as a satirical critique of a whole segregational aesthetics' (ibid).

I understand Harris to be saying here that the traditional way of thinking about artworks, as visual forms containing meaning, is well challenged by a deliberately mischievous kind of modernist art which takes a functional thing, puts it in a gallery, and says, 'this is art!' For the iron and the tacks weren't perused for internal meaning when they were part of our ordinary lives; how could they possibly have acquired any now? Such works as Man Ray's *Gift*, I take Harris to be arguing, are designed to illustrate the general futility of scanning any artwork for meaning, and then *assuming that what we find is both fixed and internal to it.*

Applying to Man Ray's work what I've said of other, more conventional artworks, I would want to make the following points in reply. Firstly, that there are two main ways we look at Man Ray's work: as decorative shape and texture (noting, for example, the curve of the metal from top down to sides, the simplicity of its full, polished face in relation to its handle, the weathered quality of its scratched and pitted surface in relation to its general smoothness, the pleasing regularity of the line of tacks and of their repeated shapes, the slight *ir*regularity of their line as well, giving a satisfying sense of the organic in the midst of the mechanical) and as stimulus to associated ideas and animal response (as when we feel the 'frankness' of its full face, the 'skinlikeness' of its slightly imperfect though smooth surface, the touchability of its spikes). If the work had an obvious narrative dimension – if it were, say, a portrait or a hunting scene – then we would be aware of this dimension too, but never to the exclusion of these other, more physical – or 'unverbalisable'? - aspects of the work. However, Man Ray's work happens to have dispensed with this dimension. Secondly, I would want to say that, in looking at the Man Ray, we are sensibly aware that there are features *physically present* in the work that are triggering our responses, although simultaneously aware that other viewers might respond to these features differently. These features contribute to our sense of its having 'content'. Thirdly, I would want to insist that our talk of 'content' is, however, at the level of interpretation, knowingly metaphorical – we do not suppose that the work is *really* a container whose lid we are lifting to reveal 'frankness' or 'skinlikeness'. Indeed, whatever could it *mean* to believe this? And fourthly, I would want to argue that what we *don't* assume is that Man Ray's work renders up its meaning via a process in which we decode 'irons' into 'domesticity' and 'metal tacks' into 'aggression' and then join the two into some suitable narrative juxtaposition. At least, many of us don't. I considered earlier some types of thinking and writing about art that *did* tend in this sort of direction. Significantly, perhaps, they have emerged from institutionalised discussion of art within university arts faculties, those bastions of the written word.

In this paper I've tried to give some idea of the ways in which Harris envisages the 'language myth' operating in relation to visual art. But my conclusion has been that a host of rather different issues are typically clustered together by Harris in his tantalisingly brief discussions of this subject. Some point in the direction of interesting and fuller accounts of the inevitable dependence of art upon the written and spoken word. Others, however, seem to make passing reference to visual art in order to illustrate a theory of human communication whose main concerns lie elsewhere. But arguably lurking underneath all of Harris's references to visual art is a dissatisfaction with the art writer's interpretive methods. I have examined two art writers out of many who seem open to criticism on this score. They are writers, I've argued, who foist onto art a way of thinking that is alien to it. I would sum up the mistake as, quite simply, the assumption that everything we experience can be said in words. I am not certain that an Integrationist theory of communication addresses this particular problem. I would suggest that, insofar as thinking and writing about art need reform at all, they need help from the art school more urgently than from a theory of communication preoccupied with the importance of language. Such a theory might identify some of the errors we sometimes make in approaching pictures, but it will not be able to describe and explain what is going on when – occasionally – we get it right.

References

Boime, A. (1995) *Art and the French Commune: Imagining Paris after War and Revolution*, Princeton, Princeton University Press.

Bryson, N., Holly, M.A. and Moxey, K. (eds.) (1994) *Visual Culture: Images and Interpretations*, Hanover:Wesleyan University Press.

Gombrich, E. (1960) *Art and Illusion: A Study in the Psychology of Pictorial Representation*, New York and London: Phaidon.

Harris, R. (1996) *Signs, Language and Communication*, London: Routledge.

Harris, R. (1998) Private correspondence with the author.

Magee, B. (1998) *Confessions of a Philosopher: A Journey through Western Philosophy*, London: Phoenix.

11 The Language Myth, Schopenhauer, and Music

George Wolf

I should like to begin by describing three aesthetic experiences, the first concerning painting, the second concerning music, and the third concerning literature.

The first takes place in a museum, where two persons, A and B, are looking at a modern painting which reveals only the merest adherence to representationalism. A, seeing nothing in it, says to B: 'Why should I like this?' B responds: 'Look at the relationships of color and shape.' Upon hearing this, A's view of the painting completely changes, enabling A actually to enjoy a whole range of modern paintings for the first time.

The second is as follows. C has heard a piece of music X a number of times, enjoying its light-hearted melodies and their modulations with slower, more serious sections, themselves characterized by strong melody. At some point C has a dream in which a barren, overcast landscape is visible, the view of which is strangely accompanied, almost as if it were a film soundtrack, by one of the sections from X. During this dream, C gets for the first time an acute sense of the extreme melancholy of the music.

In the third, D reads a foreign novel whose title contains a word which D imagines to mean 'slaughterhouse', whereas it actually means 'drinking establishment'. D enjoys the novel at some level, but cannot understand why during much of it the characters sit drinking in the front of a slaughterhouse.

I should like to offer these as typical aesthetic experiences. What I find interesting about the first is that in response to a few words a person's way of looking at a painting – indeed a whole style of painting – could be fundamentally changed in such a way that that person was newly enabled to enjoy certain works of art. What interests me about the second is the idea that a piece of music could be enjoyed on a level at which what at another time might be discovered to be a key aspect of the piece was missing. The third experience demonstrates this also, but has the additional interesting feature that a fundamental defect of the experience does not completely invalidate that experience – almost as if someone were to play a piece of music not realizing that they had misinterpreted one of the notes, but which wasn't such a horrible error as to sound absolutely like a mistake.

These, then, are possibly interesting features of these experiences. But we might go on from this point and look at the three experiences as examples of aesthetic experience in general, and ask what it is about them that makes them aesthetic. And here we may need help.

A particularly clear aid is provided by the philosophy of Schopenhauer, who devotes the whole of the last section (§ 52) of the third book of his magnum opus, *The World as Will and Representation*, to the nature of musical experience.

Schopenhauer relied heavily on Kant, so it might be worth considering a quote from the *Critique of Pure Reason* as a way of leading up to Schopenhauer's aesthetic. Here is what Kant says about transcendental idealism vs. empirical realism:

> The transcendental idealist is, therefore, an empirical realist, and allows to matter, as appearance, a reality which does not permit of being inferred, but is immediately perceived. Transcendental realism, on the other hand, inevitably falls into difficulties, and finds itself obliged to give way to empirical idealism, in that it regards the objects of outer sense as something distinct from the senses themselves, treating mere appearances as self-subsistent beings, existing outside us. On such a view as this, however clearly we may be conscious of our representation of these things, it is still far from certain that, if the representation exists, there exists also the object corresponding to it. In our system, on the other hand, these external things, namely matter, are in all their configurations and alterations nothing but mere appearances, that is, representations in us, of the reality of which we are immediately conscious. [A 371]

This quote strikes a familiar chord for us, I would suggest, for two reasons. One is that in the twentieth century we were inured by phenomenology to the idea of bracketing what we perceive, and leaving the question of its reality on one side while we try to work

The Language Myth, Schopenhauer, and Music

out just what in fact is actually appearing to us. The second reason is the extreme force, clarity and fame of Russell's and Moore's 'rebellion' against Kant and Hegel (Russell 1959: 42), which opened the field for the twentieth century's obsession with mathematical logic. In Russell's words,

> it was not only these rather dry, logical doctrines that made me rejoice in the new philosophy. I felt it, in fact, as a great liberation, as if I had escaped from a hot-house on to a wind-swept headland. I hated the stuffiness involved in supposing that space and time were only in my mind. I liked the starry heavens even better than the moral law, and could not bear Kant's view that the one I liked best was only a subjective figment. In the first exuberance of liberation, I became a naïve realist and rejoiced in the thought that grass is really green, in spite of the adverse opinion of all philosophers from Locke onwards. I have not been able to retain this pleasing faith in its pristine vigour, but I have never again shut myself up in a subjective prison. (ibid.: 48)

Nearer to us, Quine's dictum that physical objects are merely a convenient myth still echoes clearly. To use Kant's terminology, Quine is a transcendental realist because he 'regards the objects of outer sense as something distinct from the senses themselves'. Hence Quine's anxiety about establishing the status of external objects (Quine 1981: 2). In Quine's words, we 'assume' objects (ibid.), and this will include abstract objects like numbers. And hence, finally, the entire preoccupation with symbolic logic, whose ultimate function, in Quine's view, is to establish those objects over which we are prepared to quantify, or, in other words, to clarify our ontology. The reason it does this is because assuming objects is a mental act, and since 'mental acts are notoriously difficult to pin down' (ibid.), 'little can be done in the way of tracking thought processes except when we can put words to them' (ibid.) When we switch from concentrating on the thought processes and concentrate instead on words, 'then what had been a question of assuming objects becomes a question of verbal reference to objects. To ask what the assuming of an object consists in is to ask what referring to the object consists in' (ibid.) And we cannot clarify reference without regimentation, in other words constructing an absolutely clear language which shows what we are prepared to quantify over. In Quine's view, full reference comes once we have mastered the relative clause; and the regimented relative clause is none other than the quantified variable. Thus, the end point of the journey toward reference is an established language of quantification; that is, 'to assume objects of some sort is to reckon objects of that sort among the values of our variables' (ibid.: 8). Conversely, there is no reference, and hence no objects, without that regimentation, without that language of quantification.

The point about this is that Quine falls squarely into Kant's characterization of the transcendental realist. As Kant says, to repeat, 'On such a view as this, however clearly we may be conscious of our representation of these things, it is still far from certain that, if the representation exists, there exists also the object corresponding to it'. This is the source of Quine's, and the transcendental realist's, anxiety about ontology. That is to say, if we do regard the objects of outer sense as something distinct from the senses themselves, then because in sensing those objects we might in some cases be being deceived by our senses, we have to have some way of establishing ontology on a firm footing. Hence the concern, in the logical positivist's case, with verification, and in Quine's case, with regimentation.

In fact Quine goes so far as to say that deciding what there is – what there really is – is the business of serious people, the scientists and the philosophers. To quote Quine at length:

> My point is not that ordinary language is slipshod, slipshod though it be. We must recognize this grading off for what it is, and recognize that a fenced ontology is just not implicit in ordinary language. The idea of a boundary between being and non-being is a philosophical idea, an idea of technical science in a broad sense. Scientists and philosophers seek a comprehensive system of the world, and one that is oriented to reference even more squarely and utterly than ordinary language. Ontological concern is not a correction of a lay thought and practice; it is foreign to the lay culture, though an outgrowth of it. (ibid.: 9)

It is interesting to read this quote after reading Wittgenstein, because it makes us unsure whether there is serious business to be done but we lay people should leave it to the scientists and philosophers and go about our slipshod lives, or whether we should read the entire scientific and philosophical enterprise of verification and regimentation as designed to be an ivory tower language game which is merely something the slipshod are not invited to play.

The Language Myth, Schopenhauer, and Music

However this may be, the transcendental idealist does not fall into the empiricist's ontological problem because in the transcendental idealist view the objects of perception are not taken to have a reality separate from how they are perceived. Rather, they are accepted as appearance. And what things really are, what things are in themselves, is as may be but is ultimately unknowable, precisely because knowing involves conditions under which knowing is possible, and these conditions are part of our subjective situation, and do not affect things as they are in themselves. Thus, we can know what we perceive as it appears to us, but we cannot know it as it is in itself apart from all knowing.

Schopenhauer by and large accepted this position. Where he fundamentally differed from Kant was in rejecting Kant's doctrine that things in themselves are simply given to us. The thing in itself was for Schopenhauer will; but will is something that is already in us. Will exists outside the realm of phenomena, and thus is not subject to the conditions of space and time. At the same time, will is blind and is unconnected to consciousness. Consciousness for Schopenhauer was a kind of second-order outgrowth of will, a function of the brain. But the important thing was that consciousness is secondary, whereas will is primary, the ultimate reality behind appearance.

Our awareness of this blind will, our recognition that we are subject to it, is basically the source of Schopenhauer's pessimism. The world, nature, our bodies, things, are objectifications of the will, and exist in a hierarchy. Toward the high end of this hierarchy is consciousness, but even at the high, conceptual end consciousness is still tied to the will and its manifestations. And while awareness of our subjectivity to the will is accordingly a source of despair, Schopenhauer posits two domains which offer some hope of a positive outlook. One is ethics, based by Schopenhauer essentially on the idea of compassion. The other is aesthetics. Both avenues allow the possibility of escape from the subjection of the will, essentially via resignation to the will in an awareness that the will is not individual but is universal, and hence our own personal strivings and struggles come to be seen as it were as anguished revolts against the apparent despair of our being. When we come to see that our own personal will is an illusion we are then free to resign ourselves to the universal will, thus abandoning, and hence being freed from, our miserable existence.

The function of aesthetics in this picture is to achieve the greatest possible emancipation from the will by means of the purest possible contemplation and absorption into the object. This is achieved pre-eminently in the enjoyment of music, for the following reason. In Schopenhauer's view, music, existing as it does apart from any of the conceptual trappings which the other arts inevitably have to come to terms with since they have a partly mimetic basis, is the purest possible expression of the will itself. Thus, when we achieve in pure contemplation a complete absorption into the musical piece, thereby achieving an emancipation from the consciousness of our subjection to the will, what we are in fact contemplating, what we are becoming absorbed in, what we are losing ourselves in, is the will itself. Thus musical enjoyment is a paradigm of that resignation to the universal will which represents for Schopenhauer the primary hope of humanity.

There is something in this view of music which is reminiscent of Plato. However, while the influence of Plato on Schopenhauer has been pointed out, the philosophies of music of the two men are interestingly different. Plato's position is somewhat illuminated by the well-known discovery of Pythagoras concerning musical proportions. Pythagoras discovered that if you stretched a string taught between two fixed objects over a resounding surface, then depressed the string against the surface at its halfway point, the sound the string made was exactly an octave above the sound it made when plucked without being depressed. If you did the same at the two-thirds point, the sound was a fifth above the base note; and at the three-quarter point a fourth was produced. This appeared to lend support to Pythagoras' view that number was the ultimate reality in showing that number and musical proportion were intimately connected. And it encouraged the further view that musical harmony was written in nature as a fixed system. Plato took this further with the idea that certain musical forms embodied certain moral characteristics. For this reason he advocated music as one of the first two educational subjects in the republic, because it made possible the proper formation of the soul of the just man, the guardian of the state. In short, the character of the music organized the soul in a certain way.

This in at least one way is very different from Schopenhauer. First of all, Schopenhauer nowhere countenances the Platonic soul. Conversely, Schopenhauer's notion of will is absent from Plato. For Plato, different types of music embodied different characteristics. Moreover, a type of music could have an active effect on what was essentially a plastic and passive soul. There is nothing passive about the will in Schopenhauer. On the contrary, the will is a blind force which is presupposed by any kind of conscious activity, and could thus not be affected by anything else. Thus Schopenhauer has no interest in making distinctions between types of music, since what is important for him is that any music allows us to become lost – i.e. emancipated from our consciousness – in undistracted absorption in the will.

Yet there are important similarities between the two philosophers. They both agree that music has a fixed nature. It is clear that for Schopenhauer music was a form which had a definite inner meaning, and that inner meaning was the will itself. Music for Schopenhauer was a mirror of the will. Music in Plato also is a form with a definite meaning, but instead of the will it is as it were moral characteristics that are embodied by various types of music. For example, in the *Republic* Socrates asks Glaucon what the dirge-like modes of music are. When Glaucon replies that these are the mixed Lydian and the higher Lydian, Socrates says that these must then be rejected since, as he says, 'they are useless even to women who are to make the most of themselves, let alone to men' (III: 398e). He then observes that drunkenness, softness and sloth are unsuited to the guardians of the state, and asks what the soft and convivial modes are. Glaucon replies that these are the Ionian as well as again the Lydian, and Socrates in turn rejects these as useless for warriors. As for which are the desirable modes, Socrates goes right to the point. 'Leave us', he says, 'that mode that would fittingly imitate the utterances and the accents of a brave man who is engaged in warfare or in any enforced business, and who, when he has failed, either meeting wounds or death or having fallen into some other mishap, in all these conditions confronts fortune with steadfast endurance and repels her strokes. And another for such a man engaged in works of peace, not enforced but voluntary, either trying to persuade somebody of something and imploring him – whether it be a god, through prayer, or a man, by teaching and admonition – or contrariwise yielding himself to another who is petitioning or teaching him or trying to change his opinions, and in consequence faring according to his wish, and not bearing himself arrogantly, but in all this acting modestly and moderately and acquiescing in the outcome. Leave us these two modes – the enforced and the voluntary – that will best imitate the utterances of men failing or succeeding, the temperate, the brave – leave us these' (ibid.: 399a-c).

The modes, then, in Plato are musical forms that have fixed characteristics, just as the numerical proportions of harmonies are shown by Pythagoras to be written in nature. And since we are concerned here with language, it will be seen that there is an evident analogy in Plato between musical modes and names. For it is the position of Cratylus that names, if they are to be considered as real names, must possess the characteristics of what they are names of. And just as names are naturally connected to what they are names of, so the musical modes are naturally connected to moral qualities.

It is not certain whether this analogy is reinforced or breaks down when pressed further into the domain of functions. That is, should we take music and names to function similarly? It is Plato's apparent view that music was capable of shaping the soul in some way. Indeed, it is interesting to see that in some passages Schopenhauer actually seems to have taken his theory of music from Plato, as in the following passage:

> The effect of music on the mind, so penetrating, so immediate, so unfailing, and also the after-effect that sometimes follows it, consisting in a specially sublime frame of mind, are explained by the passive nature of hearing ... The vibrations of the tones following in combined, rational, numerical relations, set the brain-fibres themselves vibrating in a similar way. (1818, II: 31)

Here we have virtually unchanged Plato's view that the inner, we might say numerical, character of a piece of music enters into a mimetic relationship with the soul of the hearer which is shaped in conformity to it. But even apart from this, music would appear to have at least one dedicated function, that of entertainment, or causing pleasure upon hearing it. Bearing this in mind, we might say that in Plato music is seen as capable of putting people into the mood which a mode embodies. Thus a mixed Lydian mode will put us in a mournful mood, an Ionian mode will put us in a slothful or convivial mood, and a Dorian or Phrygian mode will put us in a brave or a temperate mood, these latter being appropriate moods for a guardian of the state. Names would not appear to have such prima facie dedicated functions.

Nonetheless, names do in a sense produce the realities of which they are names upon being uttered, and it is certainly the case that the soul is formed by speech. What names and music crucially have in common here is just this aspect: that as there is a mimetic

The Language Myth, Schopenhauer, and Music

connection between the name or the mode and the reality it embodies, so there is a potential mimetic connection between that form/meaning complex and the soul itself, which is shaped in conformity with that complex.

It may be worth dwelling for a moment on the word *name*, *onoma* in Greek. As Pfeiffer points out in his *History of Classical Scholarship* (1968: 59ff.), the division between *onoma* 'name' and *rhema* 'what is said' is first found in Plato's *Cratylus*, the Sophist Protagoras having prior to this referred to all words with the single expression *onoma*. Pfeiffer goes on to say that Plato introduced this distinction in the context of his discussion of the value of words for the knowledge of things. And indeed, in the *Cratylus* Socrates outlines just how language succeeds in giving us things. First, the vowels and consonants are sorted out according to their phonetic characteristics. This is preliminary to step one of naming, at which 'we must know how to apply each letter with reference to its fitness' (424d). And when we have applied letters to things, 'using one letter for one thing, when that seems to be required, or many letters together, forming syllables' (424e), we then combine syllables, thereby forming nouns and verbs, *onomata* and *rhemata*. Finally, as Socrates says, 'from nouns and verbs again we shall finally construct something great and fair and complete. Just as in our comparison we made the picture by the art of painting, so now we shall make language by the art of naming, or of rhetoric, or whatever it be' (425a).

Plato is even more specific in the *Sophist*, where the Stranger, considering the question whether falsity exists in speech and thought, asks how words fit together. He floats the following idea: 'Words which, when spoken in succession, signify something, do fit together, while those which mean nothing when they are strung together, do not' (261d–e). He then suggests that the signs we use in speech are of two kinds, *onomata* and *rhemata*. These are defined as follows. A verb, a *rhema*, is an expression which is applied to actions, while a name, an *onoma*, is applied to what performs those actions (262a). We then get to the crux of the matter, which is that 'a statement never consists solely of names spoken in succession, nor yet of verbs apart from names'. The Stranger says: 'if you say 'lion stag horse' and any other names given to things that perform actions, such a string never makes up a statement. Neither in this example nor in the other do the sounds uttered signify any action performed or not performed or [the] nature of anything that exists or does not exist, until you combine verbs with names. The moment you do that,

209

George Wolf

they fit together and the simplest combination becomes a statement of what might be called the simplest and briefest kind' (262b–c).

The point about all of this is that as early as Plato we have an established formal paradigm for how language links to, or rather delivers, reality, and this paradigm is dualistic in nature, consisting of one part which attaches to the thing, via mimesis, and another part through which we get knowledge of the thing. This paradigm casts a long shadow over Western thinking. But in fact the shadow already appears to have been cast by the time the noun/verb distinction emerges. The form of the shadow is really dualism itself, a dualism embodied early in Greek philosophy, where behind phenomena was posited the real, underlying, separate reality of things. This larger paradigmatic picture is reflected in Plato's doctrine of the name which gives the thing vs. the verb which, when coupled with the name, yields a completely different kind of entity, be it fitness, truth, or knowledge; and in Plato's doctrine of music which yields, when an audible musical form is produced, that wholly different kind of entity which is the moral characteristic, i.e. something in the ideal realm for the musical form in this realm to signify or deliver.

Standing in the same shadow is the Kantian doctrine of the phenomenal vs. the transcendental, taken over wholesale by Schopenhauer, and the dualism of the knowing subject and the phenomenal or transcendental object. In Schopenhauer's theory of music, the will is transcendent, blind and unknowable in itself, presupposed in all phenomenal life. Over against this is the conscious subject, a phenomenal objectification of the will, yet a conscious being striving to be freed from subjection to the will. In one sense this is an ambiguous doctrine, because the will is in effect both ultimate object and ultimate subject. It is ultimate object in being the thing-in-itself that the conscious subject is aware of without being able to know. Yet it is ultimate subject in being the absolute ground of our existence as persons, and moreover what the conscious subject merges with in the musical experience, thus dissolving the dualism of a miserable existence in the resignation to the universal will, a kind of simulacrum of death.

A consequence of these ancient and modern doctrines is that for persons living in the world, the reality of forms which they use, be they linguistic or musical, is something apart. Now it is true that the guardian of the state will be expected to shape his own real soul in imitation of the appropriate musical mode. But the point is that the moral characteristic embodied by that mode is in the first instance

The Language Myth, Schopenhauer, and Music

something separate, something 'out there', and 'not here'. The same goes for the Kantian perspective, and in a double sense. First of all, the phenomenon plays the role of object, which is thus separate from the subject. But in addition to this, there is the thing-in-itself, which is even more 'out there' in being essentially unknowable. That is, we know it is there, but we can't know it.

The result of this is that the engagement with both music and language is conceived of on what could be called an 'epistemological/ontological' model. That is, with both music and language it is a question of, on the one hand, 'what there is', which must be reached or got through to, and on the other our relationship to whatever it is, which is one of knowing, understanding, or awareness. In short, what is real is 'there', and we are 'here', having to bridge the gap between us and it by the appropriate mental posture. Even our own reality is conceived of in this way, being dealt with by such notions as 'the transcendental subject', or 'the will'. In other words, something which is implied by our existence, but from which we are essentially separate.

As in Plato's case, Schopenhauer's theory of language goes along with his theory of music. In this theory we begin with the fact that when we perceive we have representations. On the basis of these representations of perception we abstract from them, thereby deriving concepts. Now when concepts have been abstracted from perceptual representations, they cease to be perceptible. Concepts are something the mind manipulates for the purpose of thought operations. However, because concepts are not perceptible, it would not be possible for the mind to do this except for the fact that they have been 'fixed and retained' in our senses by signs, these signs being words. Thus words express 'universal representations ... never the things of intuitive perception' (1813: 148).

We can expand on this a bit. Consciousness has time as its form. Concepts, on the other hand, being abstracted from what we have been conscious of, that is, being universal representations of the objects of our consciousness, have an objective existence, but are nevertheless not in time, and thus are not perceptible. They must, then, be brought into what Schopenhauer calls the 'time-series', and linked to a representation of the senses. This is what the word does. The word, accordingly, says Schopenhauer, 'is the sensible sign of the concept, and as such is the necessary means of fixing it, in other words, of presenting it vividly to the consciousness that is tied to the form of time, and thus of establishing a connexion between our faculty of reason, whose objects are merely general universalia knowing neither place nor time, and consciousness which is tied to time, sensuous, and to this extent merely animal' (1813: 66).

We have to follow one more strand here. Schopenhauer praises Burke's *Inquiry into the Sublime and Beautiful* for Burke's statement that the words of speech are 'perfectly understood without giving rise to representations of perception, to pictures in our head' (ibid.: 67). However, Burke draws a false conclusion, in Schopenhauer's view, in saying that 'we hear, apprehend, and use words without associating any representation with them' (ibid.). We do associate representations with words, counters Schopenhauer, it is just that not all representations are images of perception. Some representations are concepts, and indeed the ones that are concepts are precisely those that need to be expressed by words. Now comes the interesting part. Because words communicate concepts, which are different from representations of perception, all hearers of a narrated event, for example, will therefore receive the same concepts. However, Schopenhauer says that 'if subsequently they wish to make the event clear to themselves, each will sketch in his imagination a different picture or image of it, and this differs considerably from the correct picture that only the eyewitness has' (ibid.) Now, if one of the hearers then narrates the event to someone else, he does so on the basis, not of the concepts he received from the original narrator, but of the concepts which he has abstracted from the picture in his imagination which was a kind of unpacking of those original concepts. Schopenhauer concludes that the narrator 'who is matter-of-fact enough to stick to the concepts imparted to him, and to pass these on to the next person, will be the most trustworthy reporter' (ibid.)

It would be difficult to come up with a clearer version of the view that one's language is a fixed code. Returning to music, the reason this art was special for Schopenhauer was that the other arts were tied to a greater or less degree to conceptual matter, and thus provided distraction from the central function of art, which is to liberate the consciousness from subjection to the will. Music achieves this liberation to the greatest degree precisely because it does not have a conceptual component, but is a direct mirror of the will itself. Interestingly, this, rather than setting music apart from the code-bound nature of conceptual communication, in fact constrains it even more closely by making the experience of music a direct code for the will. In other words, there might be a hope of coming up with our own pictures on the basis of the concepts we have received from literature or painting, thus 'misinterpreting', but at least breaking away from the what the code decrees. With music, though, this is not possible if musical communication is efficacious: it can only deliver one thing, from which there is no escape.

Stepping back now from this mini-exposition of Schopenhauer's philosophy, we might consider such a conception as comfortably situated in the nineteenth century, a point from which we have now definitively moved on. Yet we in fact find it alive and well in perhaps the most important recent statement on the subject, Roger Scruton's book, *The Aesthetics of Music*, in which Scruton says the following: 'A philosophy of music offers neither psychological explanations nor critical recommendations. It attempts to say what music is, prior to any explanation or amplification of our musical experience' (1997: 35). And later on we get a kind of epitome of Scruton's aesthetics in a passage where he says:

> The aesthetic experience is a lived encounter between object and subject, in which the subject takes on a universal significance. The meaning that I find in the object is the meaning that it has for all who live like me, for all members of my 'imagined community', who share our 'first-person plural' and whose joys and sufferings are mirrored in me. As Kant puts it, aesthetic judgement makes appeal to a 'common sense': it frees me from the slavish attachment to my own desires. I come to see myself as one member of an implied community, whose life is present and vindicated in the experience of contemplation. (1997: 460)

These quotes from Scruton will allow us to draw together some of the diverse threads of the preceding discussion. The point they have been leading up to is this. At the core of the Western epistemological paradigm is a dualistic view of the global reality in which we find ourselves as living persons. That is, there are the phenomena we see, feel, smell, hear and taste, and there is what these objects really are, what they are really made of. And this latter is not itself phenomenal, but is transcendent. At some point this core view emerges in the doctrine of the *onoma* and the *rhema*, and ultimately in the dual notion of the subject and the object. The *onoma/rhema* distinction is in one sense sharper, because what names attach to is clearly one kind of thing, while what we say about them is clearly another kind of thing; whereas when we arrive at the subject and the object – especially in their Enlightenment and post-Englightenment manifestations – it is clear that we have a dichotomy, but not always clear just what attaches to which half of the dichotomy. Hence Schopenhauer's ambiguous 'will', which in one sense is a super-subject and in another a super-object. But the same goes for Kant's 'transcendental "I"'.

What is crucial about this paradigm as regards the philosophy of music is that the *onoma/rhema*, subject/object model encourages the requirement that things like music be defined in terms of it. In other words, if there is something called music, then it must be something, and what it is has then to be susceptible to the style of explanation of everything else. The result is that music, like so much else, has been and continues to be conceived of in what I referred to as an 'epistemological/ontological' way. In brief, it is a 'something' that we 'know', or 'feel', or 'understand', or whatever other subjective act you wish to choose.

However, it turns out that the very adoption of the epistemological/ontological model creates insuperable epistemological/ontological problems, to wit, (1) who am I? and (2) what is this object? The model requires the object to be intersubjectively shareable, and so any solution to the problems, and indeed any representation of the model, will have to come up with an object that is just that. The object must be made intersubjectively shareable by fiat. Thus, for Plato the unitary forms simply must be there, for Aristotle the world and its effects on us simply must be the same for everyone, for Schopenhauer the will must be the same for all, and we subjective persons must be all equally miserable in our existence. And, accordingly, music must be a mirror of the will. Similarly for Scruton, in the experience of music the subject cannot just be me listening to this piece and feeling this feeling. Rather, I as subject have to take on universal significance, and 'the meaning that I find in the object is the meaning that it has for all who live like me'.

The trouble with this solution to the problems created by adopting the epistemological/ontological posture is that, while it attempts to account for our experience, it fails to do justice to what our experience is, or rather to what our experiences are. It is convenient for Socrates simply to assume that given musical modes will produce given moral effects, or for Schopenhauer to posit that musical movement as we experience it mirrors the movement of the universal will, or for Scruton to suggest that atonal music has anxiety as an inherent characteristic (1997: 306). But, to return to the examples offered at the beginning of this paper as typical of aesthetic experience, none of these philosophical positions can change the fact that for different people, music, art and literature are different at different times.

I should like to propose as axiomatic to musical experience a principal akin to what T. S. Eliot said in reference to Dante, which is that 'genuine poetry can communicate before it is understood' (1950: 200). If we do take the examples I cited at the beginning as typical, then one thing they show is that there is more than one way to enjoy a work of art. That is to say, I can enjoy it even if there is something about it which I later see I was unaware of or about which I was completely mistaken. I might enjoy a piece of music in mixed Lydian mode and not feel mournful. But the point is that this would not invalidate the experience I did have.

One way toward characterizing the way we really experience music would be to recall Schopenhauer's code-view of language. According to Schopenhauer, words attach to concepts, not to perceptual representations, and language operates by transmitting concepts. Schopenhauer asks: 'While another person is speaking, do we at once translate his speech into pictures of the imagination that instantaneously flash upon us and are arranged, linked, formed, and coloured according to the words that stream forth, and to their grammatical inflexions?' (1818, I: 39). His answer is no; what happens instead is that what someone says to us is immediately apprehended, unclouded by perceptions. The reason for this is that what are being communicated are 'abstract concepts, non-perceptive representations, formed once for all and relatively few in number, but nevertheless embracing, containing, and representing all the innumerable objects of the actual world' (ibid.)

Now unlike words, music is in Schopenhauer's view non-conceptual. So that when it comes time to account for how music communicates, the word-model is not available. However, with this model removed Schopenhauer cannot simply say that music communicates by evoking perceptual representations. He cannot say this because he is committed to a code view come what may by virtue of adhering to the larger epistemological/ontological model. In other words, if we are hearing subjects, then there has to be an object which we are hearing, and moreover there has to be something which makes us identical as hearing subjects.

Be this as it may, however, it is still simply a fact that different people experience music in different ways at different times. But if we accept this, then in Schopenhauerian terms music is indeed communicated to us by virtue of our perceptual representations. The only remaining problem is that we are still haunted by the question of what it is that we are perceptually representing to ourselves, and/or what it is that is causing these perceptual representations. In other words, in clinging to a scrap torn from the epistemological/ontological model – that scrap being the notion of perceptual representation, which is one mechanical part of the whole apparatus – we are still burdened with an epistemological/ontological problem. But it is a problem which is not part of our experience.

To return, then, to Eliot's dictum about poetry, how can we make sense of it with reference to music? We use the word 'understand' less in the sphere of music appreciation than we do in that of literary appreciation, so we are tempted to say: 'Great music communicates before – what?' We need to imagine the case in which we hear for the first time a piece of music which later will come to appeal to us. But here our axiom seems to break down completely. The fact is that we often hear pieces of music which we only come to like subsequently after several hearings. So in this sense it may be that the music communicates nothing until such time as we come to like it. On the other hand, something being communicated may be the only basis we have for ever hearing the piece again. In other words, unless something has come through we may never make the effort to listen to it again.

In any event, let us now imagine that the moment has come when we are listening to a piece of music which we like. What is the experience? Part of the experience is listening: we want to pay attention to what we are hearing. If I hear a piece of music which bores me, I am likely to start paying attention to something else. Listening can bring with it an absence of other activity; so we might profitably call listening itself a kind of activity – indeed just the kind of activity requisite for enjoyment. (On the other hand, we should bear in mind here that I am perfectly capable of listening while I drive.) Now while I am listening I may notice that a passage in the piece I am listening to is a deliberate quotation of a passage from another piece of music. Or I may notice that a certain passage is a return of a melody from an early part, but that in this passage the notes and the tempo have been altered. Or I may notice a number of other things. My experience of another piece of music may not be like this, but may instead consist in a certain sense of exhilaration at a certain moment, when I may even get shivers up my spine (this being a real sensation). Or it may be a brief, sharp sense of atmosphere, mood,

The Language Myth, Schopenhauer, and Music

or even place and time. At another time, I may experience a desire to hear a specific piece of music, or I may over a number of days notice myself being preoccupied with a certain piece or passage which I am just too lazy to put on; but when I do finally put it on, and then afterwards go about my business, the preoccupation has vanished. In another case I may find myself singing a part from one piece. In another, at a certain part of the piece I may not be able to resist getting up and making conducting gestures to an empty room. Or I may dance. I may also sit down at the piano and try some chords with a certain idea in mind, discovering that a definite progression develops which I like. Or I may sit down and play a piece I know well. Or I may while I am doing something else simply vaguely imagine the piece being played while hearing nothing at all.

This attempt to characterize some typical musical experiences brings back two points. The first, to repeat, is that, having come face to face with the problems of the epistemological/ontological model, we ought to entertain as genuine the option of jettisoning that model as a paradigm of explanation. The second point is that all of the offered examples of musical experience, and doubtless many more, are legitimate examples of that experience, but also differ quite markedly one from another.

As for the first point, it connects to a larger theme, which is whether we should accept Schopenhauer's and Scruton's view that listening to music involves being freed from 'the slavish attachment to my own desires', that is, being abstracted in general from the process of our daily lives while we inhabit the safe sanctuary of contemplation which is aesthetic experience. Prima facie there is already a flaw in this view, which is the idea that the context of my enjoying or in some way experiencing music does not form part of the fabric of my daily existence. If I put on a piece of music when I go home after work, this is not escaping from my life, but actually living it: it is part of how I live, not separate from how I live. I may like work but it tires me; or I may hate work but I need the money. In either case, I have every intention of keeping the work going, and perhaps part of how I do that is to mix it with listening to music. I actively pursue both things. Indeed, I may listen to music while I work.

One objection to this might be that the actual listening is a way of escaping the kinds of things I feel when working, or whatever else it is I do in my alleged real life. Now if, in order to listen, what I need is the absence of distraction which will enable me to tune in to the wavelength of the universal soul, then perhaps what we are doing is escaping the storm and stress of daily existence. But if we reject this picture – and I am basing my argument here on the notion that it does not in fact conform to our experience – then we realize that the frames of mind, or however we characterize our experience of music, which we get into when having a positive musical experience, are of no value or interest unless we conceive them as having a place in the realest world we can imagine. In other words, when we have an experience of music, the purport of that experience is that this is the way the world either is or can in fact be; such an experience is a way of actually being in the world here and now, not of escaping from misery and going to heaven.

To recapitulate briefly, then. First, the problems of the epistemo-logical/ontological model ought to function as an invitation to us to abandon that model; and indeed abandoning it is easier once we see that the model is written not in nature but merely in Plato and Aristotle. Secondly, even a cursory examination of our musical experiences is sufficient to show that the 'contemplation model' is much too limited to do justice to the ways in which we enjoy music. Moreover, when we see that the contemplation model is essentially parasitic on the epistemological/ontological view, it makes it easier to abandon that model as simply no longer good enough. But if we do, that is if we let go of our attachment to the idea that musical experience is basically a matter of contemplation, i.e. that it is basi-cally a way of communicating with the transcendental realm, then we may find ourselves asking, 'Well, what is musical experience in fact?'; and this may lead us to ask, 'Just what is going on when this thing called 'music' is happening?'. And when this happens, we see that we are looking for a different kind of answer to the question 'What is music?'

The kind of answer we are now looking for involves questions like 'What is actually happening here?' Questions like this invite answers like these:

The composer Arnold Schoenberg over a period of time thought up and wrote down notes which he planned as and called his Chamber Symphony. In 1906 he sent his manuscript to the pub-lisher, who then committed it to type, which resulted in a number of identical copies of the work. These began to be bought and distrib-uted, during and after which time musicians gathered, each with a copy of the score, and were directed by a conductor as, owing to their training, they played their instruments according to what they saw on the page. On one occasion, musicians played this piece in a

The Language Myth, Schopenhauer, and Music

building built for the purpose of comfortably housing such a group along with another group who were meant to sit and listen to what the musicians were playing. This event, which involved coordinating the movement and non-movement of these individuals, was followed by some of those who were expected to sit quietly and listen taking out their house keys and blowing through them in such a way that a shrill whistle was produced. Others made loud clapping sounds; others engaged in fist fights; and still others were seen to climb over several rows of seats in order to box the ears of an offending party sitting in front of them. This event involving musicians and audience was repeated a number of times in different places, with varying results. Upon the development of sound-recording technology, on one or two occasions musicians and a conductor performed the piece while recording equipment was capturing the sound. After this, the recording was transferred to records which could be played on a record player, enabling a listener to hear the piece which had been recorded. A number of people purchased these records, put them on their record players, and listened to the piece in a room of their house. Some enjoyed the music, some found it interesting, some noticed technical musical features of the piece, then noticed even further features upon subsequent listenings, some hated it and never listened to it again, some hated it but had to listen to it many times never wavering in their hatred, and some hated it, had to listen to it many times and came to like it.

This description could go on to at least book-, if not encyclopedic, length. In fact it might never stop. However, it doesn't need to stop for it to be evident that music is all or perhaps none of the things in such a description. The bottom line is that a description like this does not need to 'capture' music, because the need to 'capture' music in a description or definition is nothing but a symptom of the epistemological/ontological posture, which we have rejected. In other words, we reject Scruton's pronouncement, already cited, to wit: 'A philosophy of music offers neither psychological explanations nor critical recommendations. It attempts to say what music is, prior to any explanation or amplification of our musical experience' (1997: 35).

Instead, I would propose the following two counter-positions. First, if we reject the epistemological/ontological model, then there isn't anything that music in fact is. Second, as far as we real people in the real world are concerned, we already know what music is, and don't have a problem identifying it: it doesn't need to be defined.

219

But what, then, can we contribute as analysts of the situation? The answer has already been given, and is that the project being entertained here is to shift attention from the transcendental to the actual; and in the actual we see what a transcendental approach precludes, which is that the reality of music, like all of reality, involves more than one thing happening at once. This is the essential feature of what we are after. When a bow is drawn across a string, this is not an isolated event, but is a coordinated – what has been called an 'integrated' – event. Any music worthy of the name brings a lot of factors together. But whether a given event, or thought, or object, is music is for anyone to say.

References

Eliot, T. S. (1950) *Selected Essays*, New York: Harcourt, Brace & World.
Hamilton, E. & H. Cairns (1961) *The Collected Dialogues of Plato*, Princeton: Princeton University Press, .
Kant, I. (1781) *Critique of Pure Reason*, transl. N. K. Smith, London: Macmillan, 1929.
Pfeiffer, R. (1968) *History of Classical Scholarship from the Beginning to the End of the Hellenistic Age*, Oxford: Clarendon Press.
Quine, W. V. (1981) *Theories and Things*, Cambridge, Mass.: Harvard University Press.
Russell, B. (1959) *My Philosophical Development*, London: George Allen & Unwin.
Schopenhauer, A. (1813) *On the Fourfold Root of the Principle of Sufficient Reason*, transl. E. F. J. Payne, La Salle, Ill.: Open Court, 1974.
— (1818) *The World as Will and Representation*, transl. E. F. J. Payne, 2 vols., Indian Hills, Colo.: The Falcon's Wing Press, 1958.
Scruton, R. (1997) *The Aesthetics of Music*, Oxford: Clarendon Press.

Index

Abry, C. 87, 98
aesthetic, -s 22, 145, 185, 187, 190,
    198, 201–2, 205, 213, 215,
    217
anti-realism 109–116
Arbib, M.A. 60, 82
arbitrariness 85, 92, 148–9, 155
Aristotle 11–14, 16, 18, 44, 55–6,
    67, 80, 142, 187, 214,
    218
art, -s 20, 22, 183–220
    function of 212
    non-verbal 22
    of music 201–20
    visual 183–200
Aslin, R.N. 88, 99
Atiyah, P.S. 180, 182
attitude 1, 50, 67, 77, 183
    propositional attitude 104–5,
    107
Austin, J.L. 58, 81

Bacon, F. 13
Bal, M. 192
Barker, S.F. 144, 157
Baugh, J, 134, 137
Beckman, M. 91, 99
Beethoven, L. van 22
behaviourism 100–1
Bellini G. 194–7
Bindman, G. 175
biology, -ical 20, 22–3, 60–3
biomechanical 8
Blackburn, Lord 163
Bloomfield, L. 26, 39, 57
Boime, A. 190–2, 200
Brouwer, L.E.J. 144
Brown, G. 76, 81
Browne-Wilkinson, Lord 172
Bryson, N. 192–3, 200
Burke, E. 212
Burke, K. 77, 81
Burton-Roberts, N. 86, 95–8
Bynon, T. 28, 39

Cabbala 148–9
Caillebotte, G. 190–1
Cameron, D. 49–50, 52–3
Carr, P. 3, 96–8
Carter, R. 42, 53
Chomsky, A.N. 84, 93, 95–8
Churchland, P. 100, 104–5, 116
code 6, 18, 20, 22–3, 34, 36, 44–6,
    55–7, 65, 85, 93, 98, 113,
    149, 213, 215
    codification 20, 34–5, 70
    decoding 2, 22, 92, 148, 199
    encoding 2, 22, 84, 91–3, 97–8
    fixed code 6, 22, 32, 44–5, 55–7,
        65, 70–1, 78, 84, 91, 112–3,
        162–7, 169–70, 177, 181,
        183, 187, 192, 212
    genetic 22–3
Coleman, J. 91–2, 98
Commission for Racial Equality
    173–5
common sense 3, 44–5, 100–2, 106,
    167, 213
communication 2 *et passim*
    acts of 32, 67
    channels of 13
    communicative competence 57–8
    communicative relevance 69
    episode of 46
    experience of 46
    means of 62
    mind-to-mind *see* pattern-
        transference
    miscommunication 76
    musical 213, 215
    myth of 6–7, 15, 17, 21–3, 57–8,
        140, 156
    non-verbal 62
    pictorial 186, 191–2
    public 43
    purpose of 61–2, 64–5, 191
    training in 49–50
    visual 186
    with the transcendental 218

Index

community 1, 15, 21, 26, 136, 140
comparative reconstruction 25, 28
complementary sequel 72–3
complex vs. simple 56–8, 61–2, 68, 70, 76
  complex adaptive systems 62, 65, 80
computer 11, 112
context 33, 42, 44, 47, 50, 71, 156, 184
  context-free, context-neutral 2, 35, 165, 180
contractualism 21, 143, 153, 157
convention 22–3, 43, 58, 66, 71, 77, 80, 84, 93, 96–8
corpus 63, 65–6
  corpus linguistics 65
creativity 35, 81
Crowley, T. 52–3
cultural fossil 1, 3, 13

Damasio, A.R. 61, 81
Daneš, F. 56, 81
Dante 215
Dantzig, T. 146–7, 157
Darwinism, 135
Dascal, M. 56, 81
Dauncey, P. 144
Davis, D.R. 4
Davis, H.G. 21, 80–1
Dawkins, R. 22, 24
definitions 1, 47, 173–6, 219
Dennett, D. 109–12, 114, 116
Denning, Lord 161, 167, 170–2, 174–5
Descartes, R. 11
determinacy 52–3, 55–6, 64–5, 132
  fallacy of 56, 132
  of linguistic sign 52–3
Devlin, K. 141, 157
diachronic linguistics 28, 30–2
dialect 4, 42–3, 123, 135
dialectology 123
dialogue 56
  dialogic action game 58–81
  dialogic interaction 60

dictionary 4, 39, 47, 49, 170, 175–6
  visual 189
DNA 22–3
Docherty, G. 91–2, 97–8
Durkheim, E. 21

education 20–21, 41–53, 132, 206
Eichenstein, Z.H. 148–9, 157
Eimas, P.D. 86, 98
Einstein, A. 150
eliminativism 100–16
Eliot, T.S. 215–6
Ellis, A. 44
emotion 22, 77
empiricism 150, 153, 202, 205
epistemology, -ical 17, 29, 211, 214–9
ethics 205
ethnicity 126–31, 135, 173–9
ethnisme 126–31, 135
etymology 4, 32
evolution 60–1, 143
  of communication 60–1
  of *homo sapiens* 143
  of language 60–1
  of the universe 61

facts, types of 94–5
Falk, J. 43, 53
Fishman, J. 123
Fodor, J. 107–9, 113, 116
folk psychology 21, 100–16
form
  change of 32
  invariance of 7, 47
  knowledge of 7
  linguistic *passim*
  musical 206–8, 210
  phonological 86, 91
  stigmatized 48
  variation of 42
formulaic expressions 50
Foulkes, P. 91–2, 98
Fraser, Lord 174, 179
Frege, G. 144, 154
Freud, S. 191
Friederici, A.D. 87, 99
Fromkin, V. 42–3, 53

Index

games 20, 23, 153
dialogic action game 58–81
language game 46–7, 155–6, 177, 204
Gandhi, M.K. 1
Gell-Mann, M. 55, 57, 61–2, 66, 82
gematria 147–9
gene 22–3
generativism, -ist 28–9, 56, 84, 91, 97
Géricault, T. 192–3
gesture 60, 69, 185
Gombrich, E. 187, 200
grammar 4, 6, 43, 45, 48, 51, 93, 95–8, 154
as a collection of rules 45
universal 93, 95–8
Greenberg, J. 29
Günther, H.F.K. 132, 137

Hahn, H. 150, 157
Hale, M. 97–9
Halsbury, Lord 169
Harris, J. 95, 99
Harris, R. 3, 21, 24, 44–5, 55, 58, 60, 68, 71–2, 74, 76, 78–9, 81, 84, 91–3, 99, 101, 113–4, 131–2, 139–40, 142–6, 159–61, 166, 181, 183, 184–9, 191–2, 194, 197–200
Hart, H.L. 159, 182
Hartley, L. 43, 54
Haugen, E. 123
Hawking, S. 66, 81
Hegel, G.W.F. 203
Hintzman, D.J. 91, 99
Hirst, D. 189
Hirt, H. 127
historical linguistics 25–40
Hogben, L. 147, 157
Honey, J. 41–3, 48–9, 51–2, 54
human science 55, 81
Humboldt, W. von 128, 135
Hutton, C. 21, 134, 137, 159

Iamblichus 144–5
idealism 202, 205

idealization 42, 50, 96, 118
ideas 16–18, 20, 185
as language-dependent 18
as transferable patterns 16–17
pre-linguistic 18, 185
'simple ideas' 16
Ifrah, G. 146–7, 157
illocution 67, 72
image acoustique 18, 86
indeterminacy 35, 55–6, 64–6, 76, 78, 80–1, 165
principle of 66
individuality 50–1, 58, 65, 140
instrumentalism 109–12, 114, 144, 156–7
integrational, -ism, -ist 1, 3, 22, 47–8, 53, 63, 70, 76, 81, 84–6, 89–91, 100–1, 115–6, 144, 156–7, 162, 181, 183–4, 186, 188–9, 192, 197–8, 200
intentions 3, 21, 162, 165, 167–70, 192–3
intentional realism 107–9
intentional stance 110–2
intentional state 104, 106
interaction 12, 35, 46, 50, 60–1, 67, 77
intuitionism 152
invariance 2, 6–7, 32, 35, 47, 97, 165, 180

Jackendoff, R. 45, 54
Jackson, P. 121, 137
James, W. 102, 117
Jenson, A. 134
Johnson, S. 49
Johnstone, B. 50–2, 54
Jusczyk, P.W. 87–8, 99

Kandinsky, W. 189
Kant, I. 202–5, 210–1, 213
Keller, R. 26, 40
Kingman Report 51
Kloss, H. 123
knowledge 6–7, 13–14, 17, 20, 38, 97, 205, 209–11
of forms 7, 38
of meanings 7

223

Index

knowledge *Cont'd*
  of the external/natural world 6,
    13–4, 17
  phonological 97

Labov, W. 27, 40
Lakoff, G. 56, 82
language, -s 1 *et passim*
  ordinary 204
  standard 21, 41–53, 123
  vernacular 136–7
language community 2, 21
language myth 1 *et passim*
  as linguistic theory 31
  characteristics of 2
langue 57, 160
Lass, R. 25, 33, 40
law and language 74, 159–81
law of nature, 19–20, 141, 150
Lawrence D.H. 169
lay orientation 48, 204
legislation 19–21, 41, 133,
    159–181
Lehmann, W.P. 27, 40
Lévi-Strauss, C. 5, 15, 24
Levin, M. 120, 137
Lewontin, R.C. 120, 137
Liberman, I.Y. 89, 99
Lightfoot, D. 29
likeness 8, 11–12
Lindsay, G. 95, 99
linearity 7
linguistic change 4, 25–39
linguistic community 26, 136
linguistic historiography 25
linguistic typology 29
linguistic universals 29
linguistic variation 42–3, 50, 52,
    96–8
linguistics, 3 *et passim*
  'doing' linguistics 91
  theory of 3, 6, 31
  twentieth-century 47, 142
literacy 43–4, 84, 86–7
  alphabetic 84
literature 22, 201, 213, 215–6
Locke, J. 12–13, 16–18, 24, 44, 203
Love, N. 4, 90–1, 162, 165, 169,
    171, 174–5, 177

McMahon, A.M.S. 27–9, 31, 40
Magee, B. 19, 24, 197, 200
Martinet, A. 55, 82
mathematics 139–57
meaning 7 *et passim*
  change of 32
  indeterminacy of 64–5, 76, 78,
    80
  interactive 78
  invariance of 7, 47
  knowledge of 7
  lexical 88
  literal 172
  meaning position 68
  modes of 157
  musical 207
  pictorial 192
  picture theory of 150–1
  social 63
  types of 63, 68
memory 84, 91–2
mental ability 60
mental act 203
mental pattern 16, 45
mental state 68, 70
messages 6–8, 13, 18–19, 22–3, 60
  from God 23
  from Nature 13, 17–18
  transmission of 6–7
metalanguage 33–4, 46, 115, 153,
    156, 160
methodology 55–6, 58, 63, 65–6,
    70, 80, 136
Michelangelo 191
Milroy, J. 26–7, 29, 40, 50
mimesis 8, 22, 187–8, 206, 208–10
mind 15, 20–1, 24, 32, 45–6
  common 21
  mind-to-mind communication
    see pattern-transference
mirror neurons 60–1, 69
misunderstanding 58, 75–6, 80
models
  epistemological/ontological 211,
    214–9
  hydraulic 11
  interactional 12
  logical 5
  myths as 15

224

Index

models *Cont'd*
  of academic disciplines 62
  of communication 16–17, 22, 45
  of pattern transference 7, 11–12,
    16, 18, 22
  of sense perception 11–12
  of standard English 44
Mondrian, P. 188–9
Monet, C. 190
Moore, G.E. 203
Mugglestone, L. 44, 54
music 22, 120, 201–20
Myers, S. 91, 99
myth
  and reality 5
  and truth 5
  as cultural fossil 1–2, 13
  as model 5, 15
  characteristics of 1, 4
  Lévi-Strauss on, 5, 15
  of communication 6–7, 15, 17,
    22, 57–9
  of consciousness 103
  of natural law 19
  of Oedipus 4
  of physical objects 203
  of race 118–37
  of the gene 22
  of the social contract 21–2
  of *Volk* 133–4

names 8, 74, 148, 208–10, 213
  divine 148
  name-giver 5
  name-giving 74, 145, 209
National Curriculum 51
nationalism, -ist 44, 132, 136
native speaker 132
Neil, Lord 179
neogrammarian 28
Newton, I. 150
nominalism 144
norm, normative, -ity 36, 50, 66, 72,
  96–7, 153, 155–6

Oedipus 4
Oliver, Lord 175
open-endedness 56, 76
Oxford English Dictionary 44, 51

painting 8–9, 22, 183–201, 209,
    213
parole 32, 57
Parpworth, N. 179, 182
pattern 7–13, 15–18, 21–2, 45, 57,
    87–8, 141, 151
  action pattern 57
  lexical 88
  pattern of patterns 45
  phonotactic 87
pattern transference 7–13, 15–18,
    21–2, 57, 140, 144, 156
  and sense perception 12, 140
  as natural phenomenon 8
  iterative transference 10, 21
  lineal transference 10, 15, 21–2
  mediated transference 18
  multiple transference 10, 15
Penrose, J. 121, 137
perception 63, 86–7, 211–2,
    215–6
  and representation 211–2,
    215–6
  of speech 86–7
Pfeiffer, R. 209, 220
philosophy
  of language 15
  of mathematics 140, 149
  of mind 16, 100–16
  of music 206, 213–4
  of perception 16
  of science 140–1, 156
physics 55–6, 62, 66
  quantum 56, 66
Pictet, A. 127, 131
Pierrehumbert, J. 91, 99
Pinker, S. 19–20, 24, 143, 157
Plato 8, 12, 14, 21, 145, 206–11,
    214, 218
poetry 9, 19, 215–6
Poliakov, L. 119, 137
politics 36, 53, 136–7
  political psychology 44, 132
  political theory 20
Porphyry 145
Preston, D. 43, 54
probability 65, 67, 70, 75, 80–1, 168
proprioception 87
Protagoras 209

225

Index

psycholinguistics 4, 86
psychology 15, 20–1, 62, 100–16
punctuation 43–4
Pythagoras 144–5, 147, 206, 208

Quine, W.V.O. 203–4

race 21, 118–37, 173–9
  myth 118–37
radical internalism 84, 93, 95–8
Ramsey, W. 100, 117
rationalism 150, 153
Ray, M. 198–9
reading 21, 44
realism 14, 188, 202–4
  empirical 202
  linguistic 14
  pictorial 188
  transcendental 202–4
reality 4, 5, 17, 46, 63, 121, 141,
    144, 150, 202, 205, 210
  accessed through words 148
  and logic 152
  as unknowable 17, 205, 211
  embodied in names 209
  mathematics as expression of
    144
  mental/psychological 31,
    84–98
  musical 220
  of consonants 4
  of contradiction 5
  of dialects 4
  of linguistics 136
  of linguistic change 4, 25–39
  of linguistic units 4
  of numbers 4, 145
  of segments 84–98
  of sentences 4
  of standard English 47
  of syllables 84–98
  of vowels 4
  of words 4, 84–98
  social 141
reflexivity 34, 74
register 43–4
regularity 27, 65
Reiss, C. 97–9
religion 20, 23

Rembrandt van Rijn, H. 9
Renoir, P.A. 190
repetition 9–10, 34
representation 5, 57, 84–98, 119,
    145, 156, 211–2
  and perception 211–2
  C-representation 95
  iconic 119
  lexical 91
  mental 84–98
  M-representation 95
  of objects 202, 204
  of sounds by letters 145
  phonetic 91
  phonological 85, 88, 92, 97
  universal 211
reproduction 9–10, 22
rhetoric 19–20, 77, 209
Rizzolati, G. 60, 82
Rodman, R. 42–3, 53
Romaine, S. 123, 137
Rosch, E. 56, 82
Rousseau, J-J. 21
rule 41, 45, 53, 55–8, 64–6, 71–2,
    78, 80–1, 153, 155, 159–81
  'golden' 165
  legal 159–81
  linguistic 41, 45, 53
  morphological 65–6
  literal 163, 169, 171
Russell, B.A.W. 154, 203
Russell, Lord 170

Sapir-Whorf hypothesis 3
Saussure, F. de 17–18, 23–4, 28,
    30–2, 44–5, 57, 85, 122,
    125–31, 135, 137, 142, 168,
    177, 181, 185
Scarman, Lord 171
Schleicher, A. 128
Schoenberg, A. 218
Schopenhauer, A. 201–20
science 4–5, 11, 19–20, 22, 55–6, 81,
    139
  biological 20
  history of 56
  human 55, 81
  natural 22, 55
  physical 20

Index

Scruton, R. 213–5, 217, 219, 220
Searle, J. 68, 82, 101, 107–8, 113, 117
segment 84–98
segregational, -ism, -ist 22, 46–7, 184, 186, 188, 198
semiology, -ical 8, 192–4, 198
sense perception 11–13, 63, 140–1
sentence 2 *et passim*
 pattern of 45
 reality of 4
Shanker, S. 150, 158
Sheridan, J.T. 144
sign 7 *et passim*
 arbitrary 149
 conventional 19
 invariance of 7, 30
 linguistic 18 *et passim*
 natural 8, 19
Simonds, Lord 170, 172
Sinclair, J. 72, 82
Skeldon, A. 144
slang 44
social contract 21–2
social intercourse 23
social network 29
social theory 20
society 1, 6, 21, 23–4
sociolinguistic, -s 42–3, 123
sociology 21
Socrates 5, 207, 209, 214
somatic particularism 14–15, 18, 21, 140
sound 8, 18, 22, 63, 92–3
 sound change 28–9
speech 18 *et passim*
 speech act 58, 67–70, 72–3, 75–6
 speech circuit 45, 168
 speech community 36, 132
 speech perception 86–7
spelling 36, 43–5, 47, 49
Standard English 41–53, 123, 167
 as a dialect 42, 123
standardization 41–53, 132, 180
standard usage 176
standing for 4, 113, 142, 145

statutory interpretation 162–6
Steinthal, H. 122–6, 137
Stich, S. 100, 103, 105, 117
structuralism, -ist 28–9, 56–7, 142, 184
Studdert-Kennedy, M. 86, 99
surrogational, -ism, -ist 4–5, 113–4, 142–7, 149–54, 156–7, 184, 186–7
 psychocentric 142–4, 149, 151, 156
 reocentric 142–6, 149–50, 152–4, 156
synchrony, -ic linguistics 28, 30–2

tally systems 146–7
Taylor, J. 91–2, 99
Taylor, T.J. 4, 17, 21, 24, 45–6, 66, 80–2, 115, 117
telementation 6, 12, 16, 30, 32, 45, 93, 132, 164, 166–8, 177, 181, 184
Templeman, Lord 174, 176, 179
text 19, 21, 23, 63–4, 163–4
 pictures as 192–3
Tietze, A. 22
Tiles, M. 150, 158
Titian 194–7
token-iterative 146
Toolan, M. 20, 56, 61, 65, 70, 72, 74, 79, 82
transmission 7, 32, 45–6
Trudgill, P. 42–4, 48, 54
truth 4, 5, 18, 46, 63, 68, 74, 150, 192, 210
type-token distinction 85–6, 96, 180

Ulmenstein, F.C.U. 133, 138
uncertainty principle 56
universals 212
utterance 7, 34–5, 46, 69–70, 85–6, 184

Velleman, S. 87–8, 99
verbalism 185, 198
Vihman, M-M. 87–9, 99
vocabulary 43–4, 51

227

Index

Volk 123, 125, 132–4
Volkstum 133

Walker, M. 141, 158
Watson, J.B. 100–3, 117
Watts, E.S. 120, 138
Weigand, E. 58, 64, 69–72, 77, 82–3
Wessels J.M.I. 87, 99
Whitney, W.D. 130
Whorfian 14
will 205–7, 214
Wittgenstein, L. 5, 79, 150–6, 204

Wolf, G. 22
words 2 *et passim*
  meaning of 78
  reality of 4, 84–98
  swearwords 44
writing 2, 21, 24, 34, 42–3, 46–7,
  53, 85, 89, 119, 145, 149

Yule, G. 76, 81

Zander, M. 169, 182
zero 146

CPSIA information can be obtained at www.ICGtesting.com
Printed in the USA
BVOW03s0057070214

344192BV00007B/82/P